BLUNT

BLUNT
NIGEL PARRY

pH powerHouse Books Brooklyn, NY

BLUNT
NIGEL PARRY

INTRODUCTION
TOM FORD

FOREWORD
ROGER ROSENBLATT

DESIGN
JUSTUS OEHLER, PENTAGRAM

DEDICATED TO
MELANIE,
EMMA, AND JACK

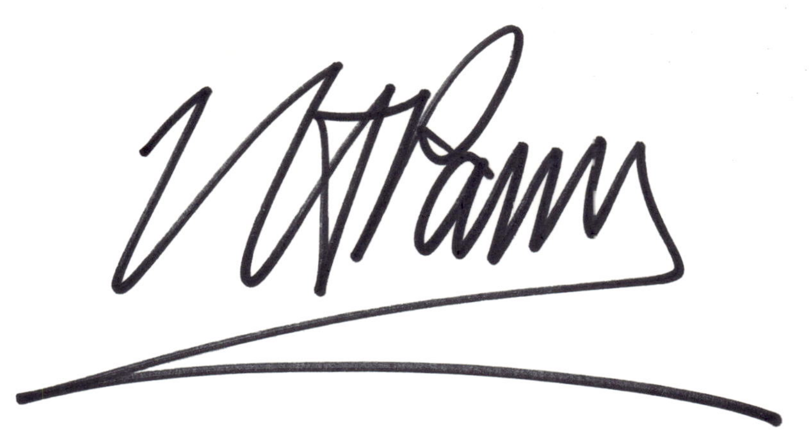

INTRODUCTION

Blunt. The very word conjures up strong, graphic images. Nigel's photographs can often seem blunt on the surface, as they usually cause a visceral reaction. They are potent. They are powerful.

I must admit, however, that I have a hard time thinking of Nigel the man as blunt. In fact he is anything but. He is sweet and kind. I think that his kindness and warmth are part of how he manages to capture something intimate from his subjects.

Of course Nigel's eye is quick and refined, and he is able to see in a way that accounts for the strong graphic quality of his pictures. He is a master of black-and-white. But there is always more to his photographs than simple graphic punch.

I am fortunate to have been photographed on numerous occasions by Nigel. I always look forward to his photo sessions, which have resulted in what I feel are some of the best photographs ever taken of me. I am difficult to photograph. I am stubborn and want to control things, and I often tend to be stiff and not give much to the camera other than my two or three well-rehearsed poses—but Nigel always manages to find a new angle or to capture something fresh.

I trust Nigel, and the trust that his subjects place in him allows him to capture something more than just their image. He has, on occasion, captured their souls.

Tom Ford

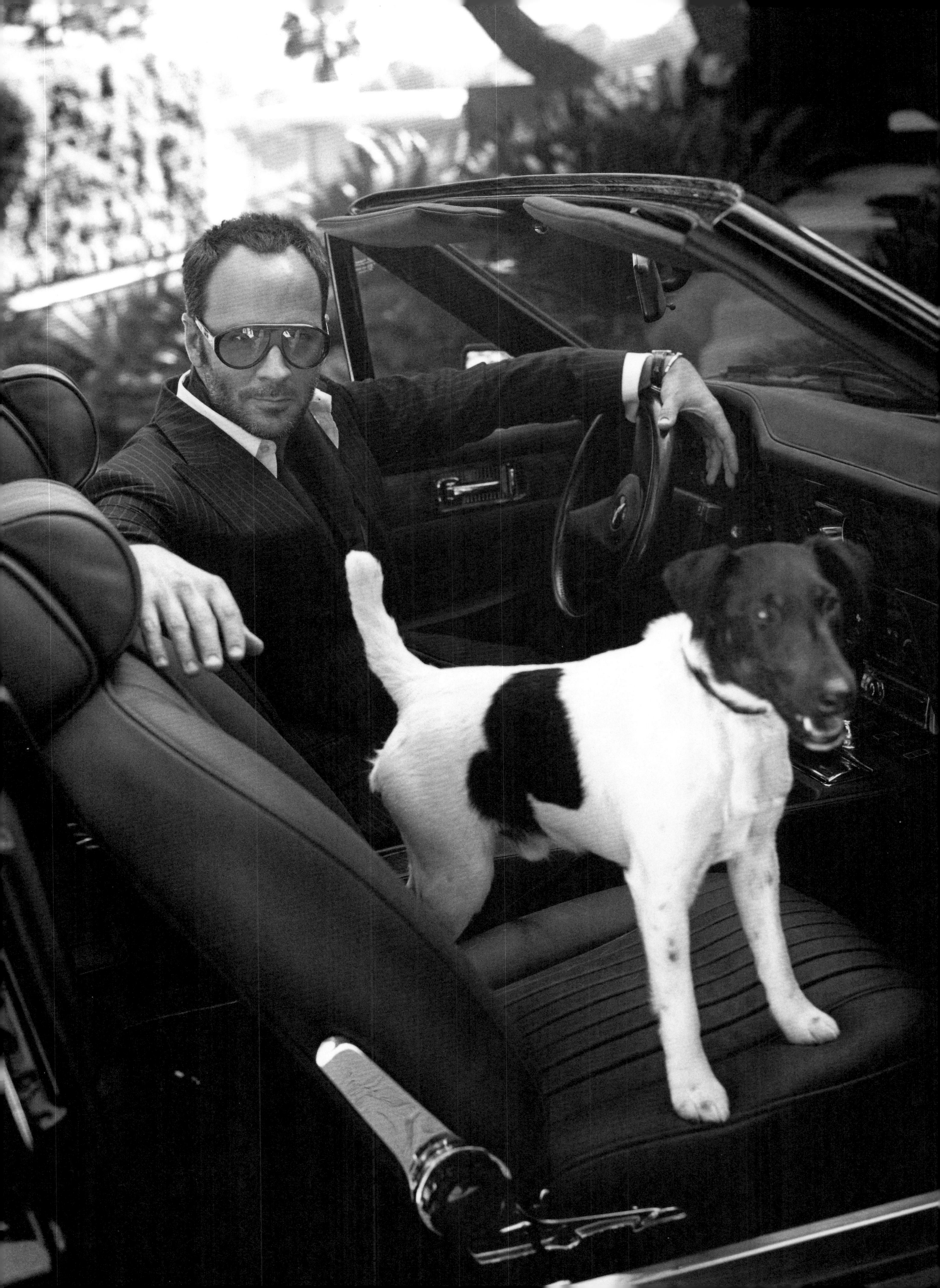

FOREWORD

Something about the light he shoots them in. And something about the way the subject fits and does not fit the frame. Tim Robbins, for instance, chinless and seemingly blasted by a searchlight. No matter how old he gets, Robbins always looks like the boy in high school whose startled innocence belies a mind capable of trouble. Or George Clooney, cut off at the hairline, one third of his face in shadow, and looking like a film noir detective who has just cracked wise. Or Edie Falco, also not quite full-headed, and shot off-center: dark clothing, white-white face, and her eyes looking for a thought that is not sad.

Most of us do not know any of these people except by their public displays, but we dimly sense who they are. Nigel Parry senses who they are as well, but hardly dimly. A photographer with a writer's imagination, Parry uses no tricks, no bizarre sets or costumes. He does not need to decorate the essential person, for the essential person is all that he is interested in. One can almost hear him instruct his subjects: If you want to smile, smile; if you want to grimace, do that. More likely he does not instruct his subjects at all, but simply waits for the one picture that shows the human being, who is essentially always strange.

Did he tell Ellen DeGeneres to look scared? I doubt it. But wait, she's biting the collar of her jacket like a child, so this is play-scare, the comedian's scare. But wait again. Why would the fluid, bouncy Ellen choose to look big-eyed and jacket-biting unless it is because she wants us to know that to be Ellen, however funny and friendly, is always a little scary? Is she kidding?

The black-and-white helps, of course—the absence of distracting color; the color thus discovered in the attitude and expression. But not all black-and-whites are the same. Parry does with faces what Sebastião Salgado does with human suffering. He makes his people appear as if they had been pared down to basics, basic black-and-white. Yet life exists in color, so it is the black and white that create the artifice. Oddly, he falsifies his subjects by making them true.

The shadows fallen on Joaquin Phoenix; the finger-pointing of Bill O'Reilly; the tangle in which Mel Gibson finds himself, so close to a natural crown of thorns. So it goes. But there are hidden people here, too. I defy you to recognize Monica Lewinsky at first sight. (I know that girl, but from where?) And George Bush, hidden in the open, the top of the head removed from the man who is in over his head.

This then is what I take to be Parry's gift. He suggests that the subjects be themselves and then he photographs the selves they cannot see, yet know are there. From the cover shot one might conclude that Paul Giamatti thinks of himself as a horrifying clown, a potential monster. But like nearly everyone who shows up here, he is merely beautiful.

Roger Rosenblatt

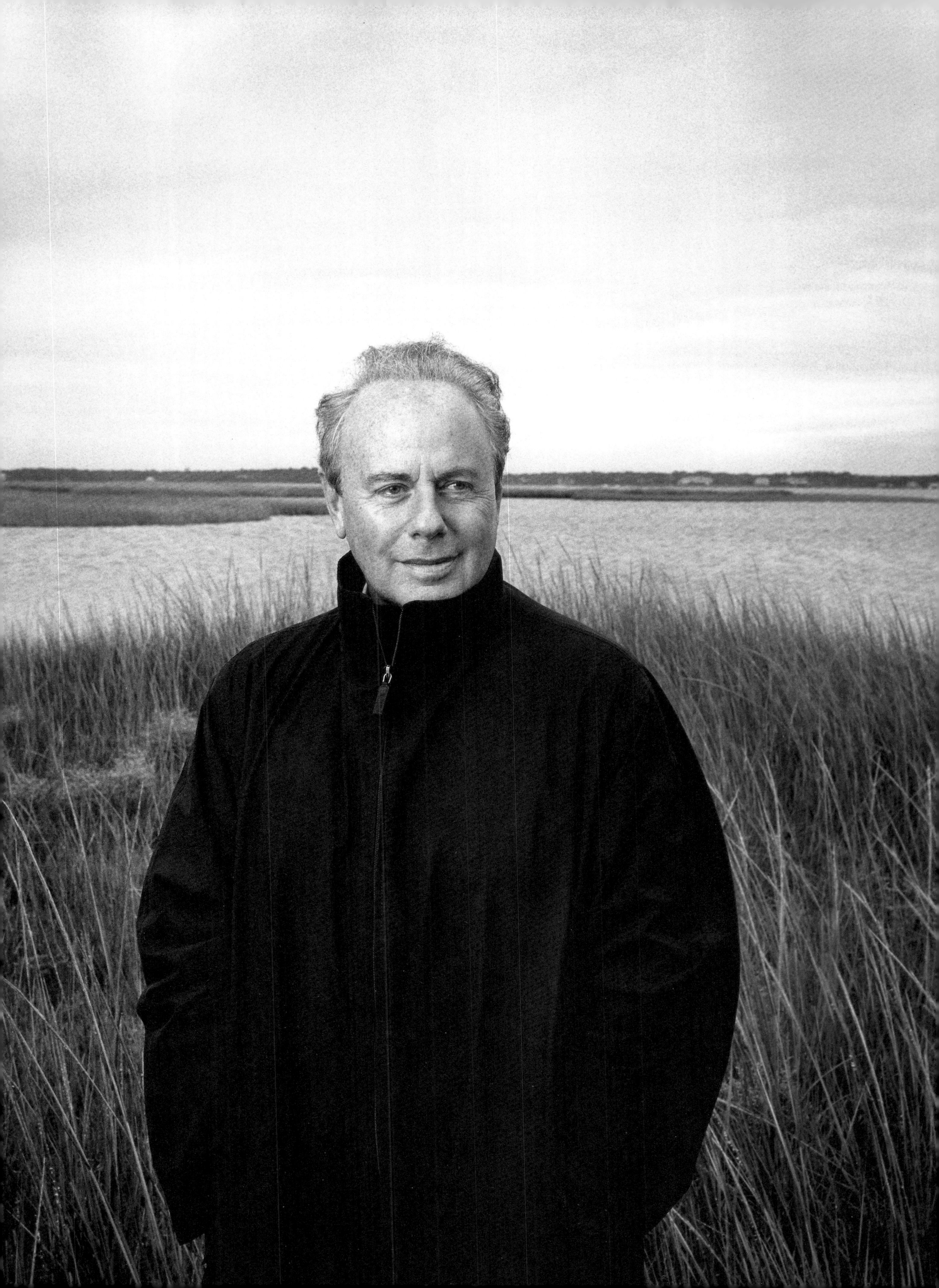

IS THIS THING REALLY REAL?

50 CENT

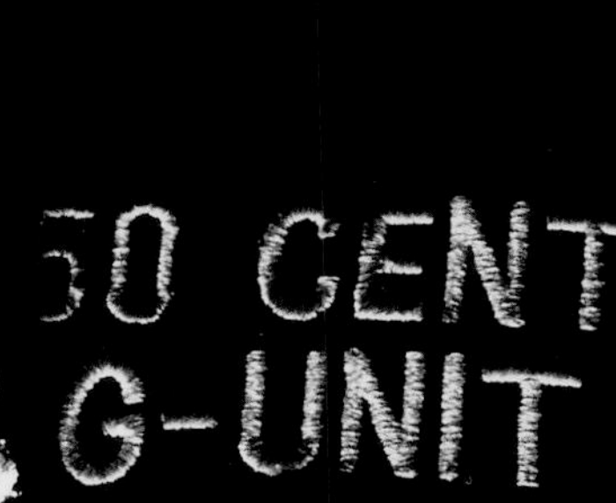

50 CENT
G-UNIT

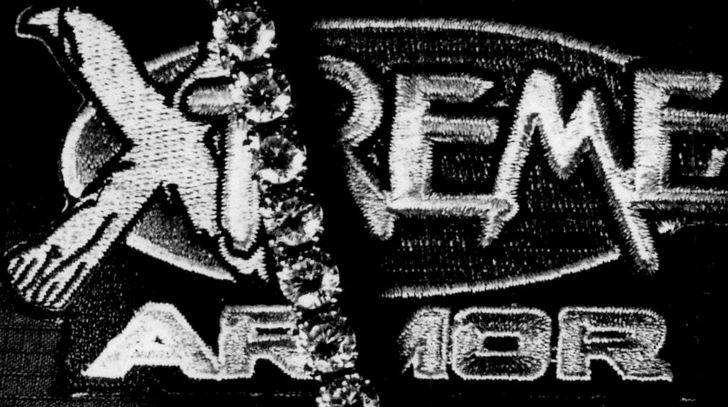

XTREME

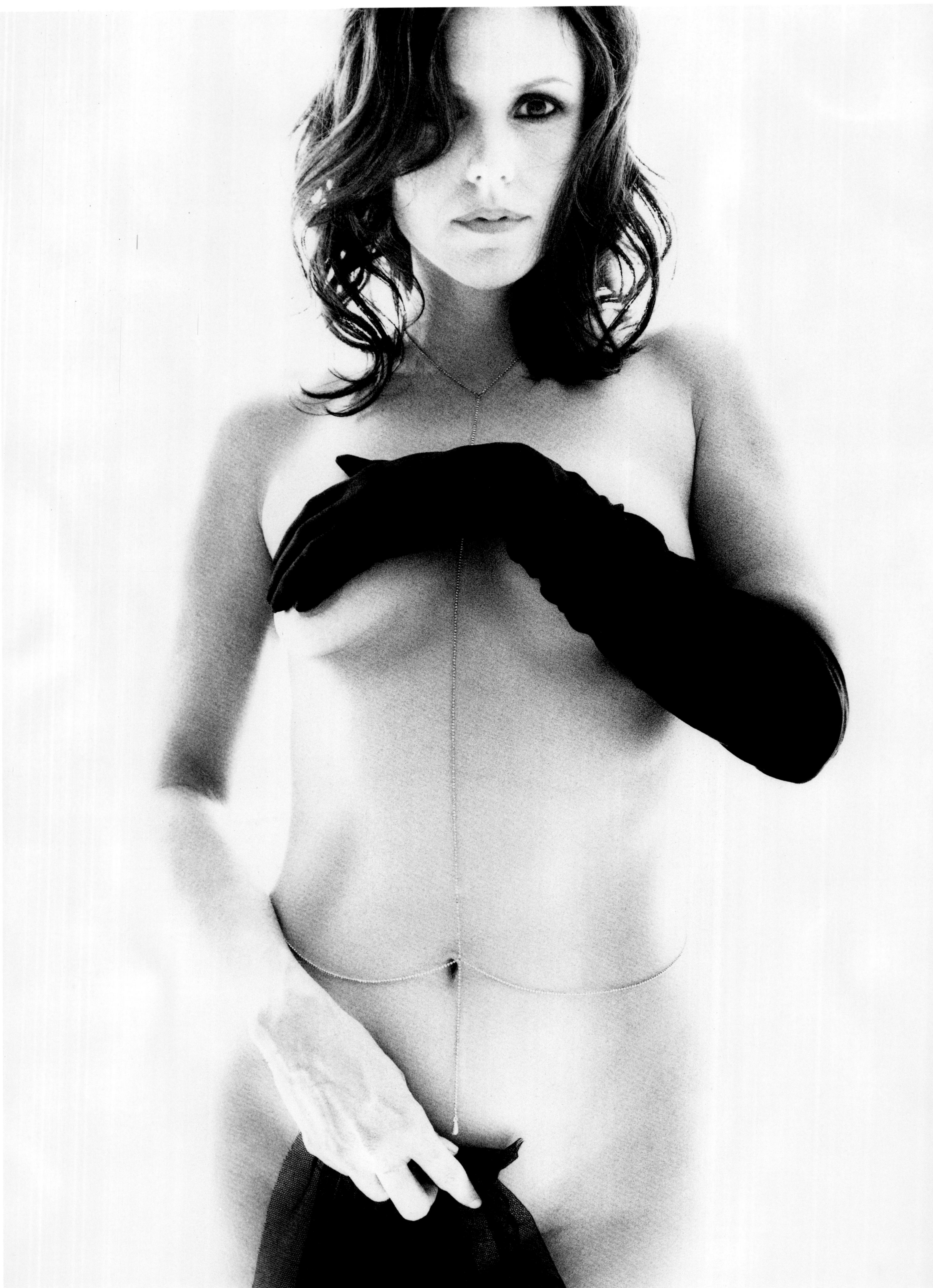

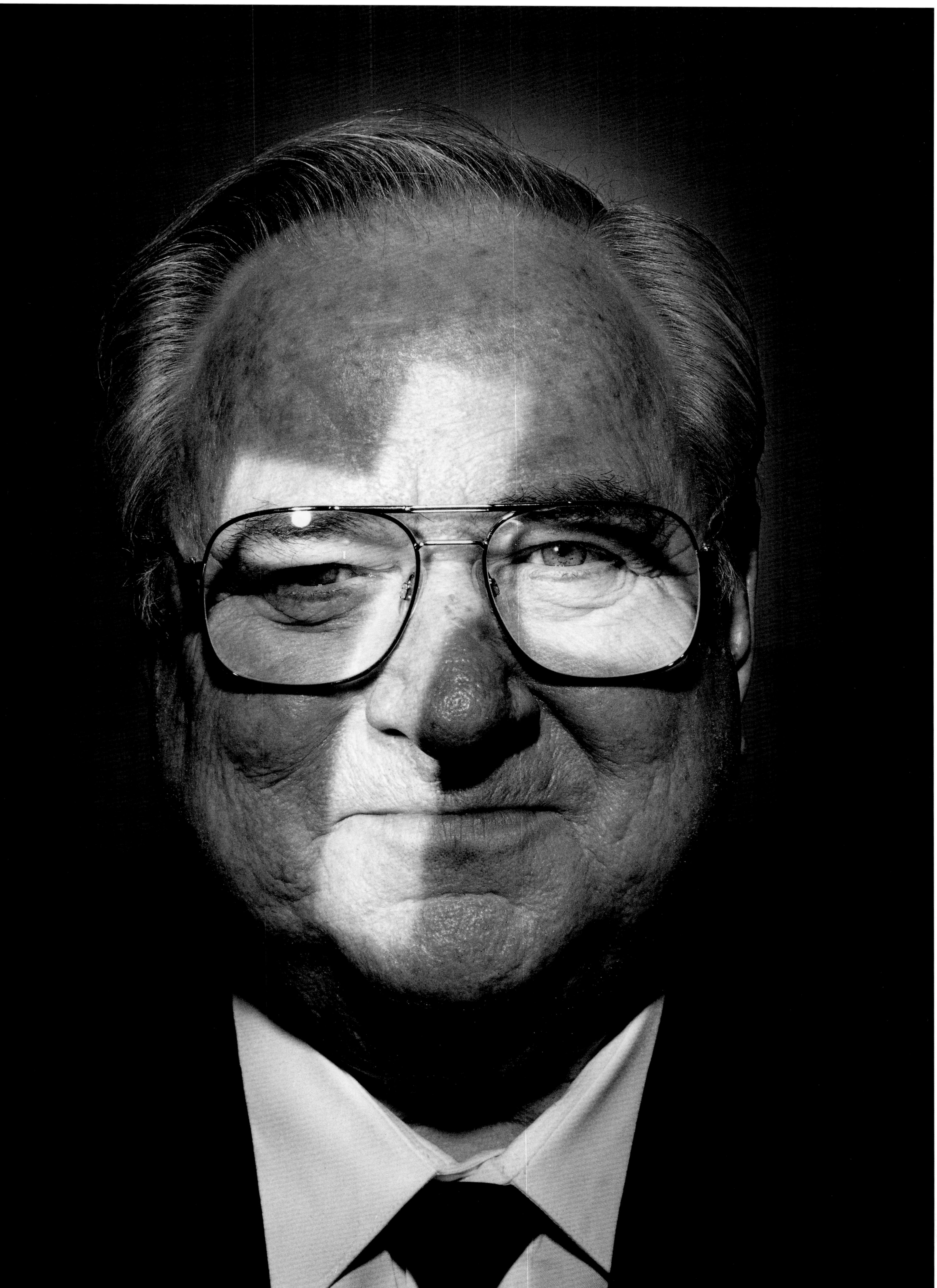

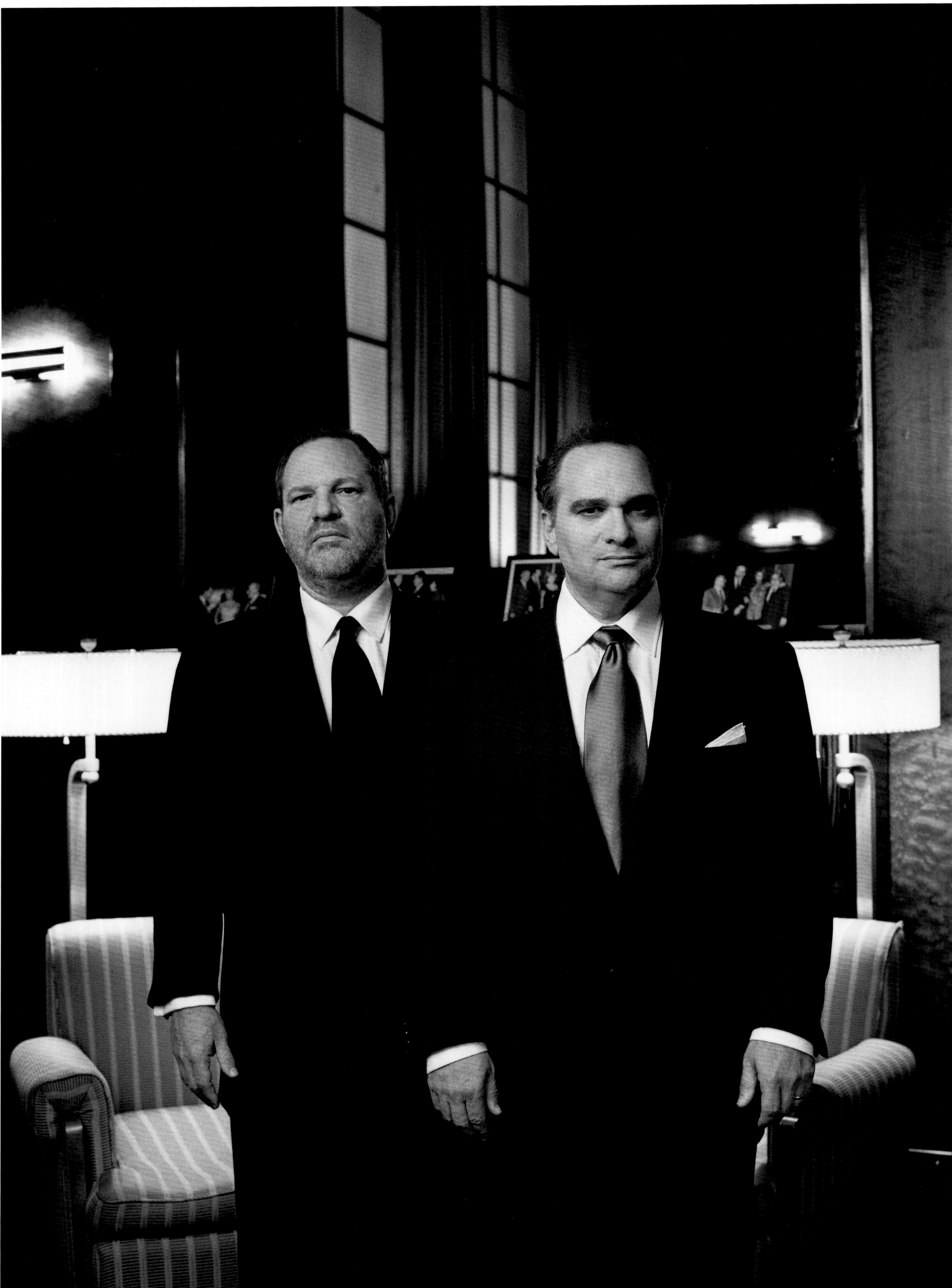

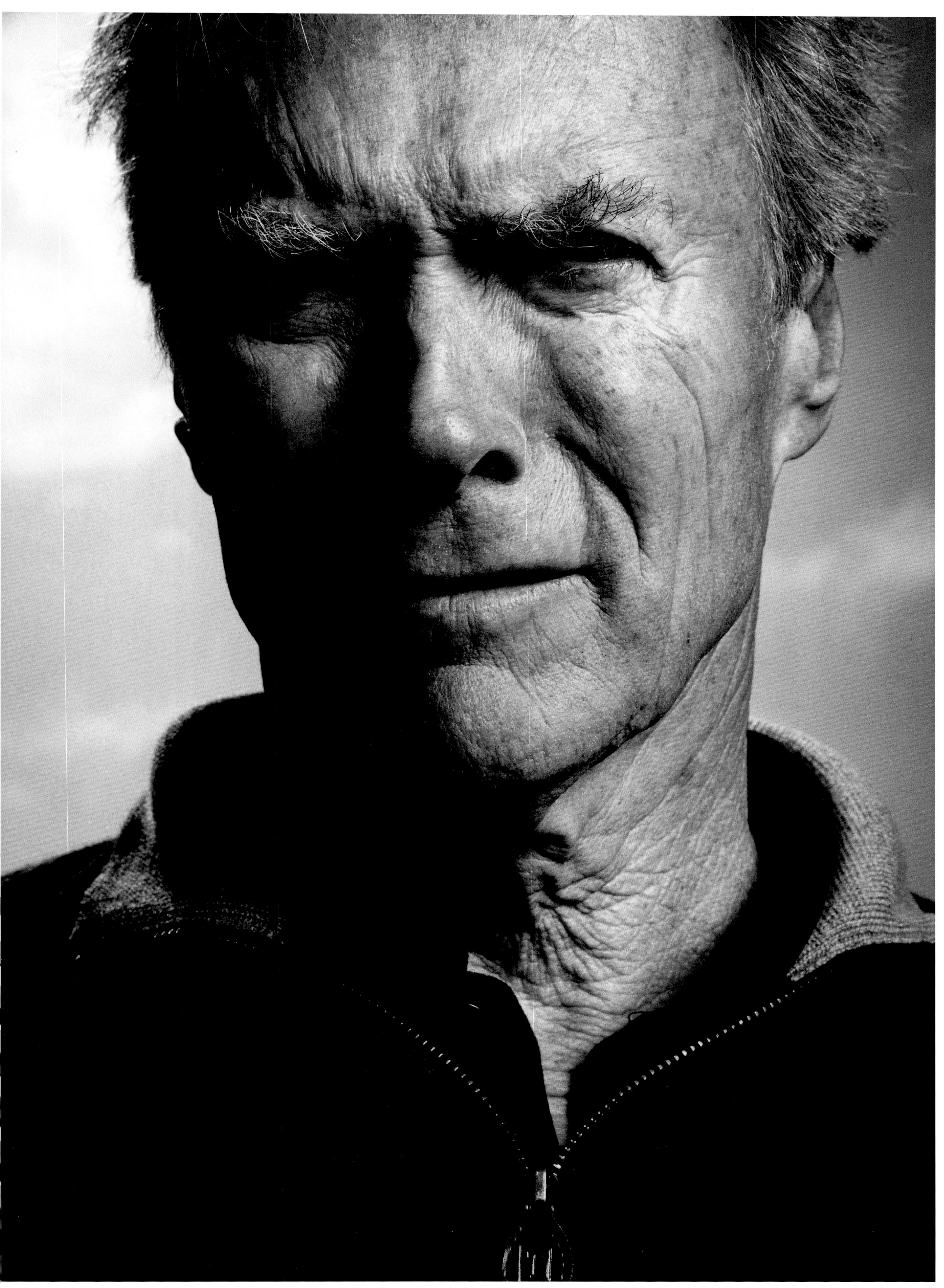

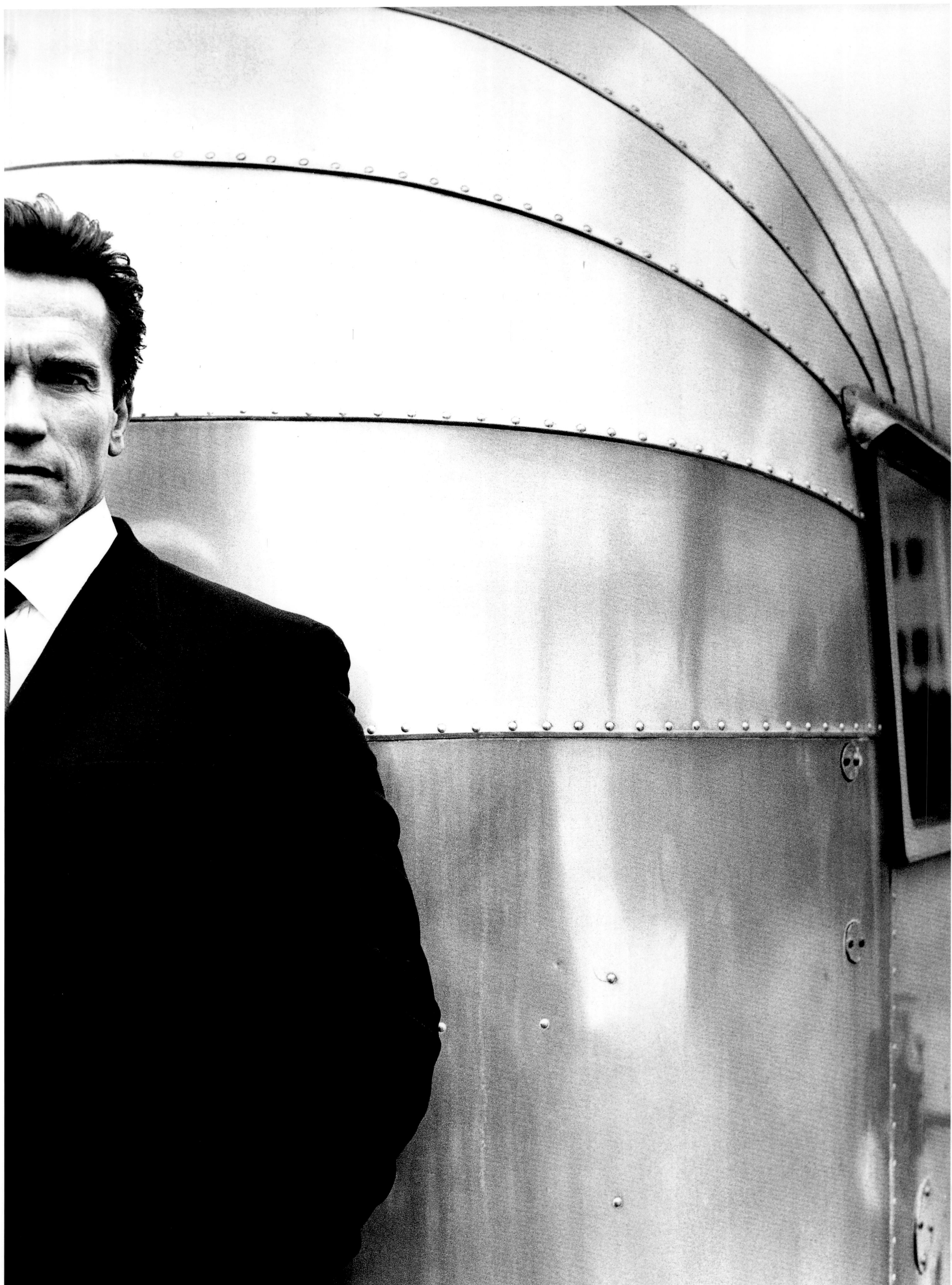

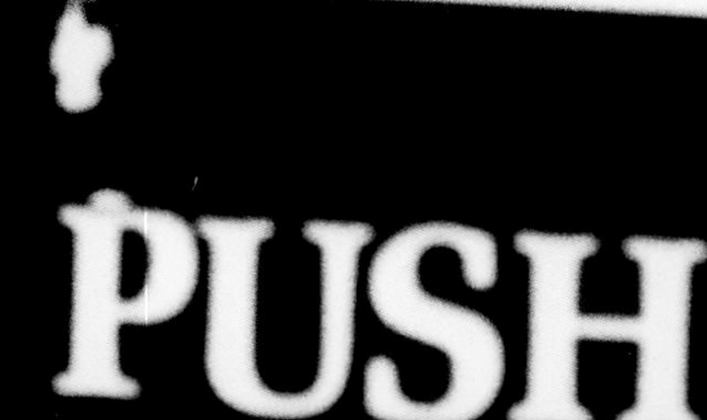
PUSH

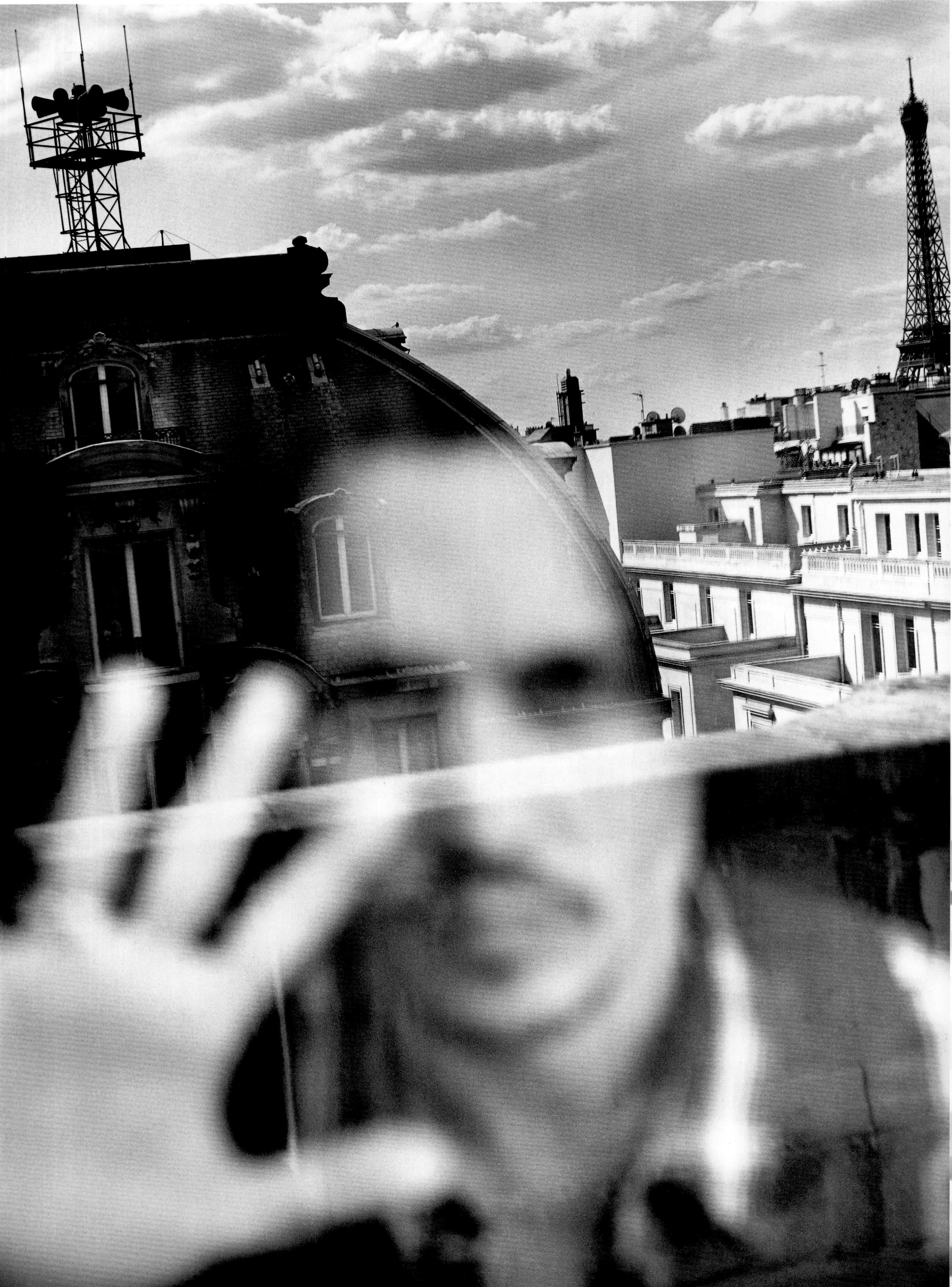

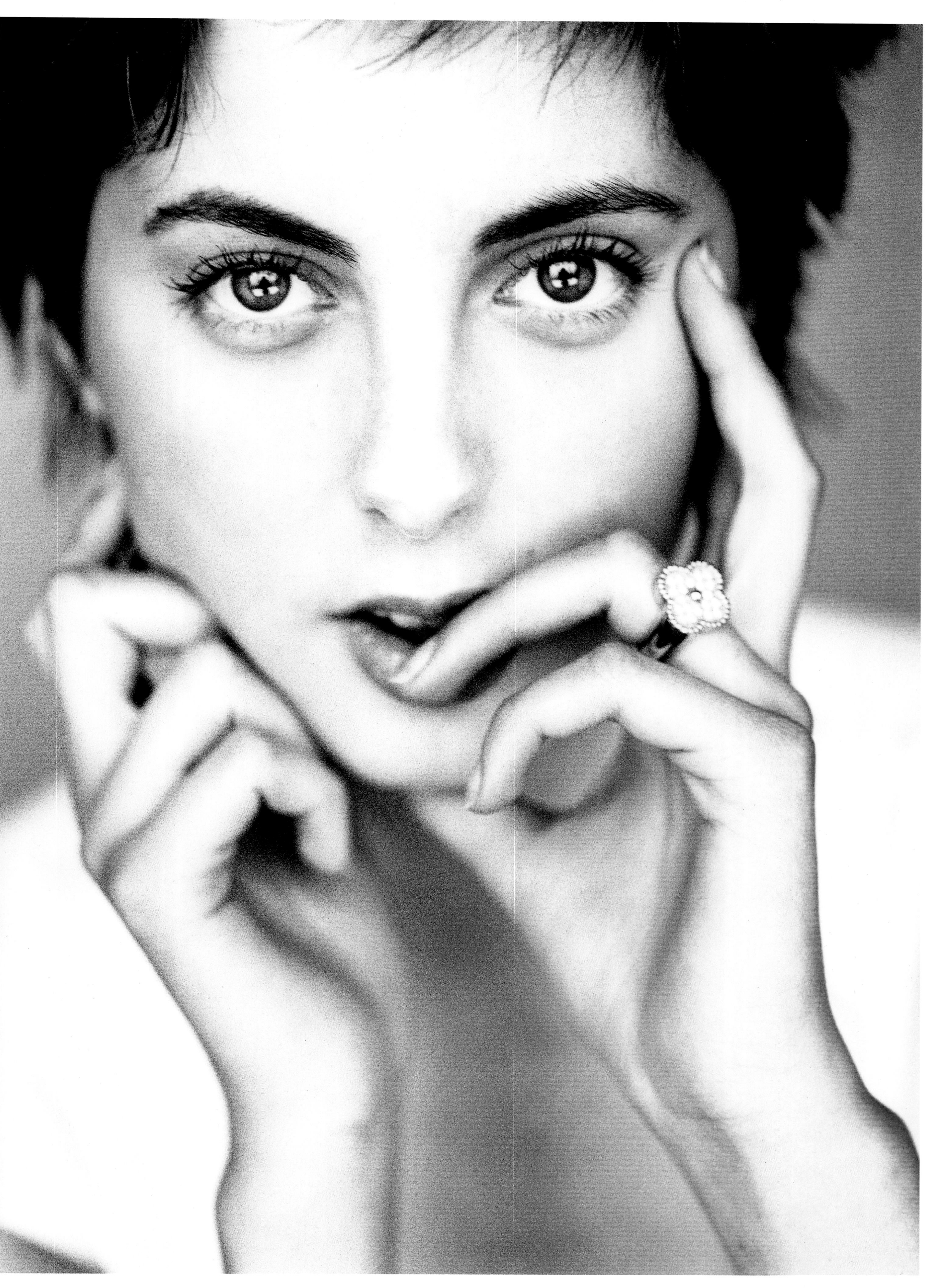

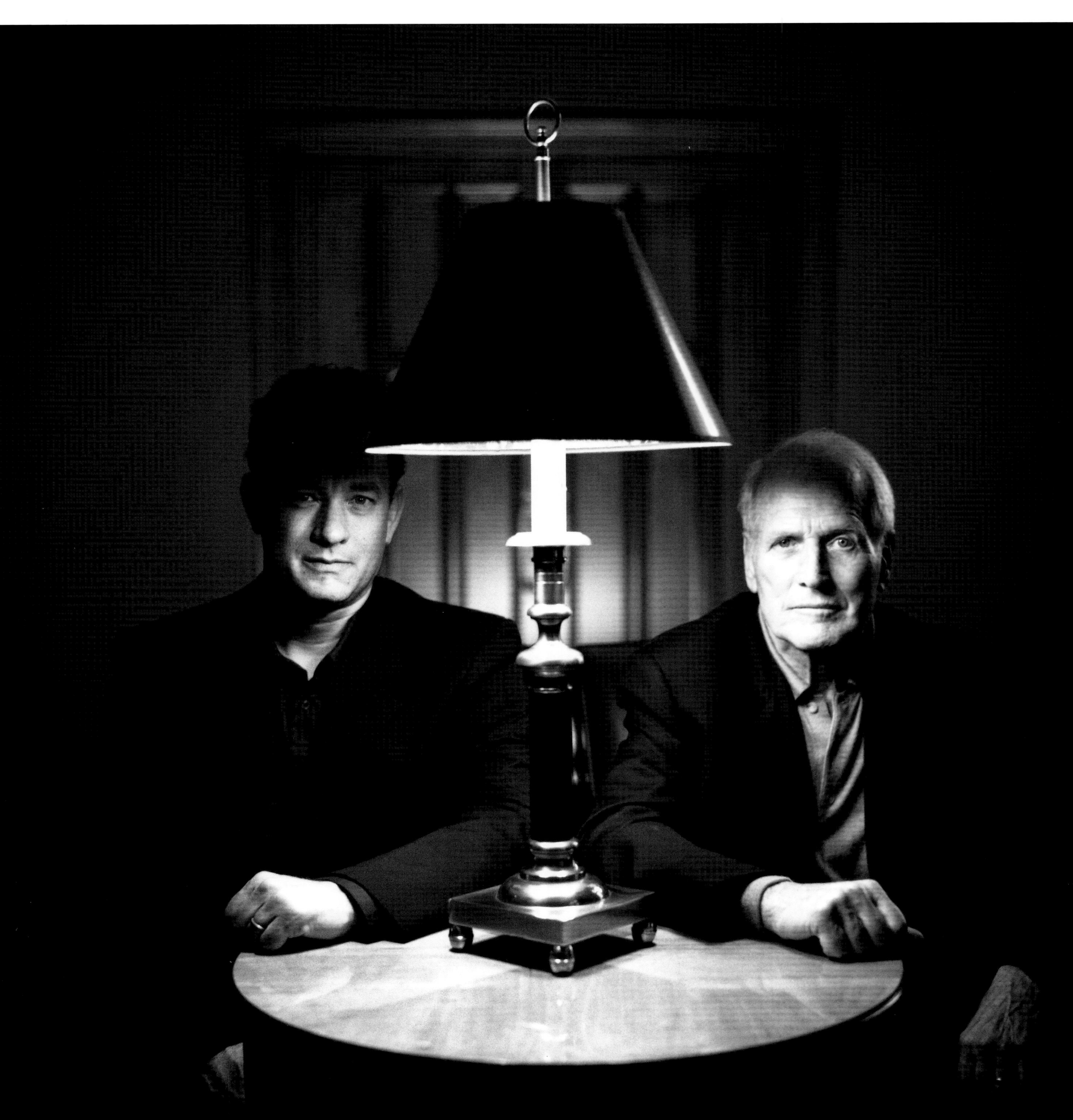

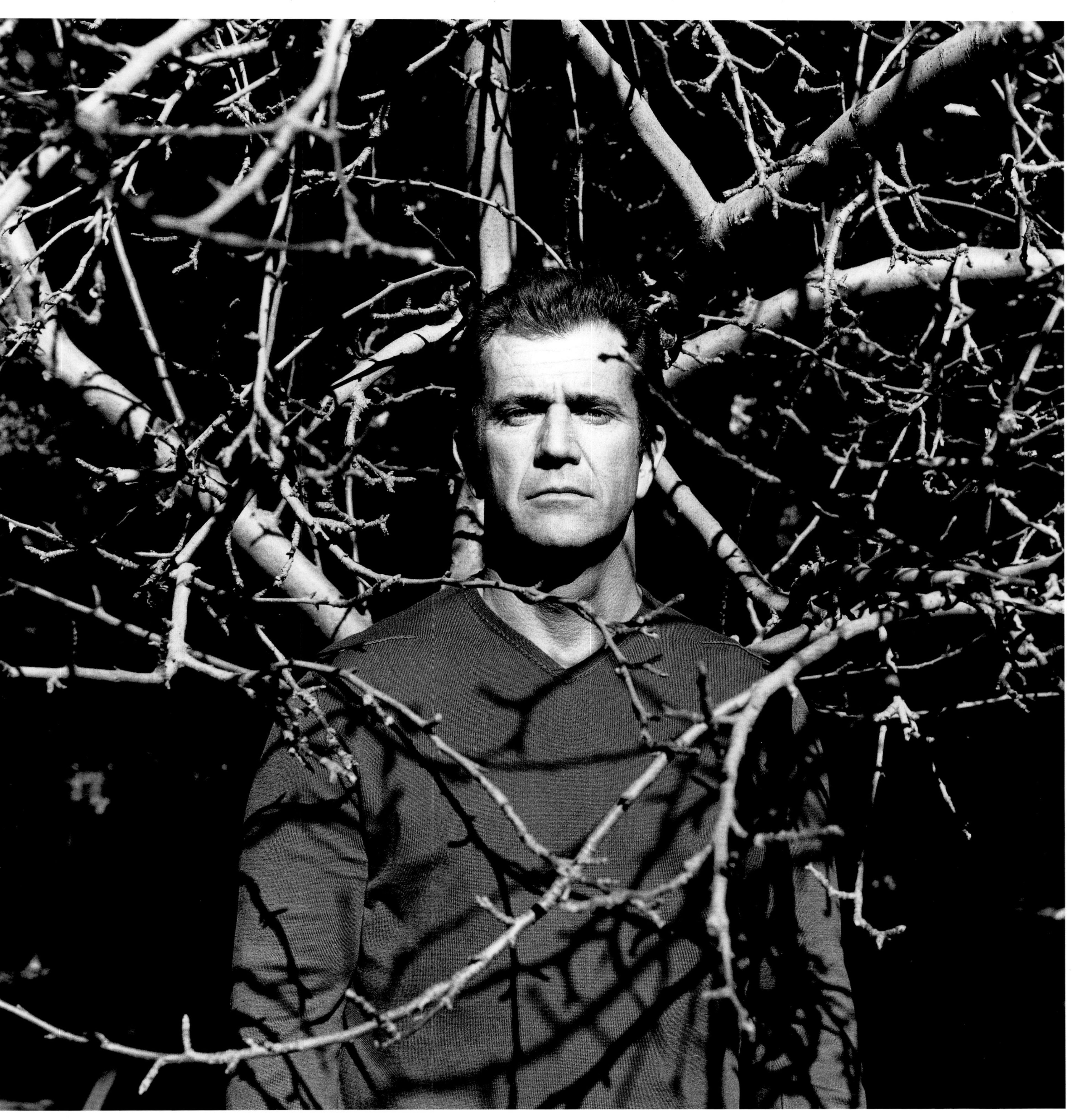

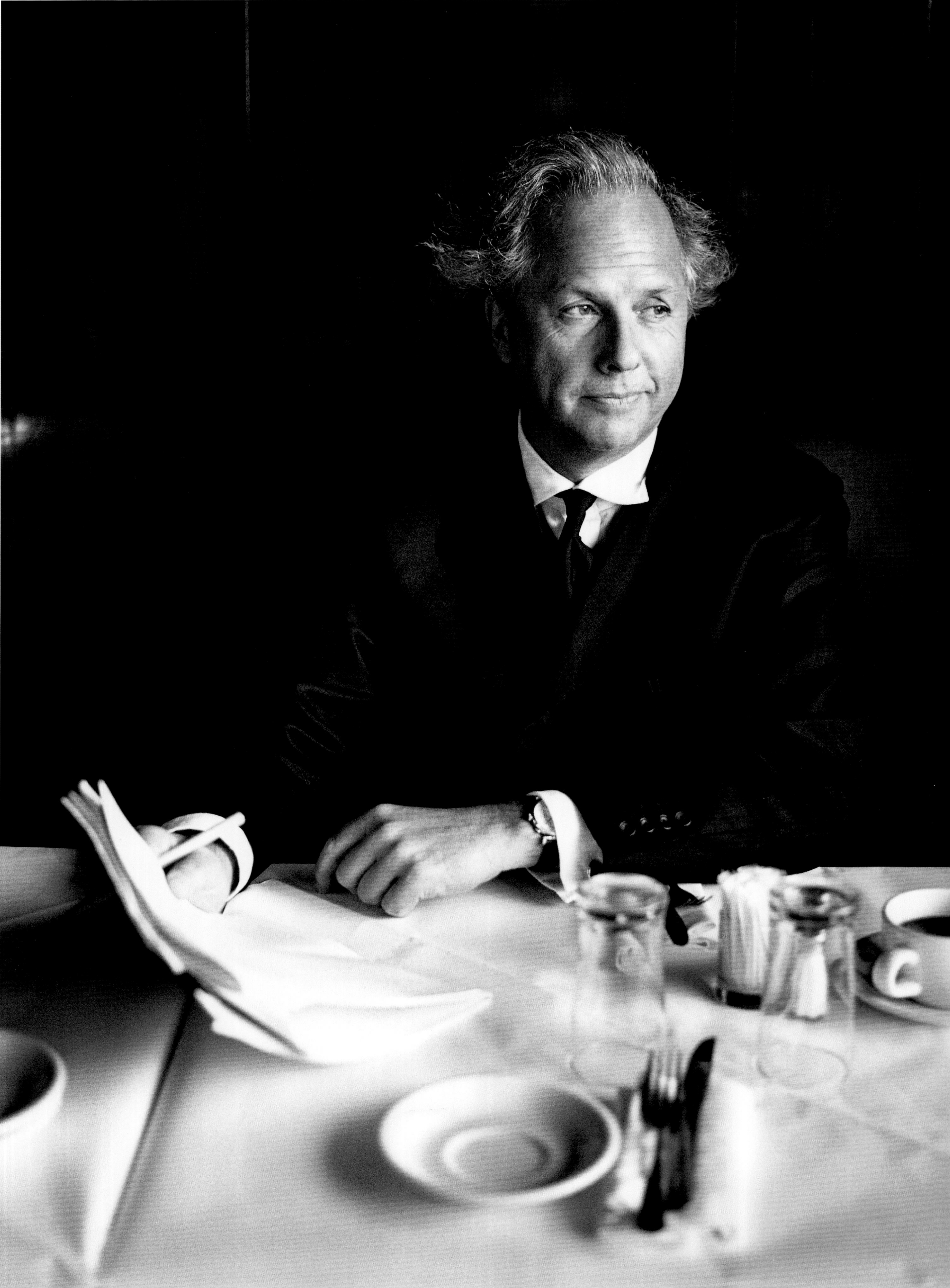

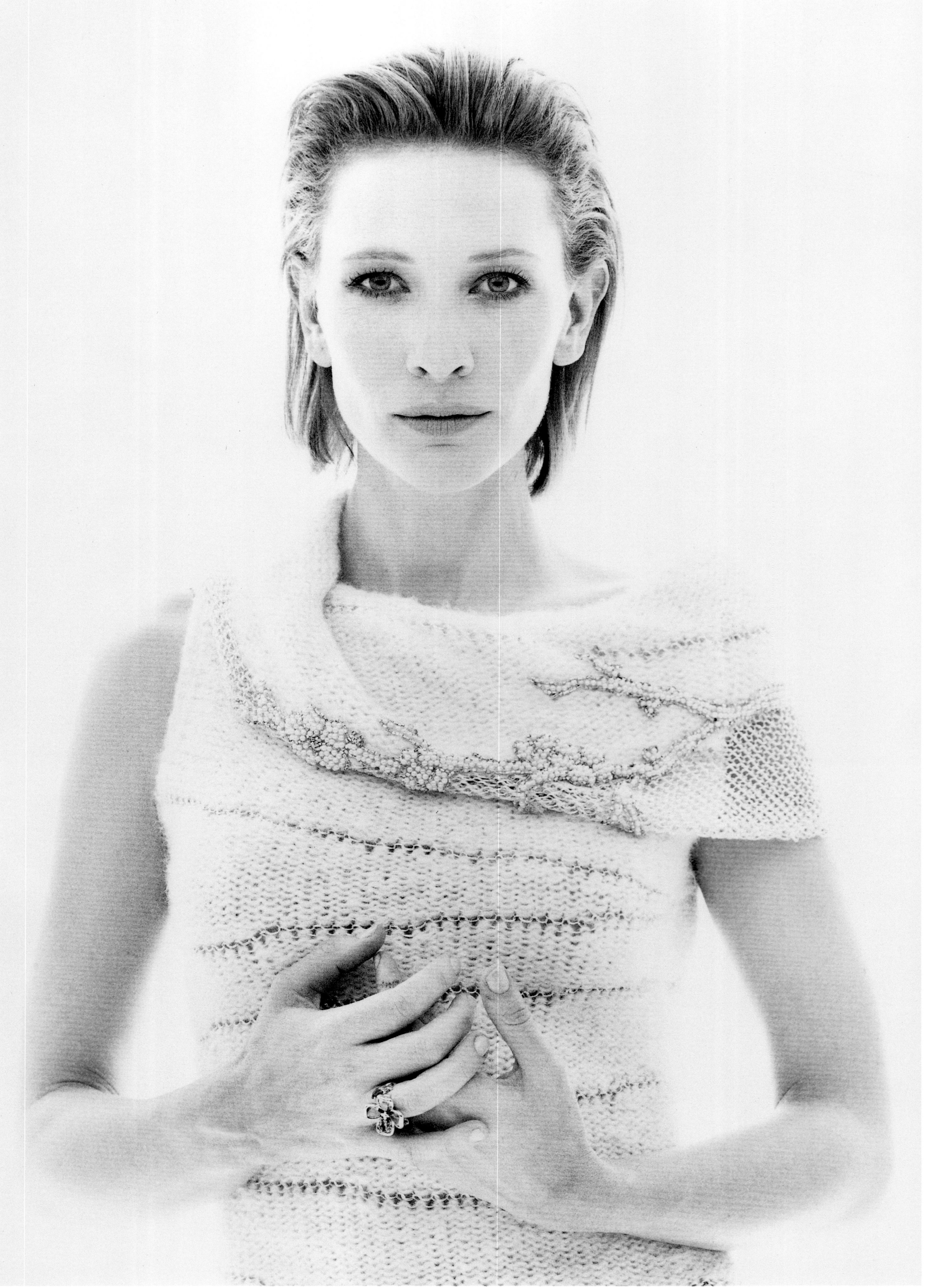

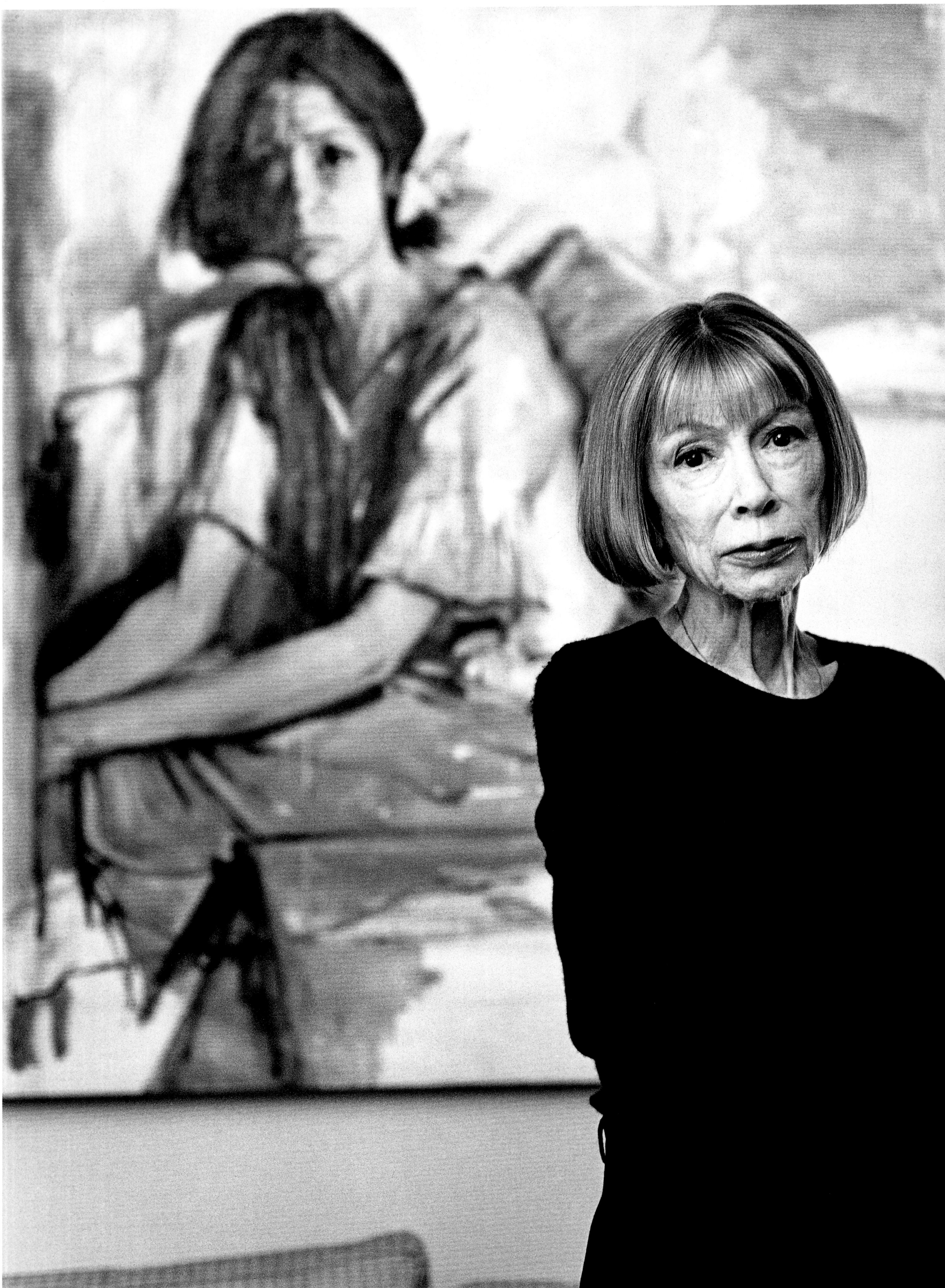

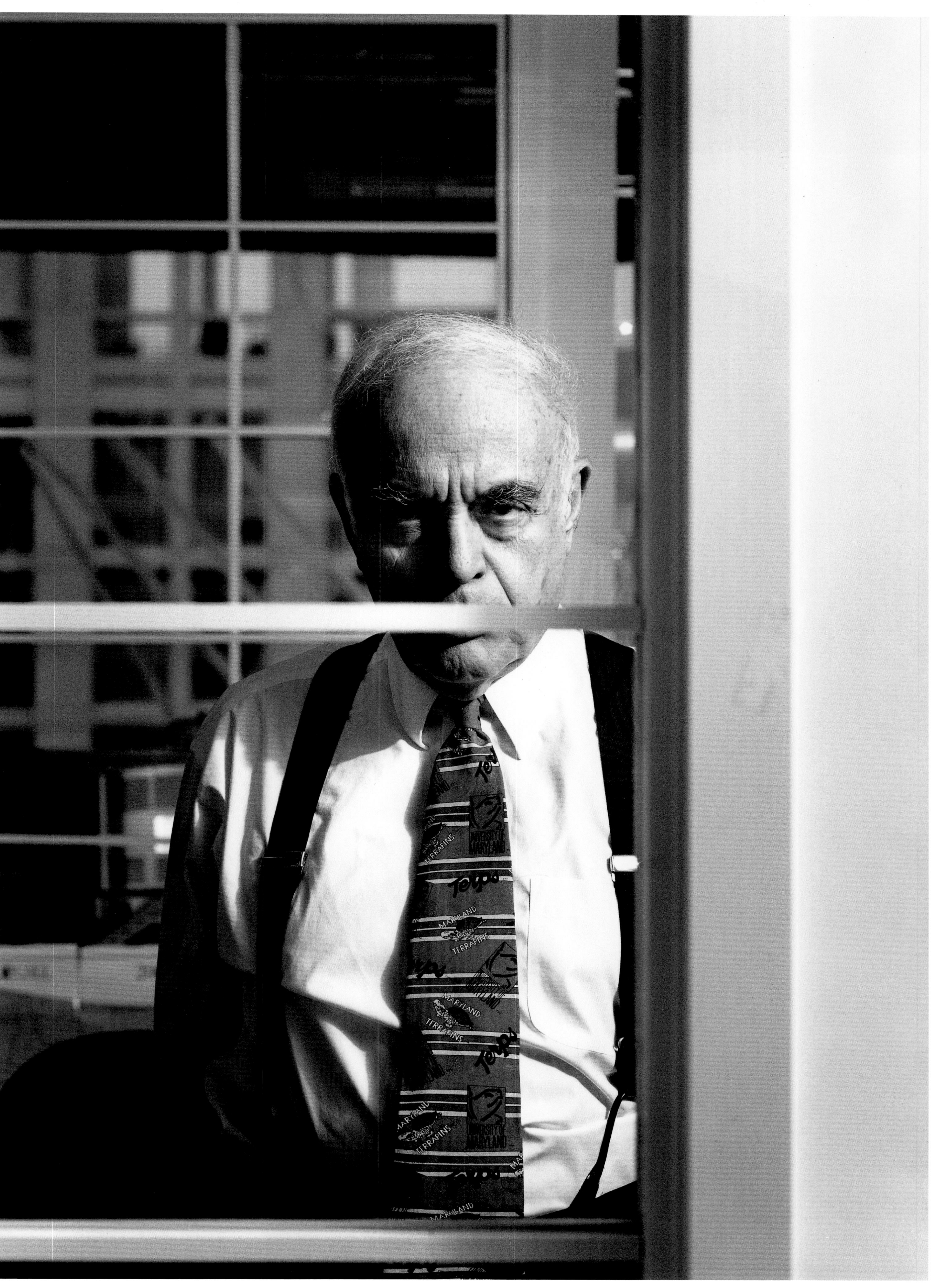
Terps
UNIVERSITY OF MARYLAND
TERRAPINS
Terps
MARYLAND
TERRAPINS
MARYLAND
TERRAPINS
Terps
MARYLAND
UNIVERSITY OF MARYLAND
TERRAPINS
MARYLAND

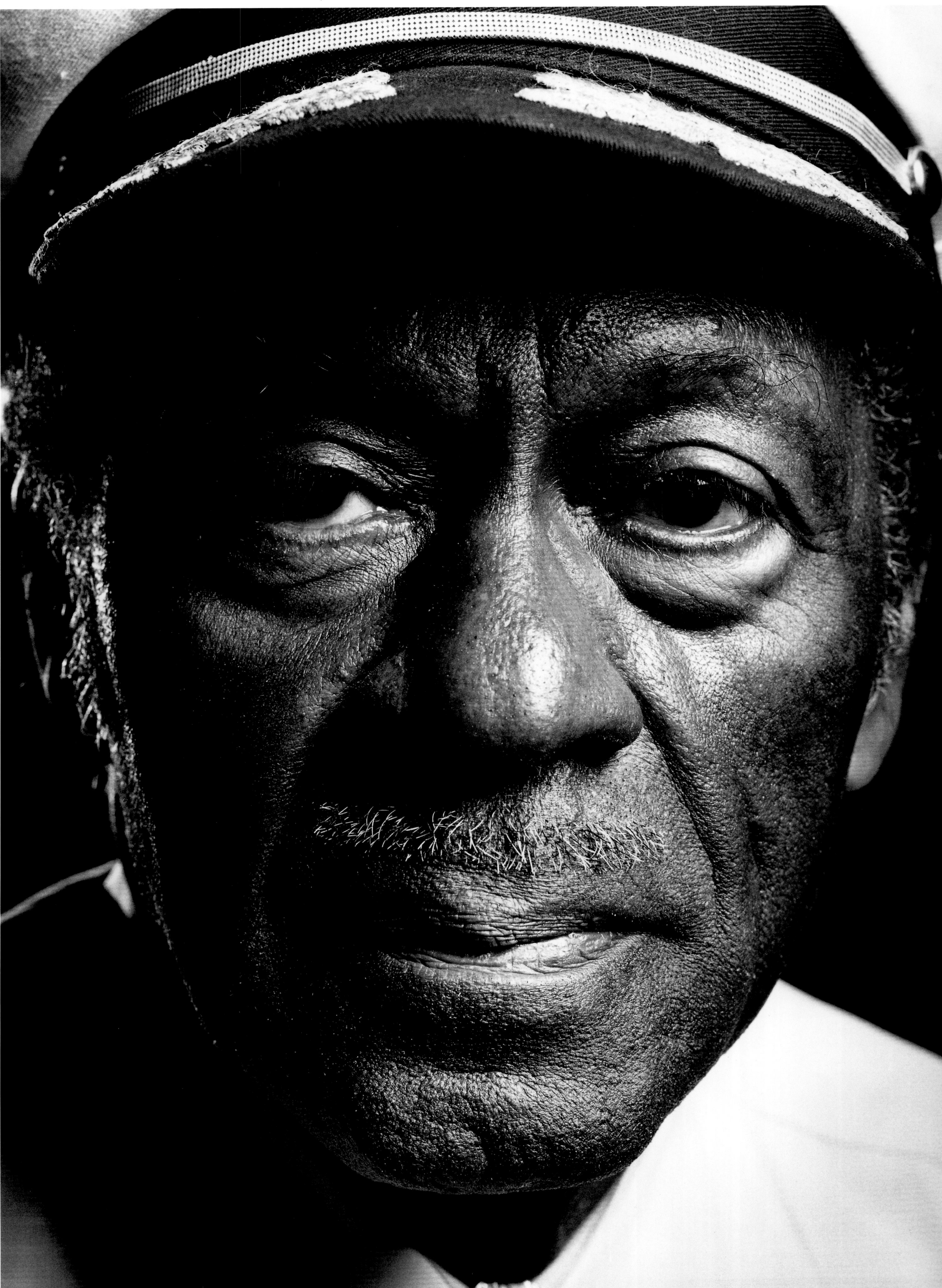

PORTRAITS ON PREVIOUS PAGES

50 CENT

MARY-LOUISE PARKER
JERRY FALWELL

THE WEINSTEINS
CLINT EASTWOOD

ARNOLD SCHWARZENEGGER
PAUL WOLFOWITZ

JOHNNY DEPP
EVA AMURRI

TOM HANKS & PAUL NEWMAN
MEL GIBSON

GRAYDON CARTER
CATE BLANCHETT

JOAN DIDION
ROBERT NOVAK

CHUCK BERRY

LET'S ROLL!

TODD BEAMERS' LAST WORDS TO HIS WIFE LISA
FROM UNITED FLIGHT 93, 9/11/2001.

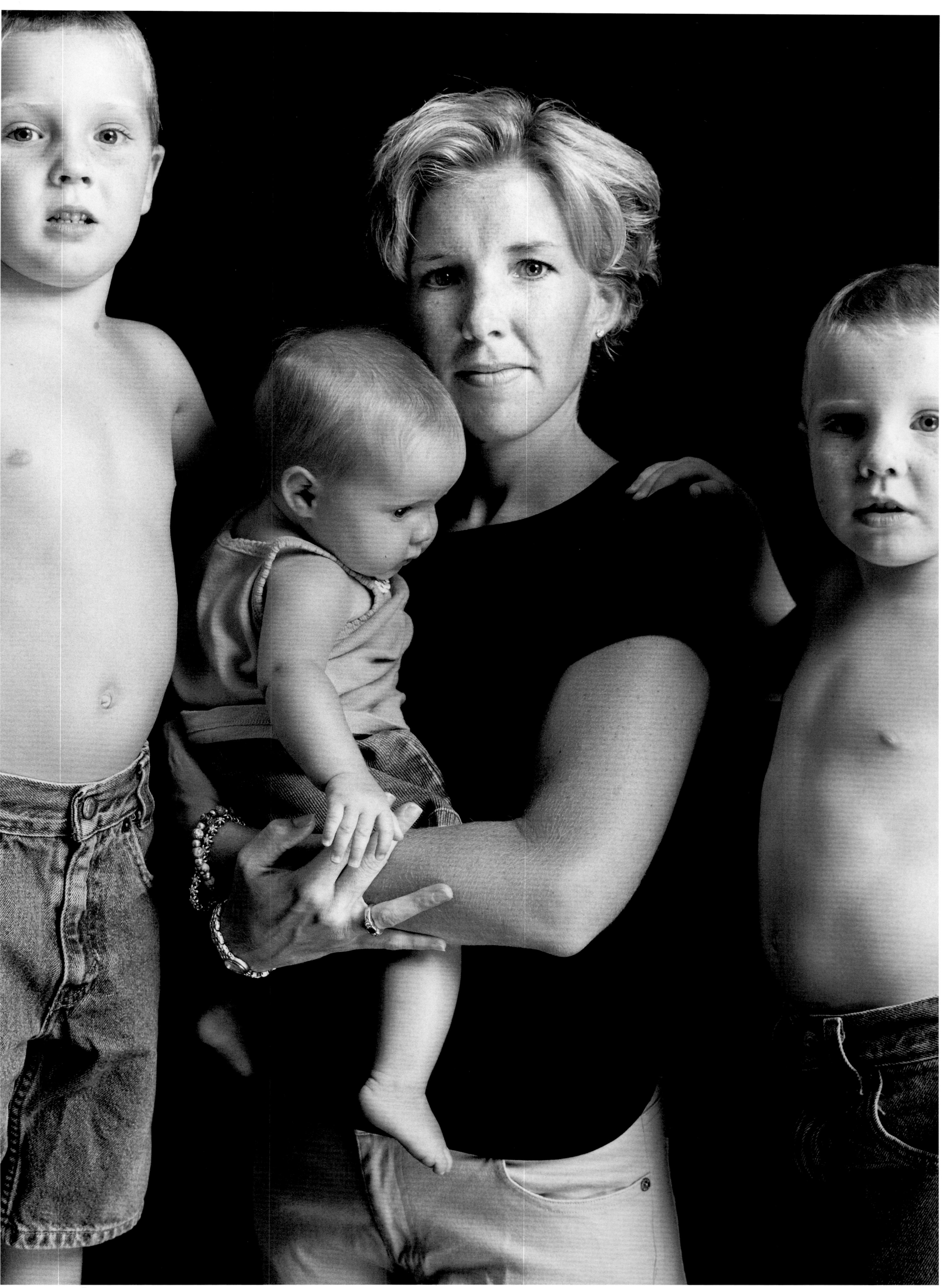

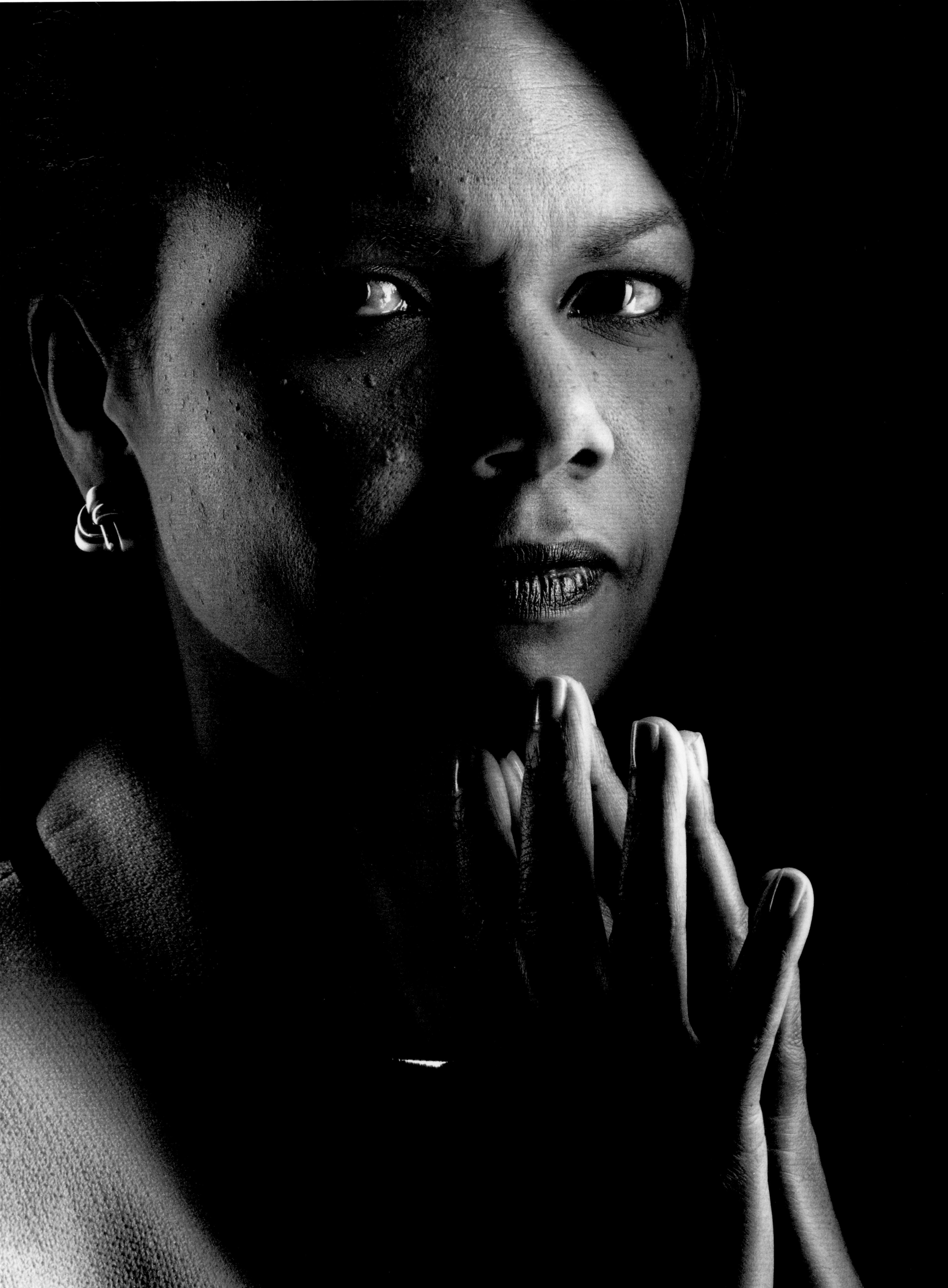

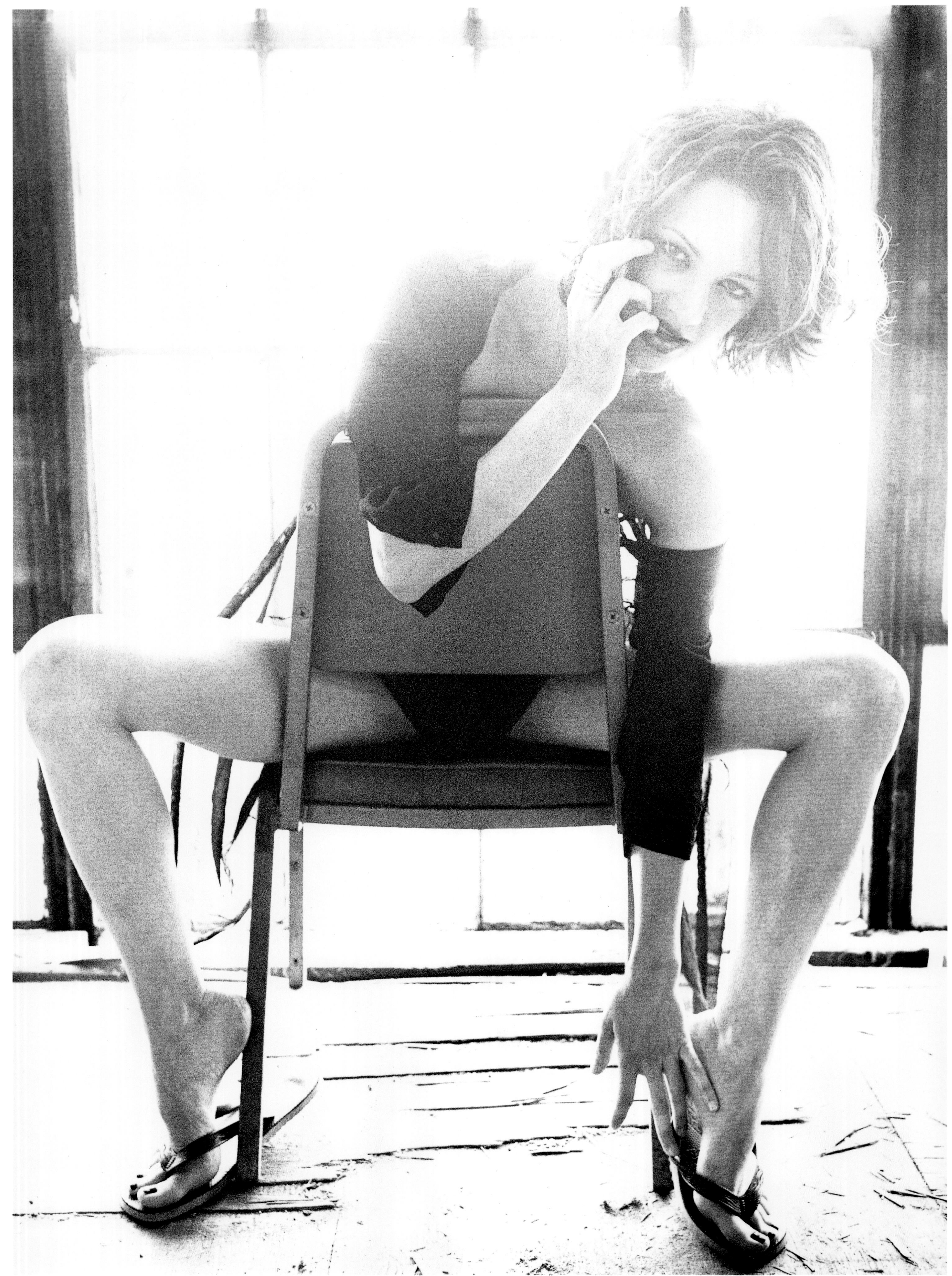

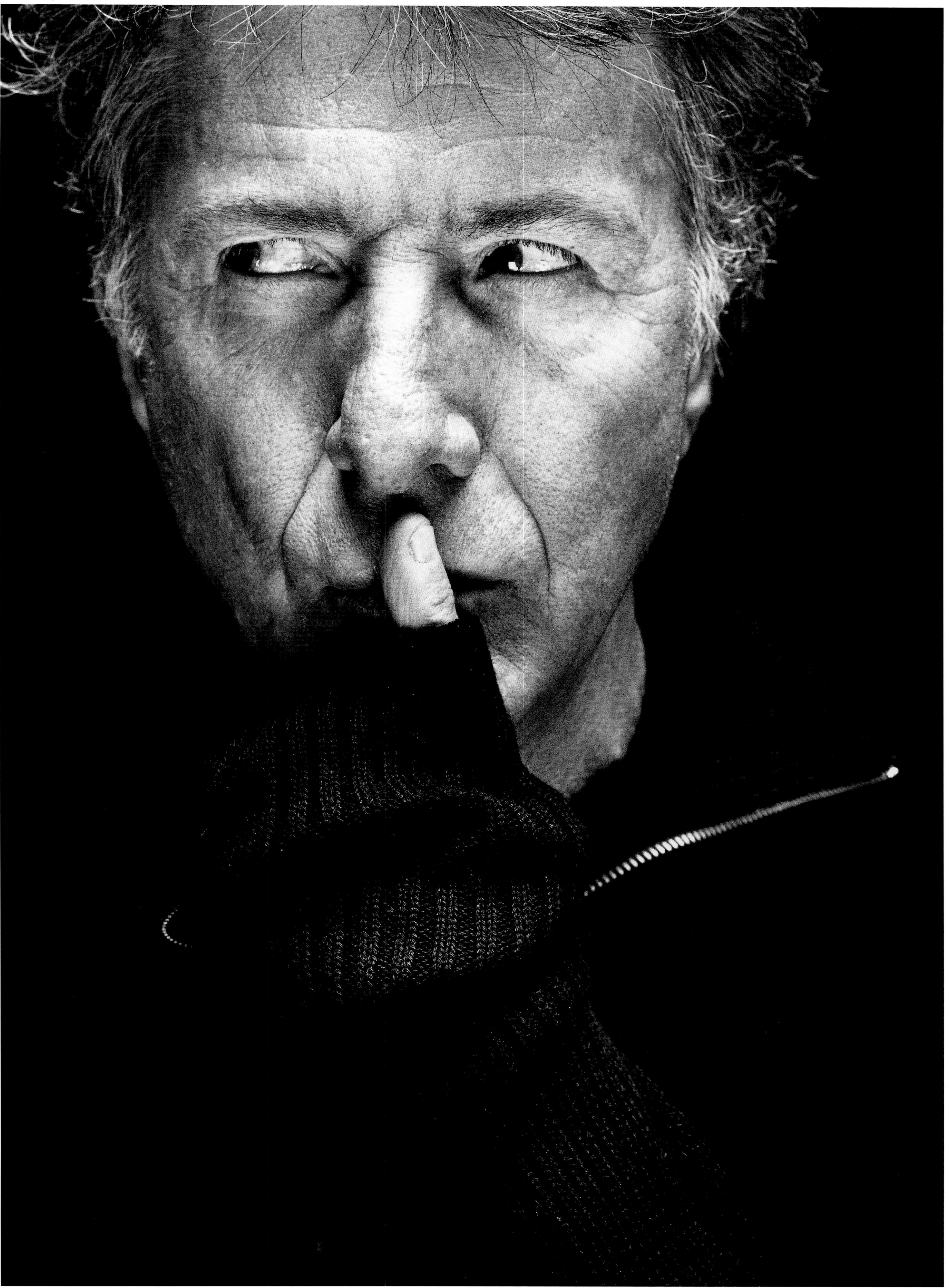

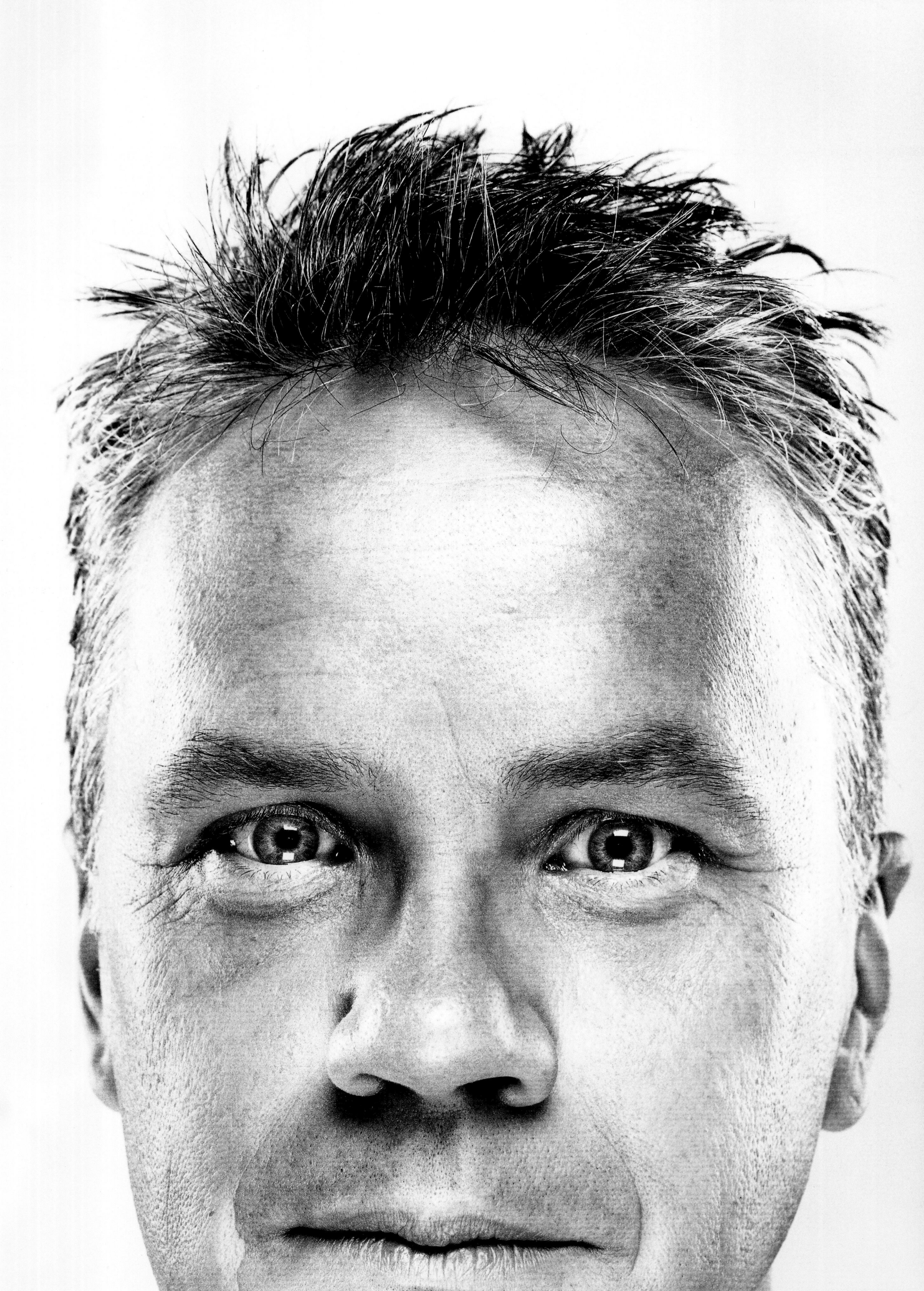

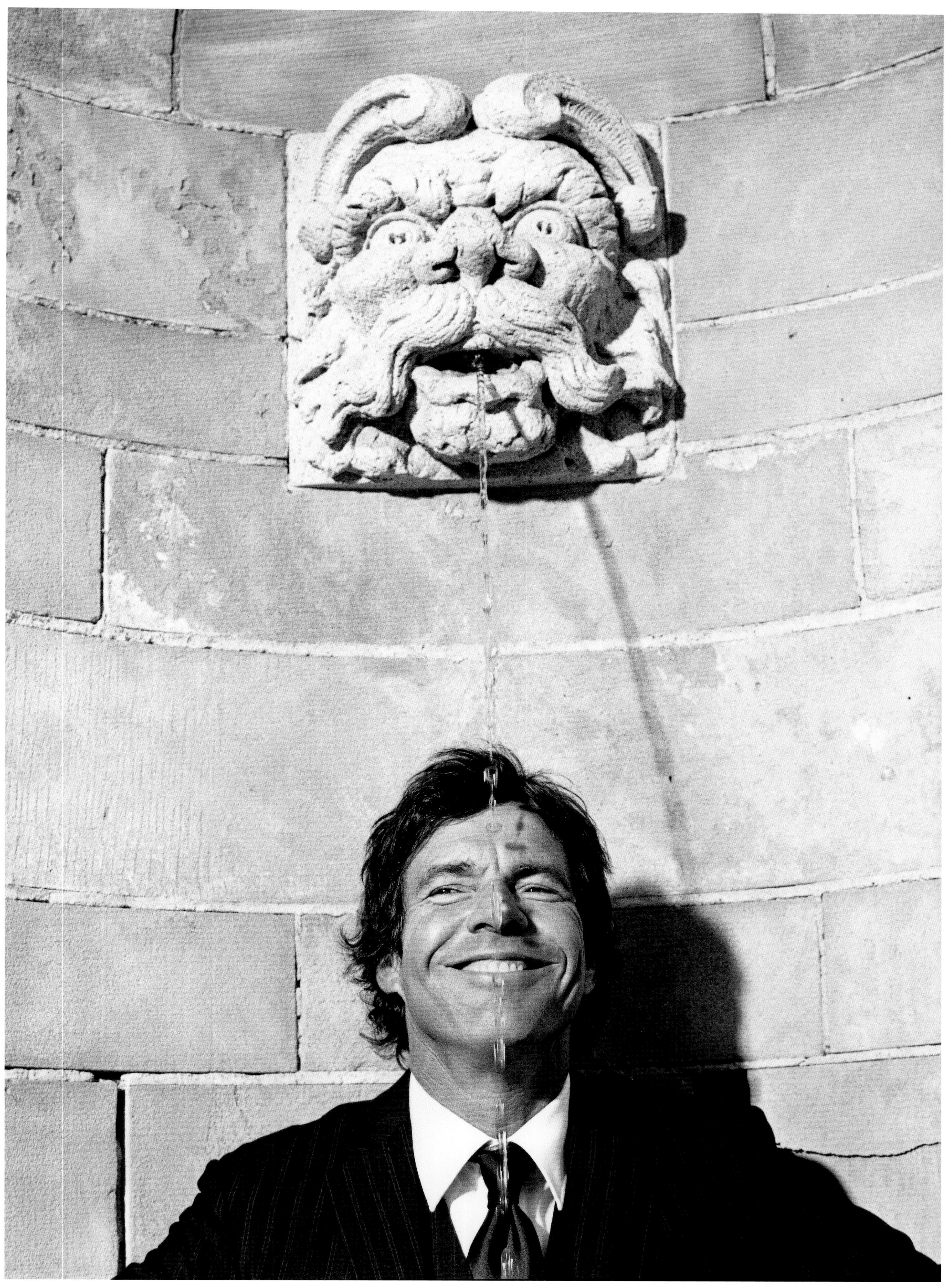

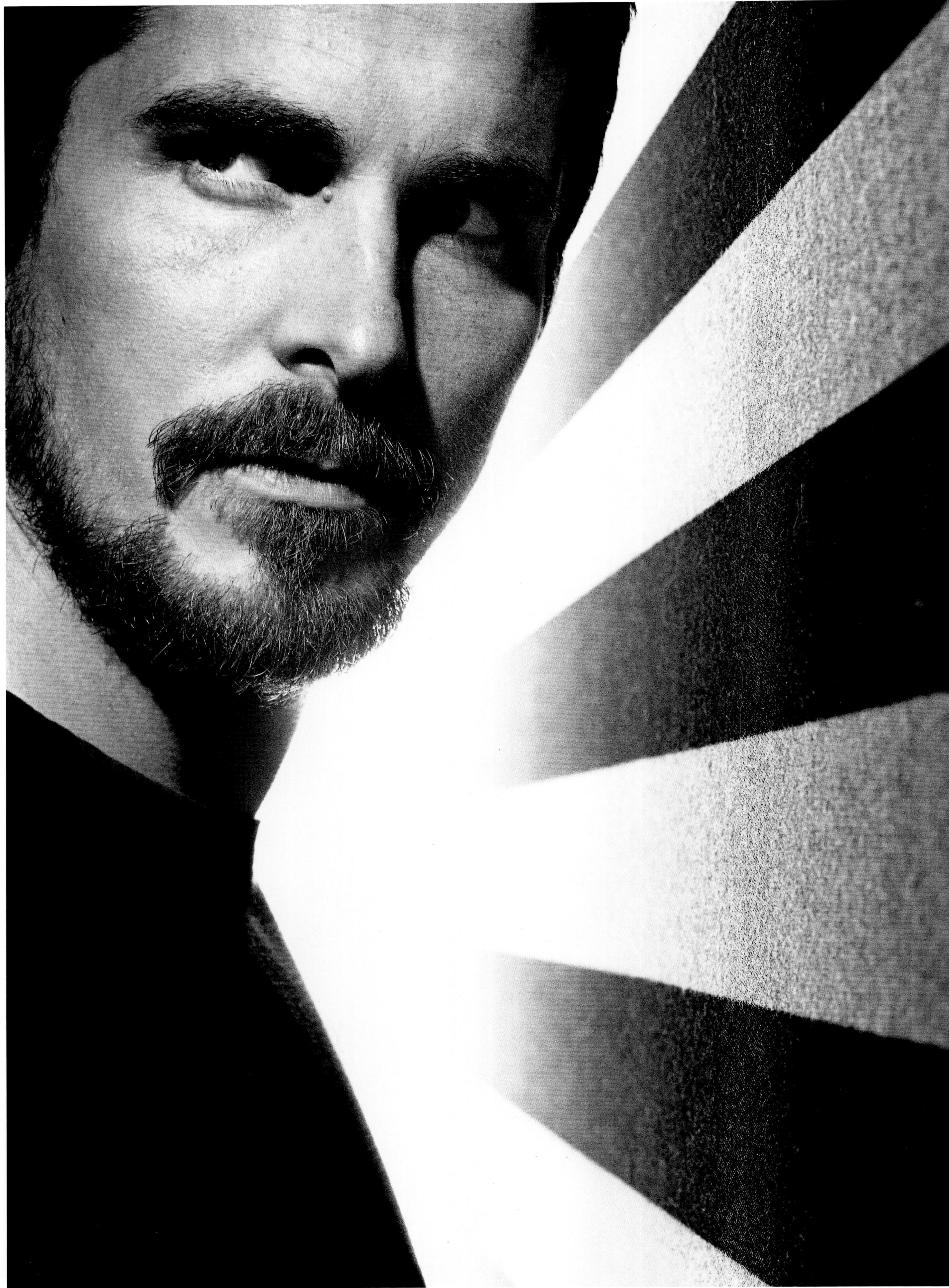

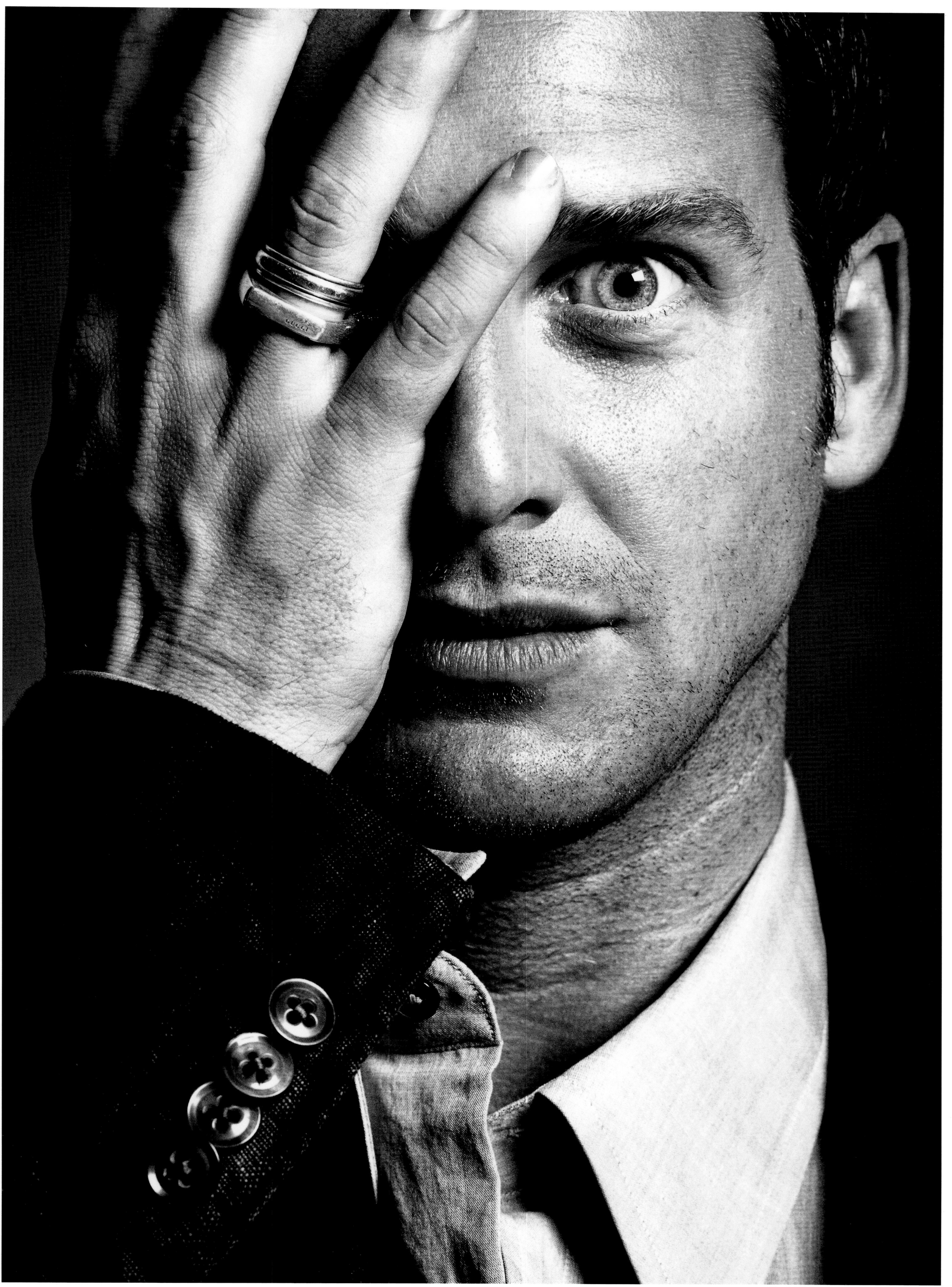

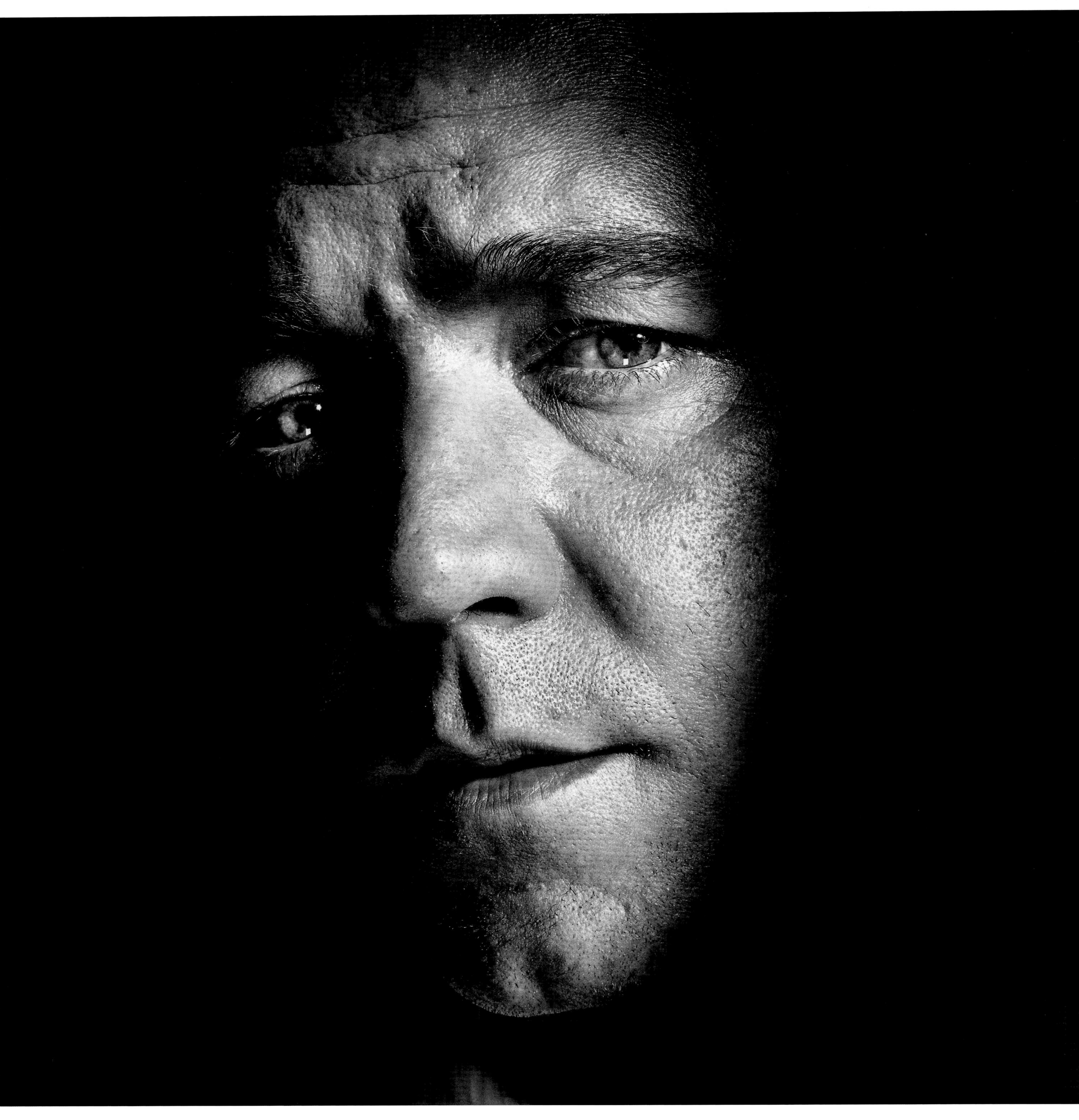

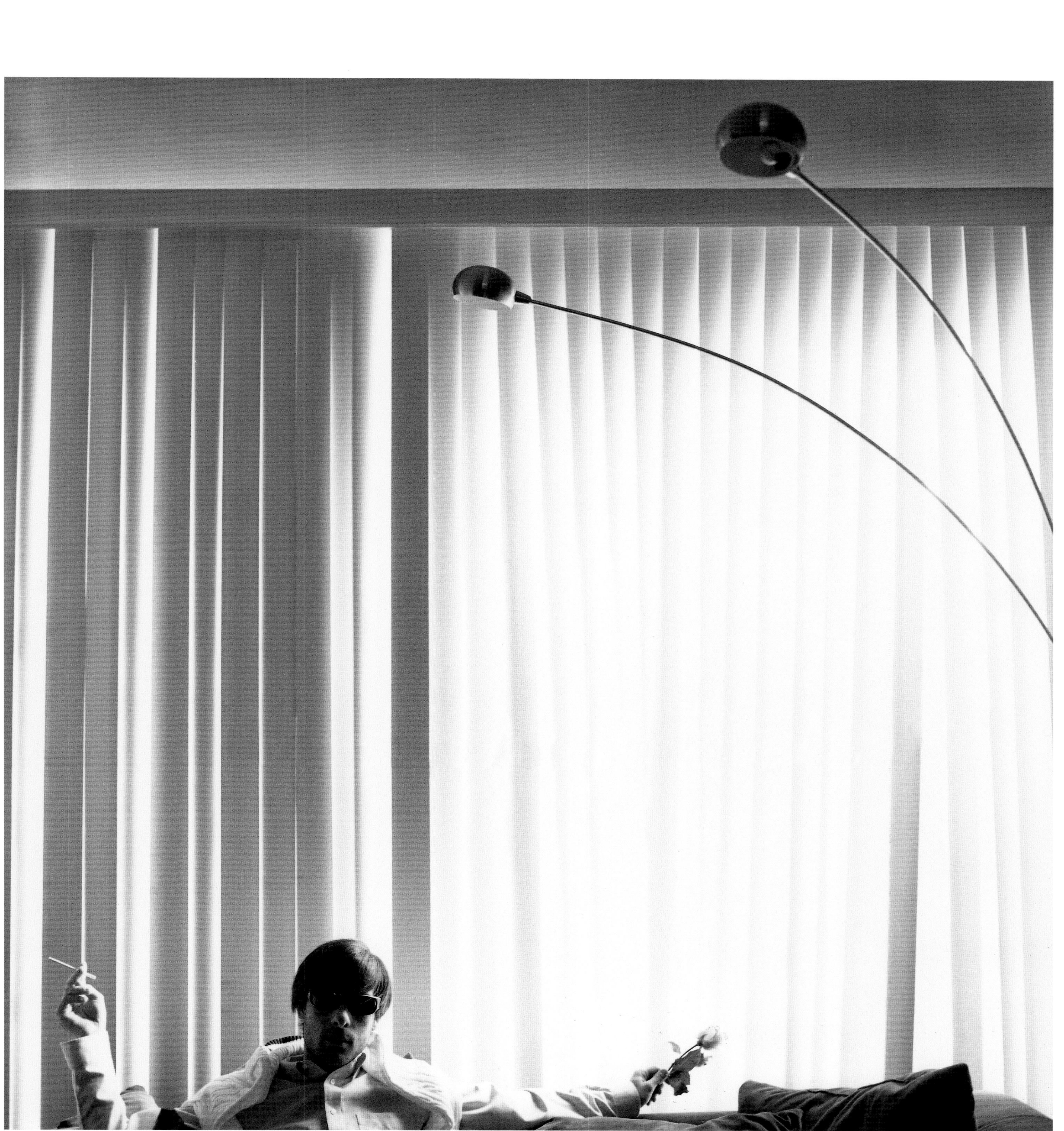

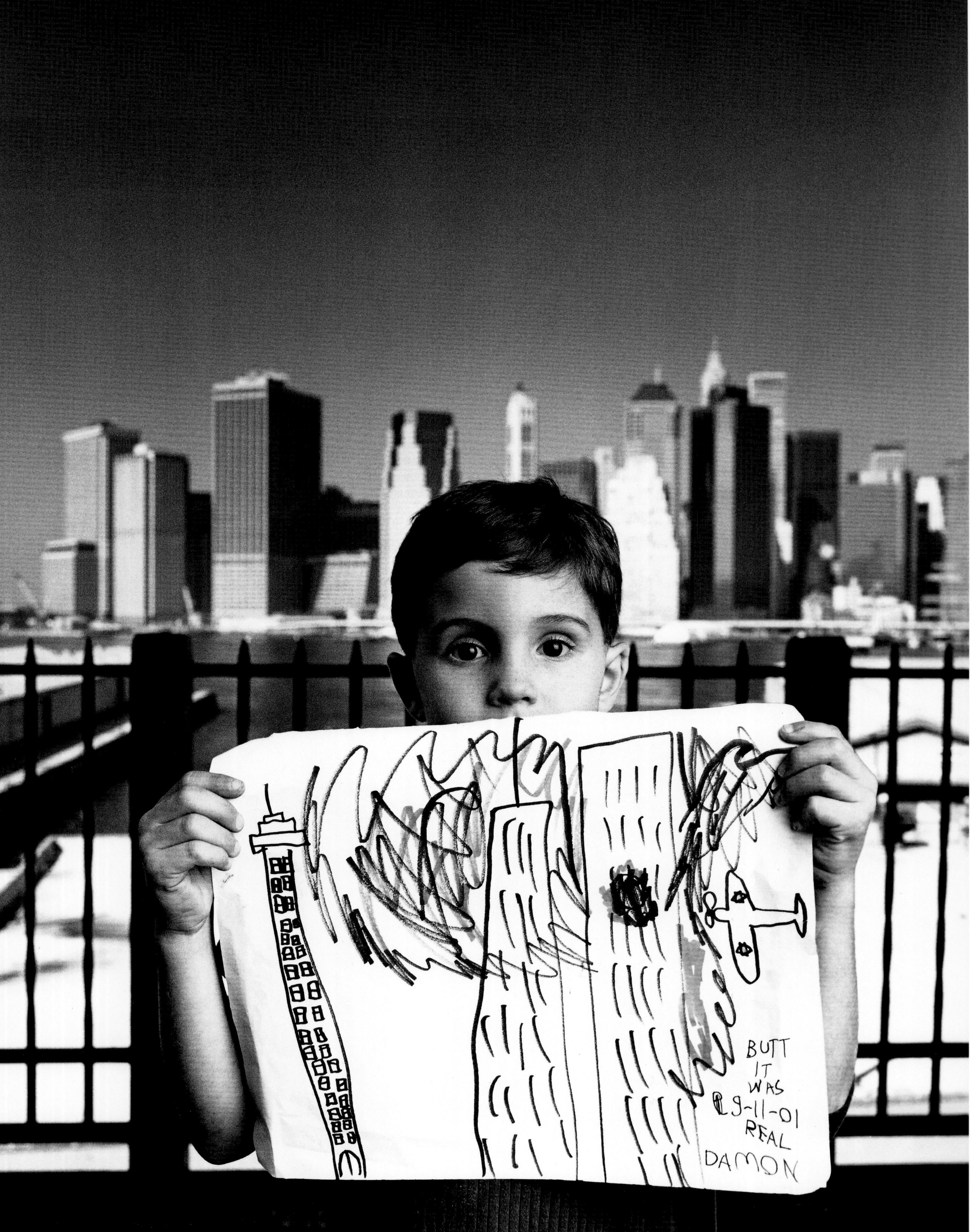
BUTT
IT
WAS
9-11-01
REAL
DAMON

PORTRAITS ON PREVIOUS PAGES

LISA BEAMER & FAMILY

CONDOLEEZZA RICE
ALICIA KEYS

ASIA ARGENTO
DUSTIN HOFFMAN

TIM ROBBINS
DENNIS QUAID

CHRISTIAN BALE
JOSH LUCAS

RUSSELL CROWE
JASON SCHWARTZMAN

DAMON SMITH

GOOD MORNING... FINE PAIR OF SIDEBURNS YOU GOT THERE NIGEL.

GREETING BY THE LEADER OF THE FREE WORLD, PRESIDENT GEORGE W. BUSH.

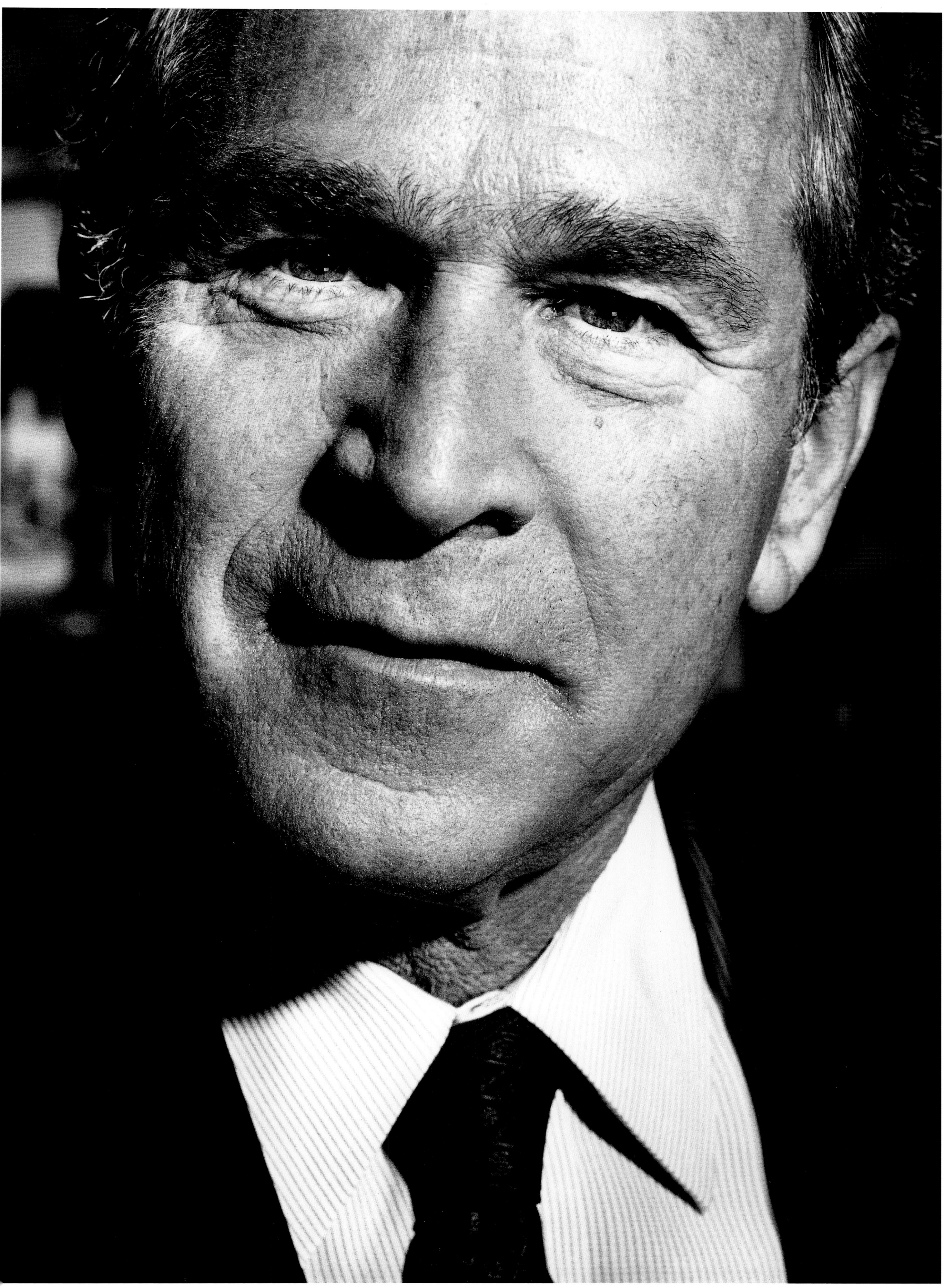

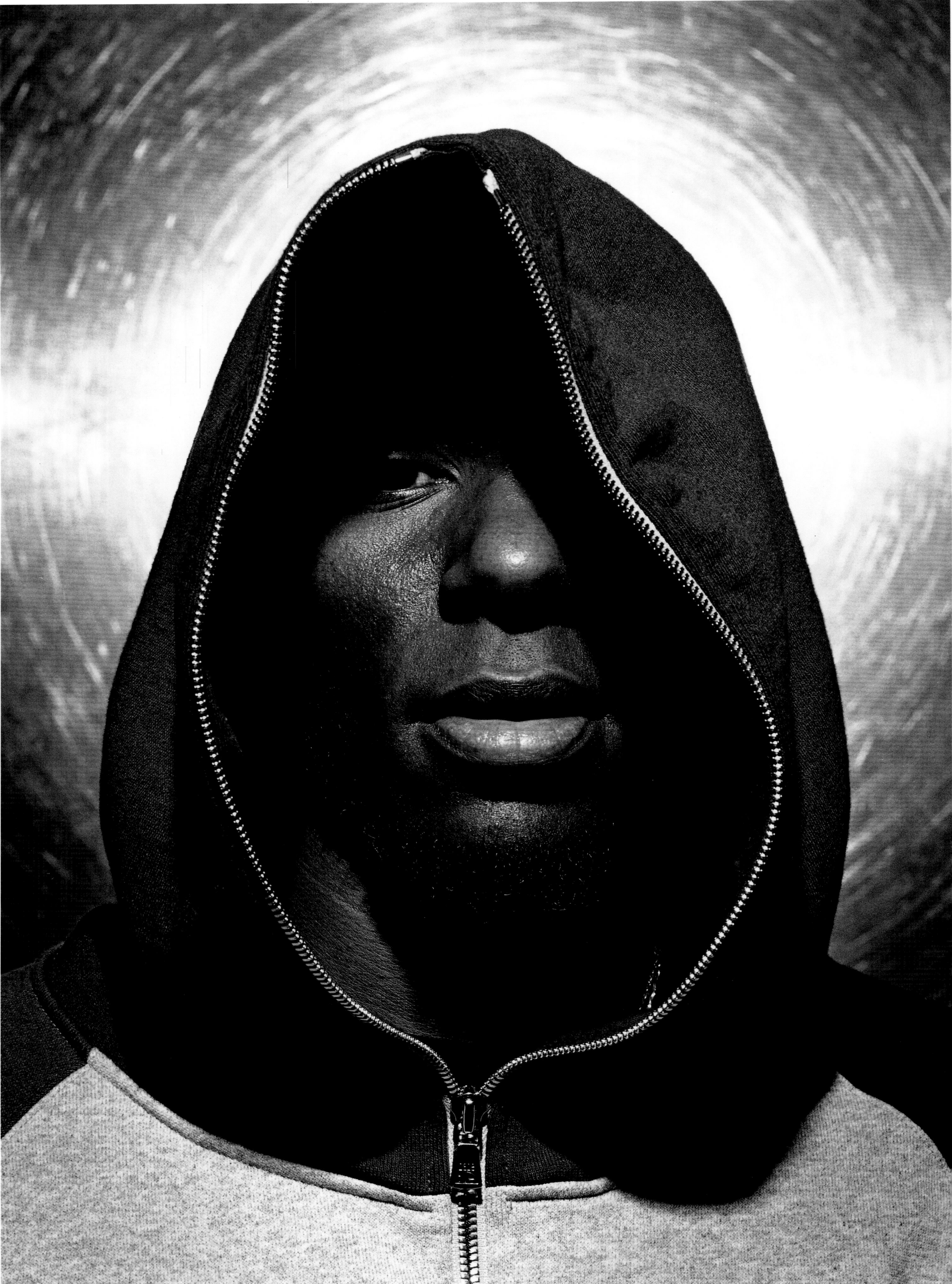

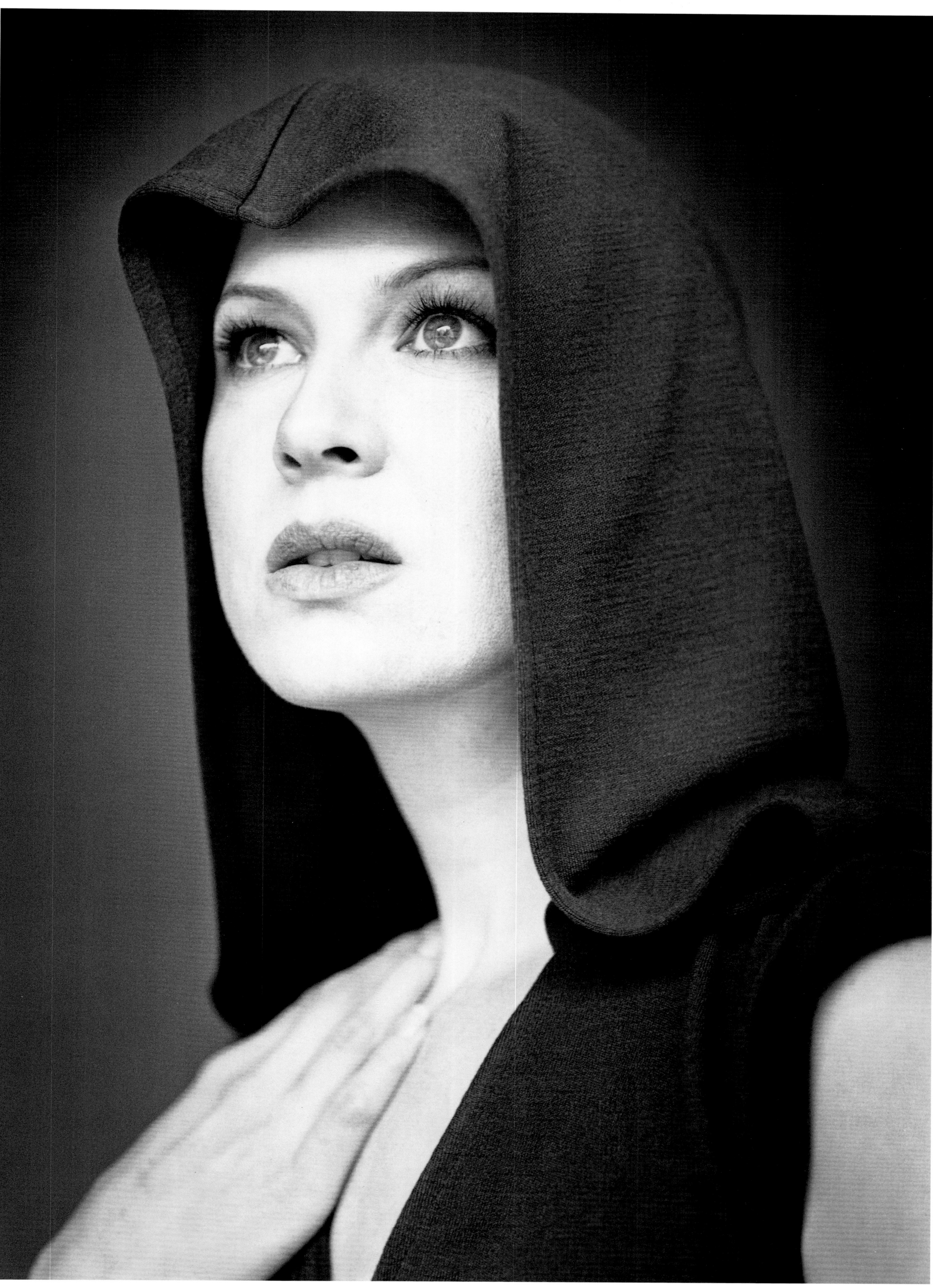

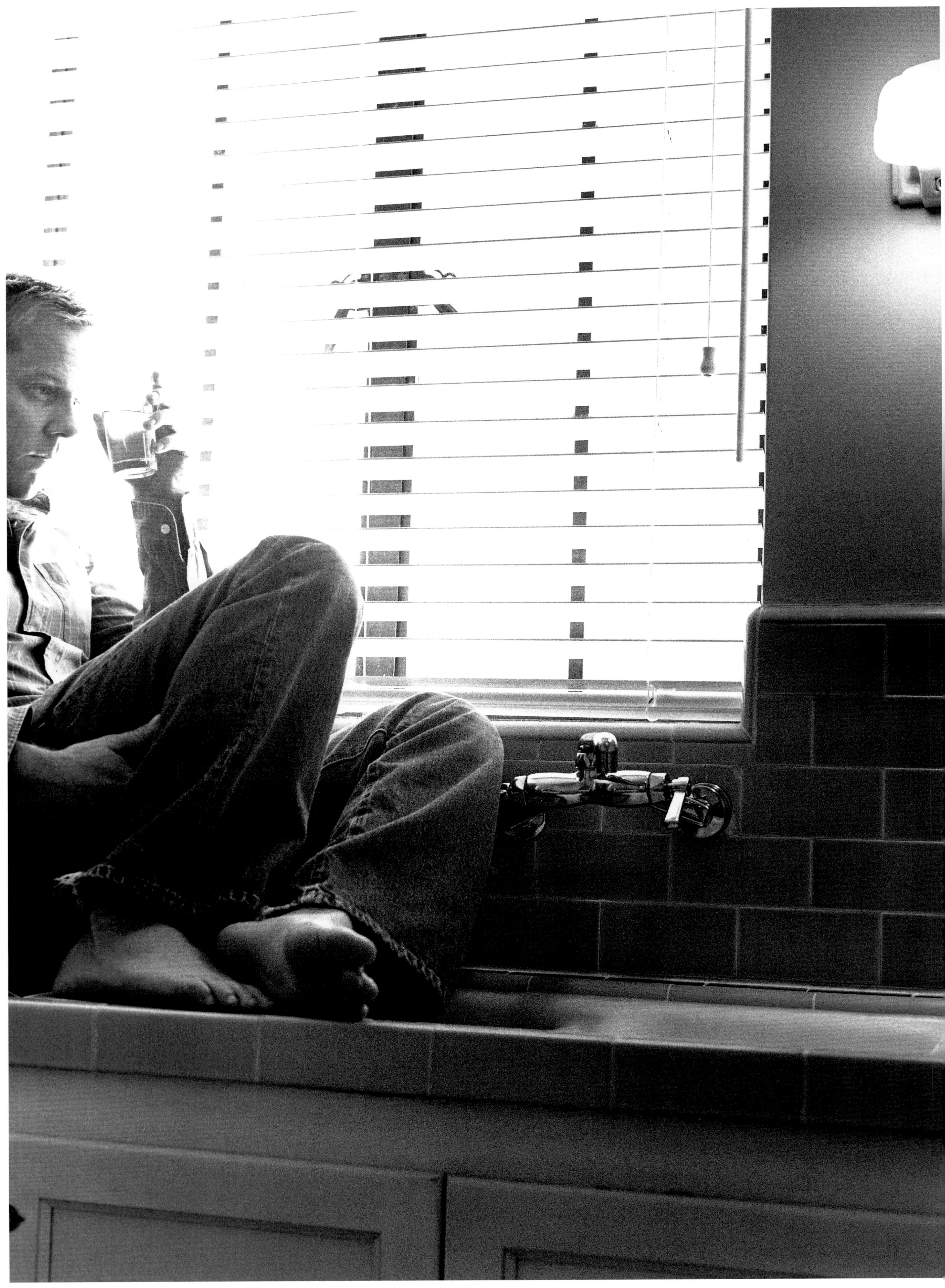

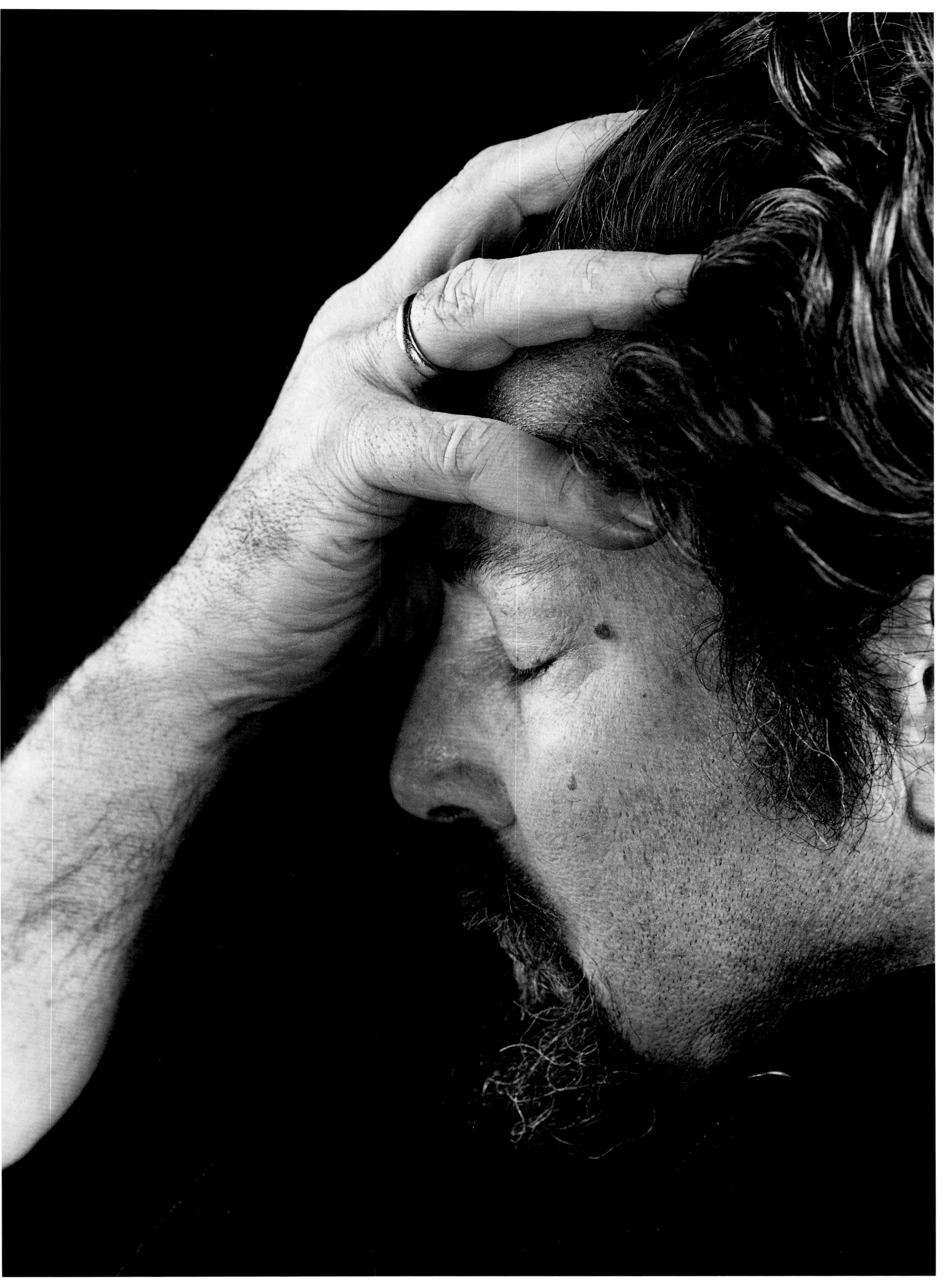

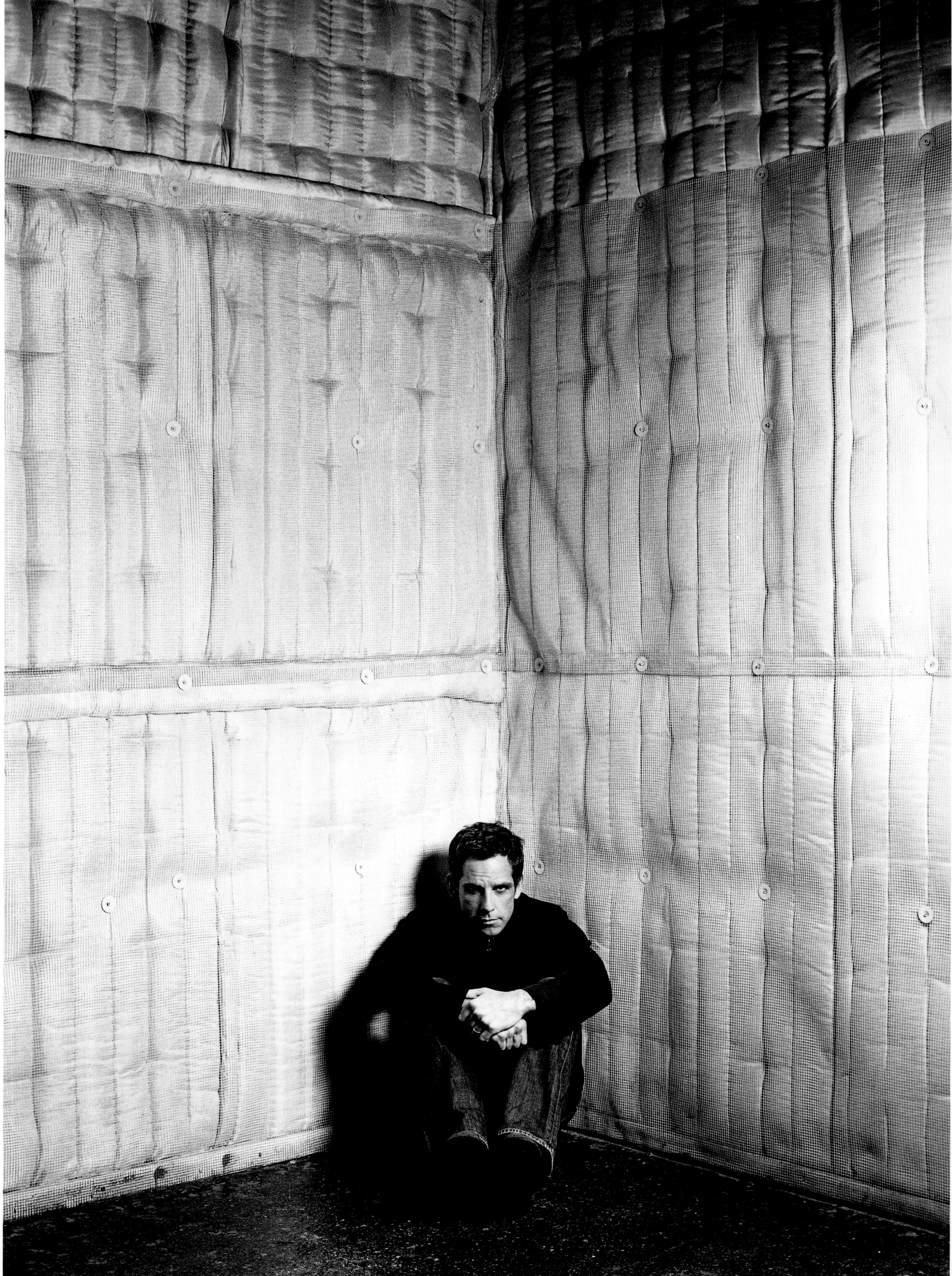

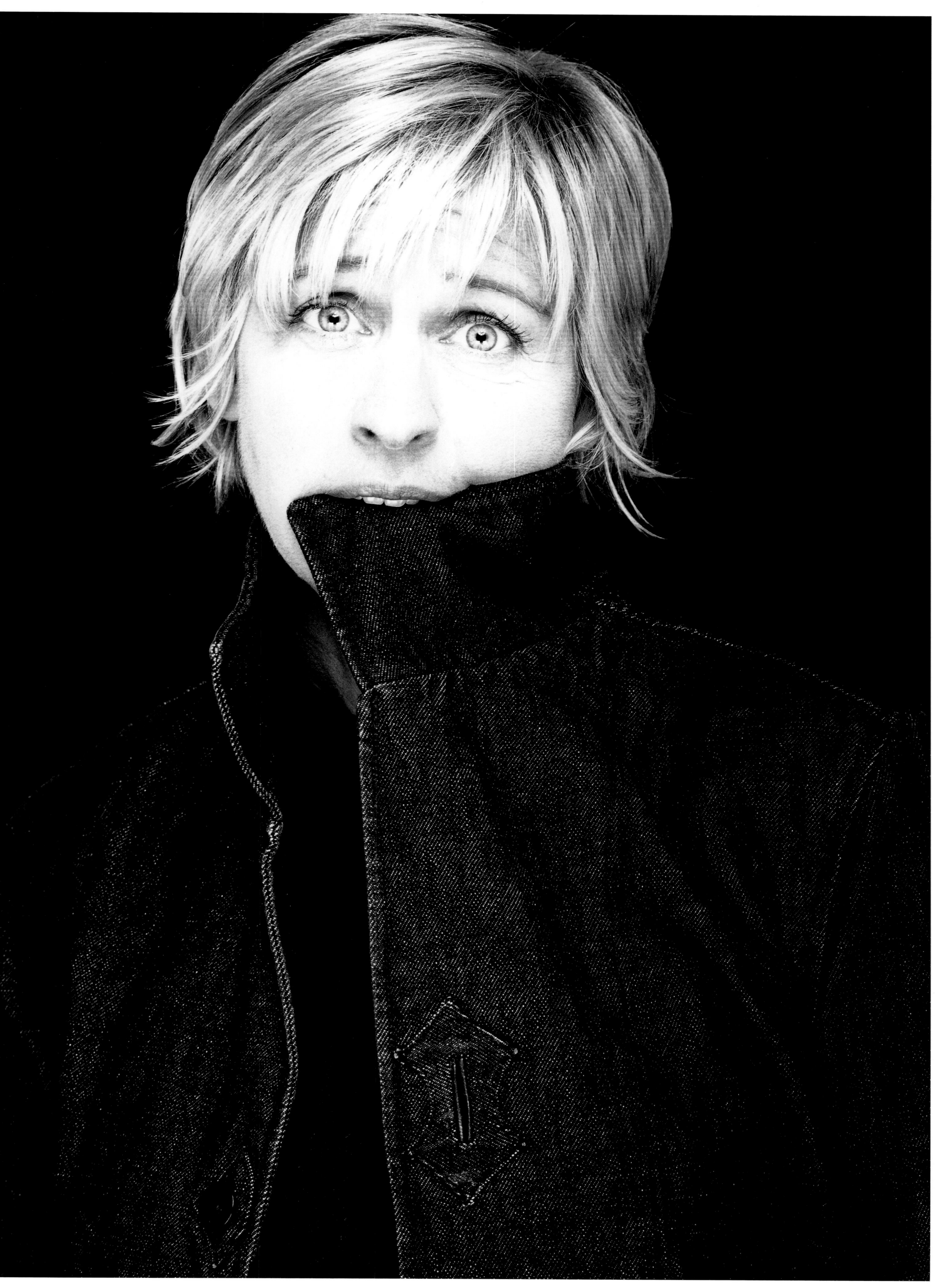

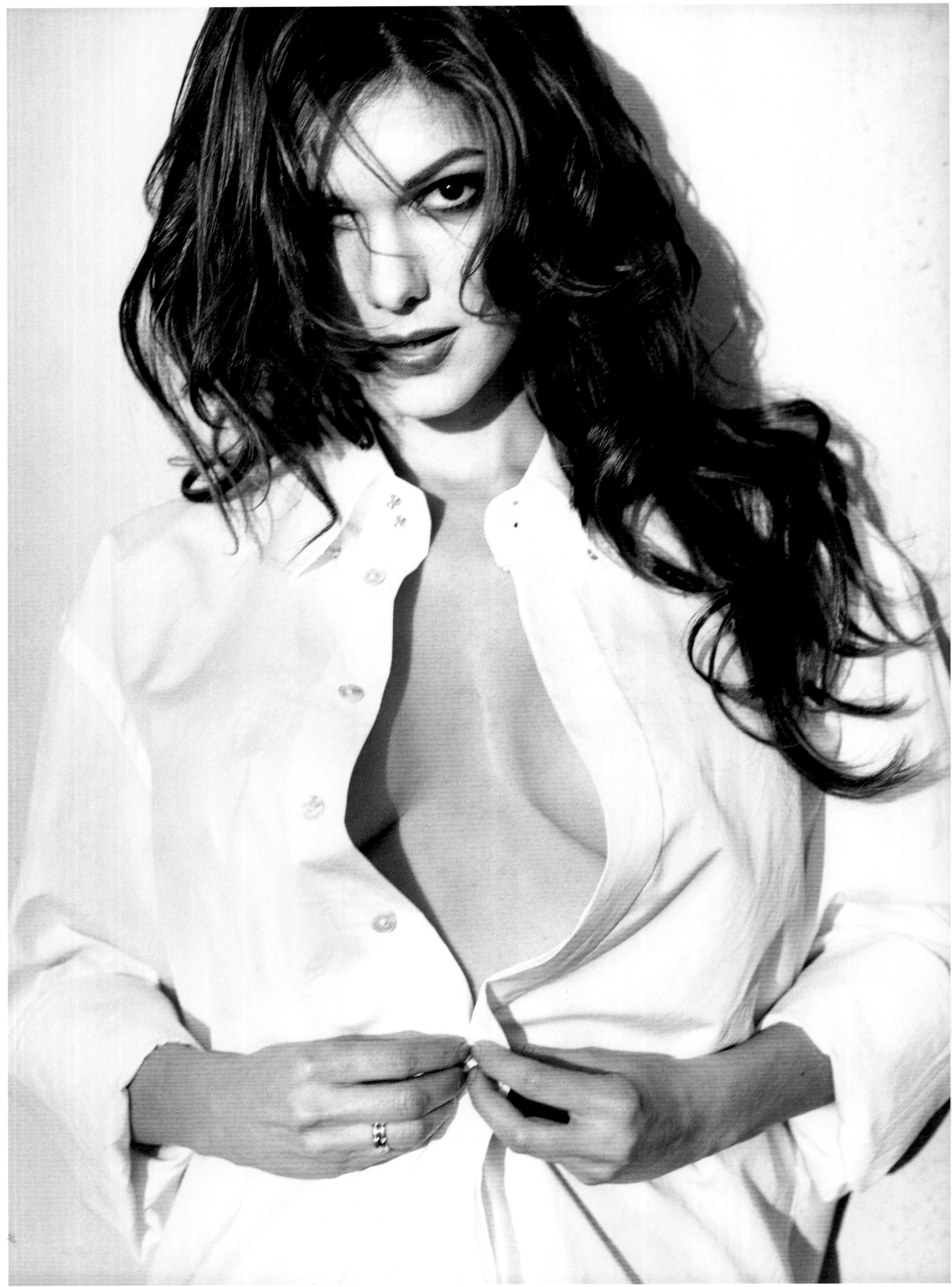

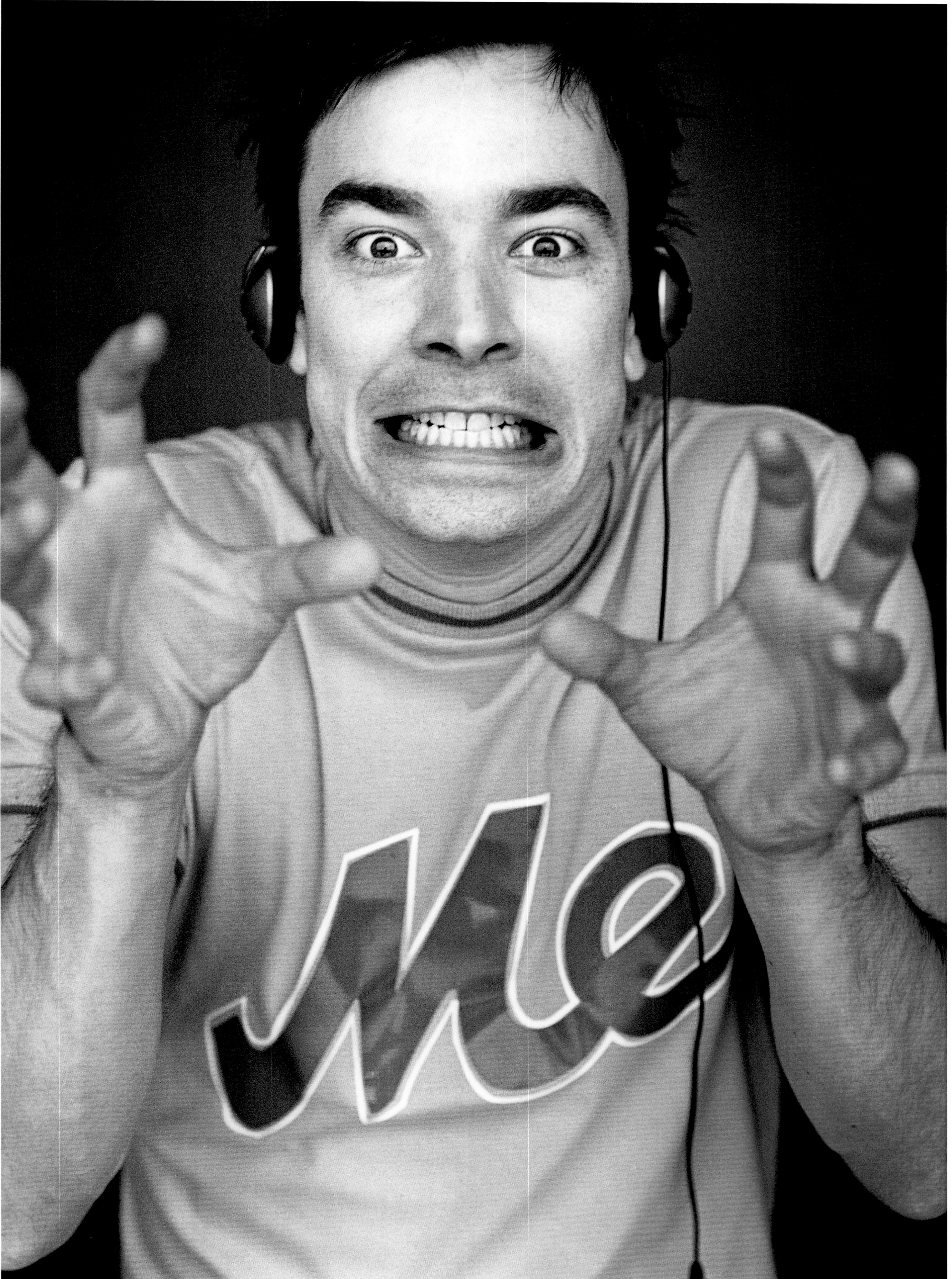
Me

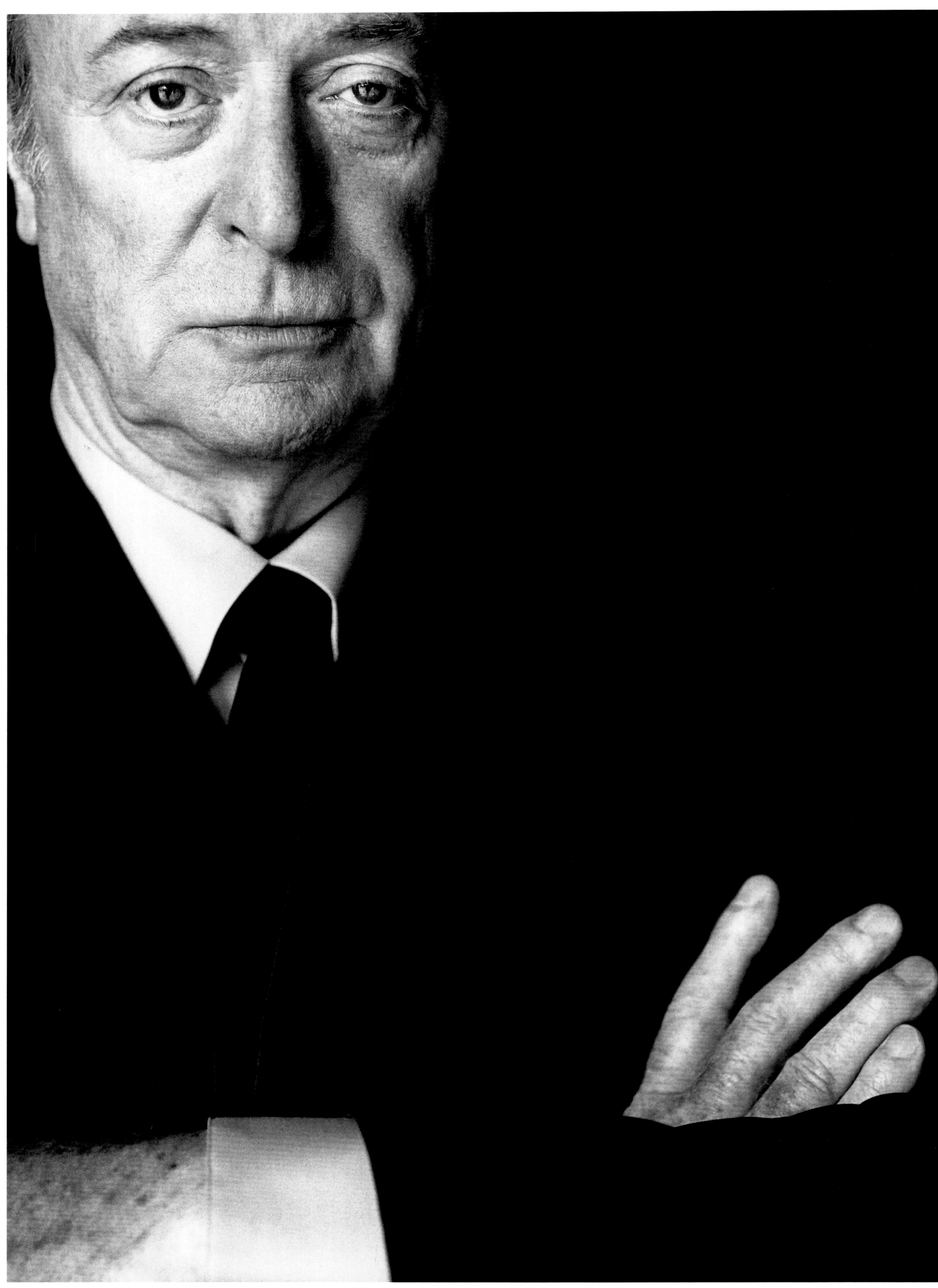

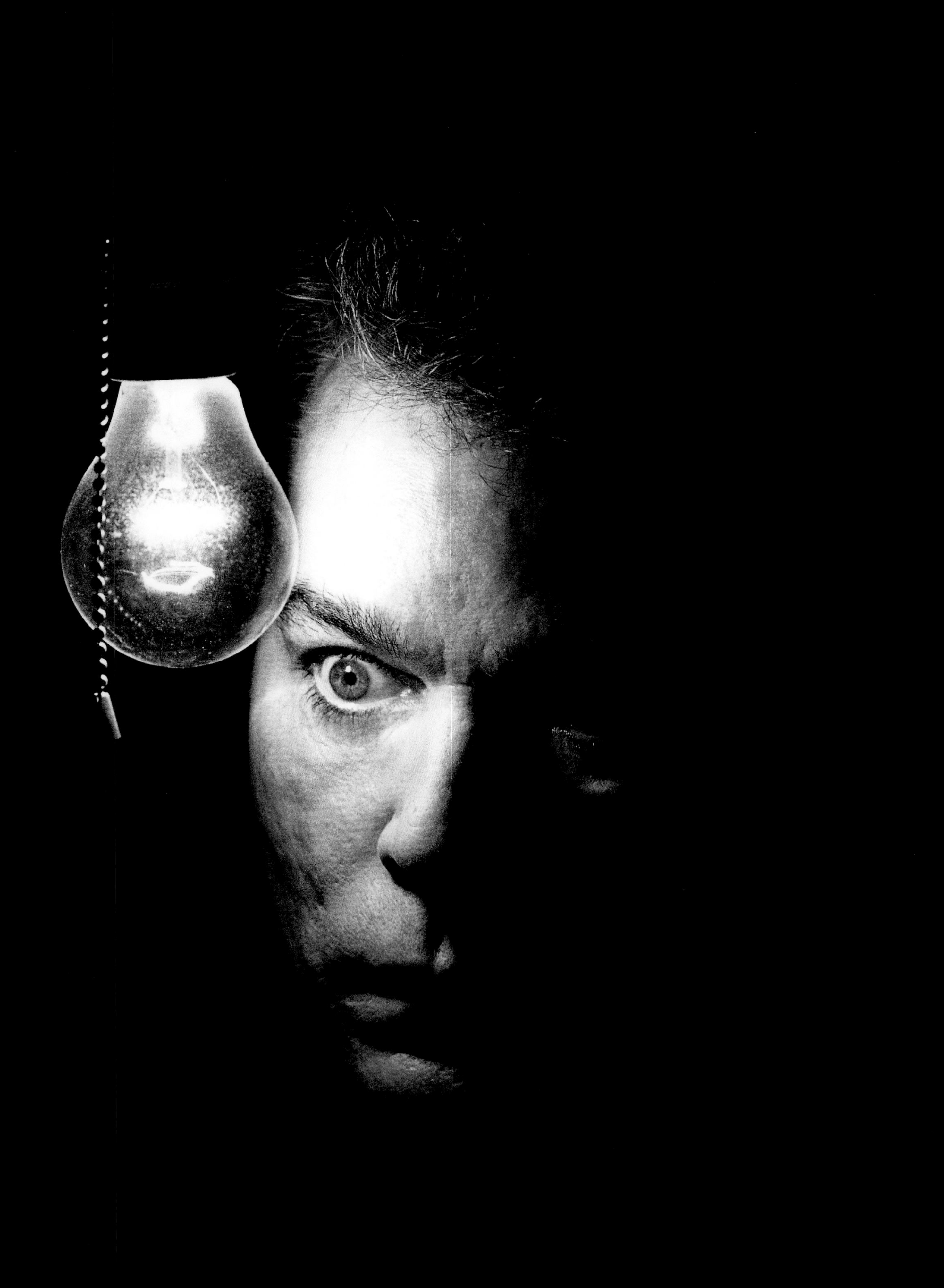

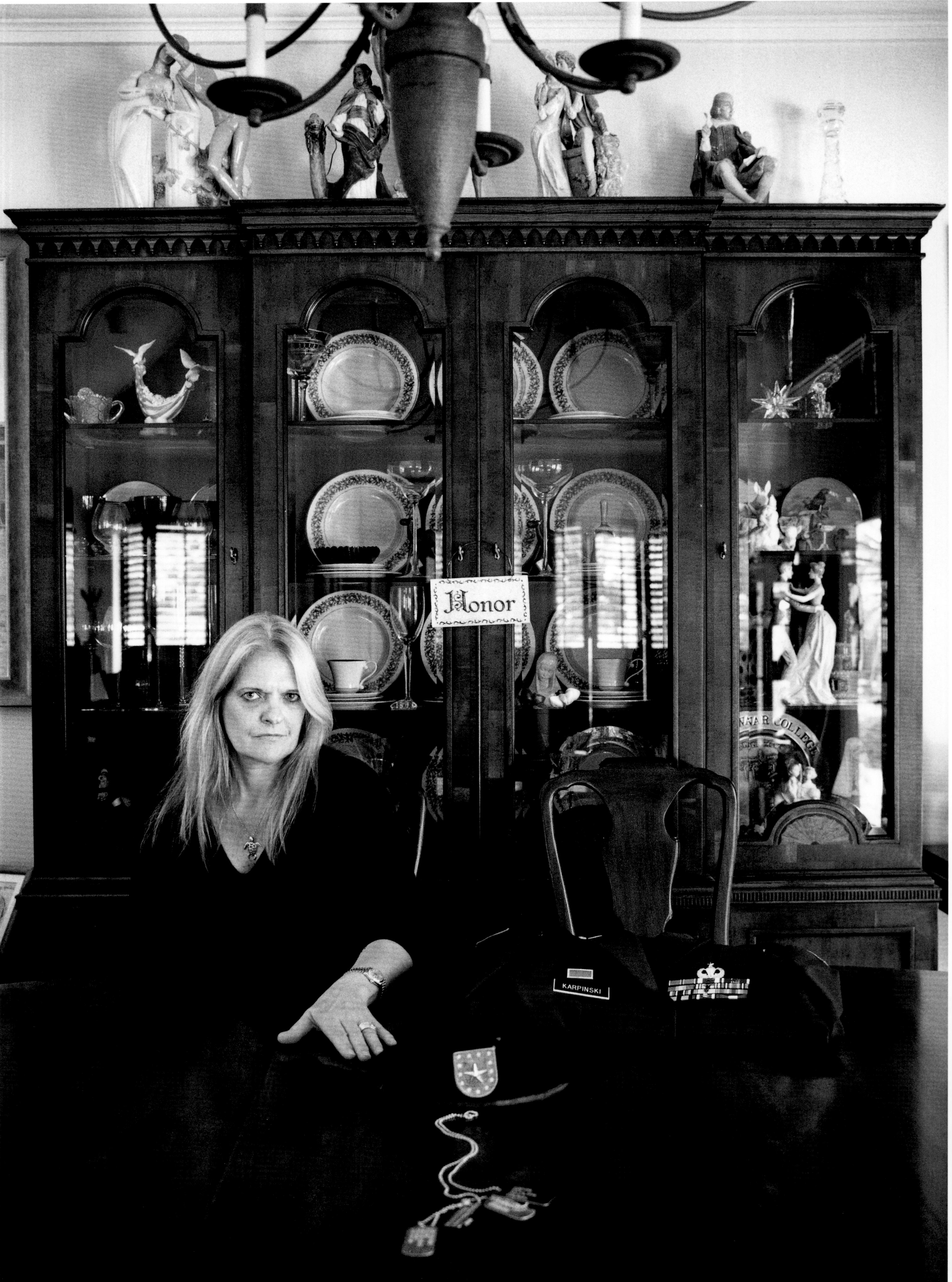
Honor
KARPINSKI

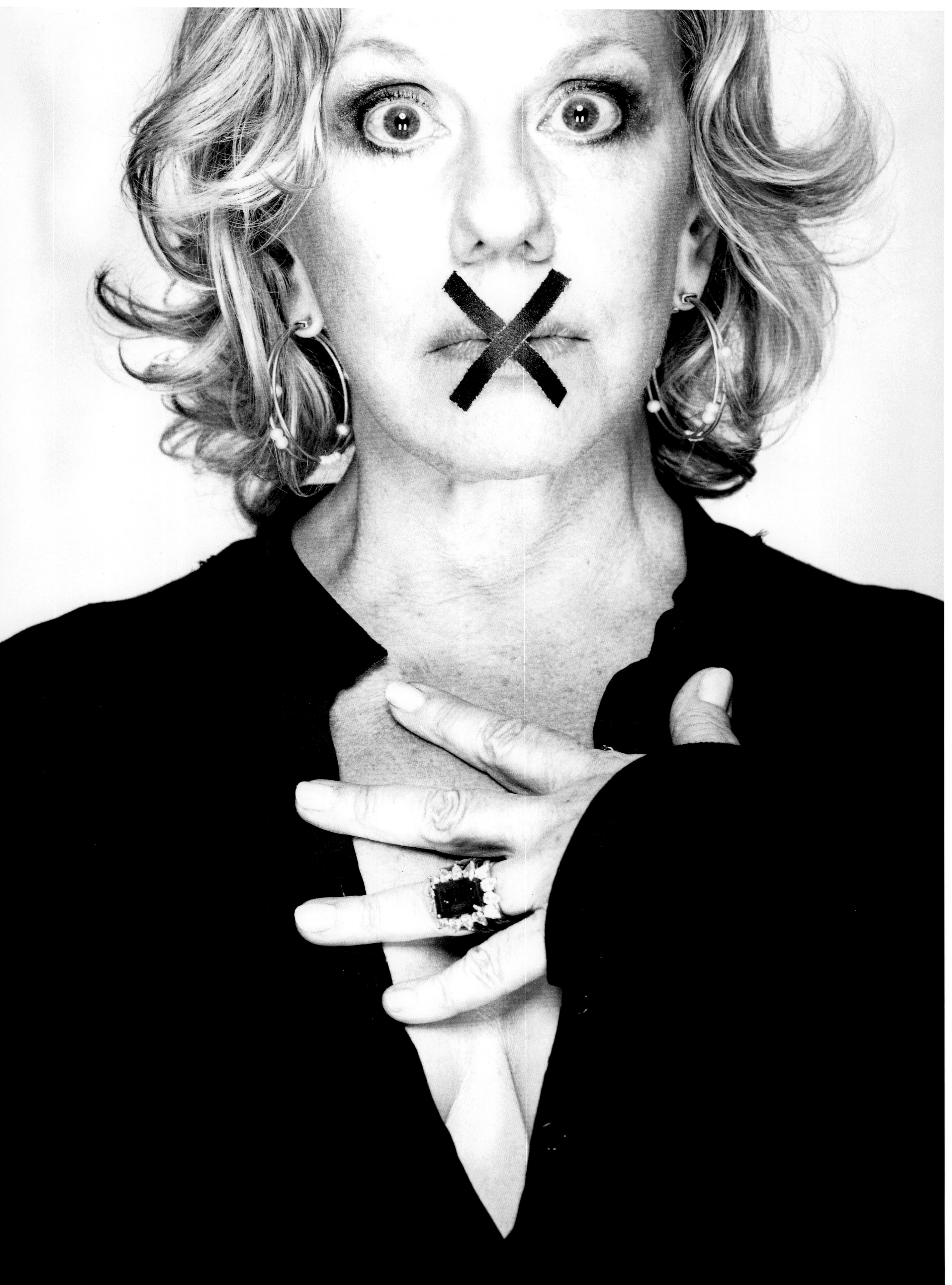

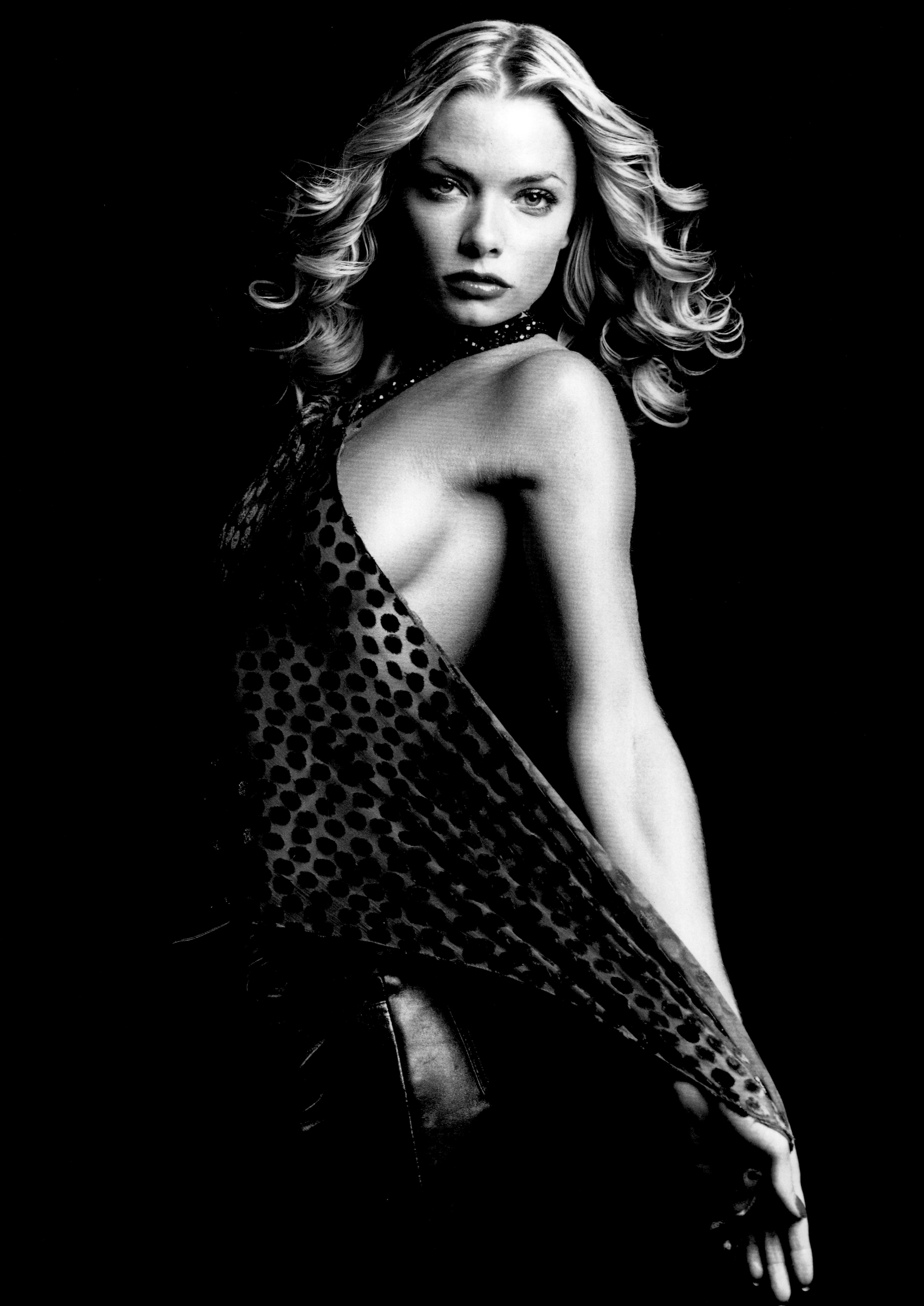

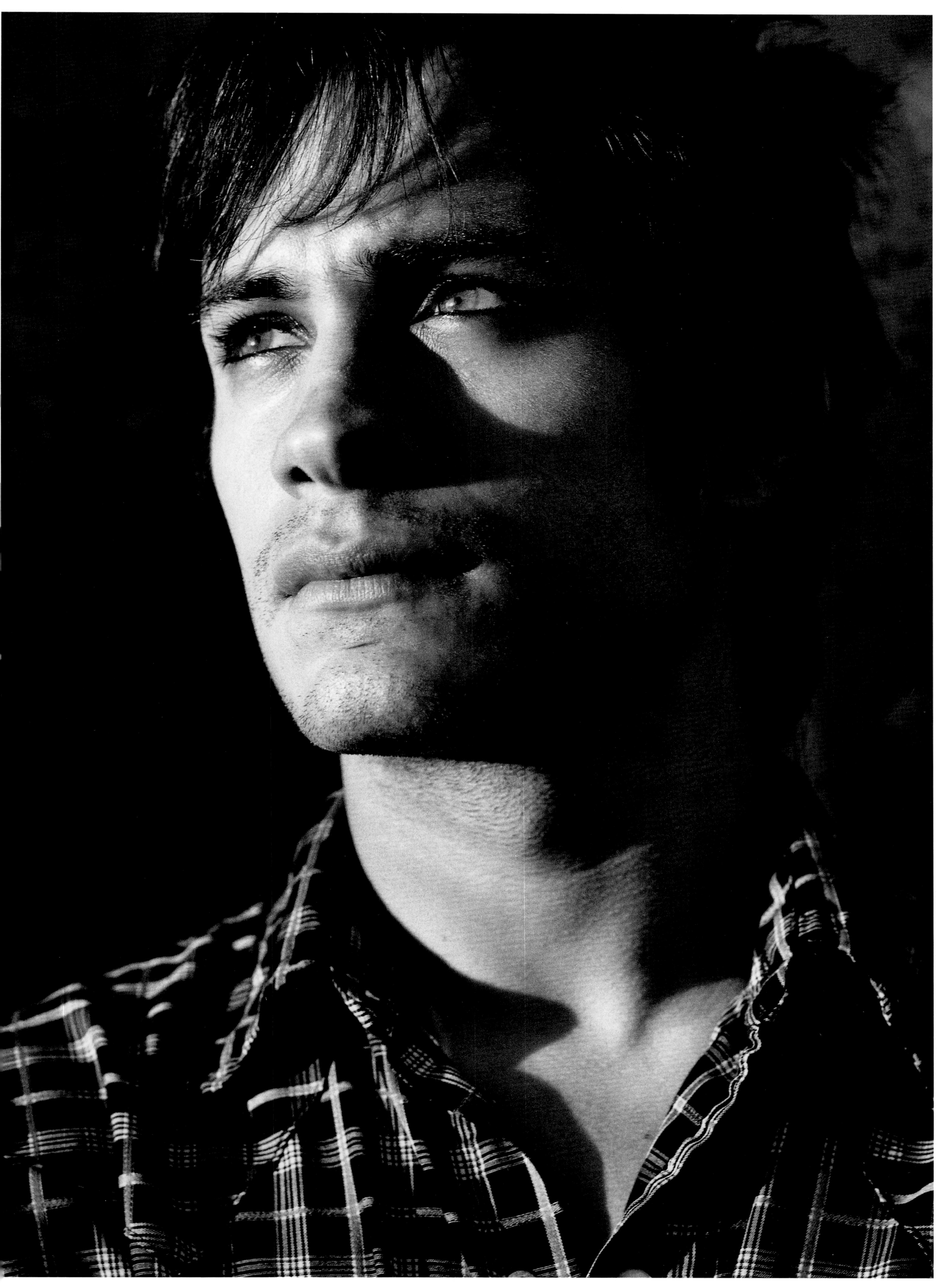

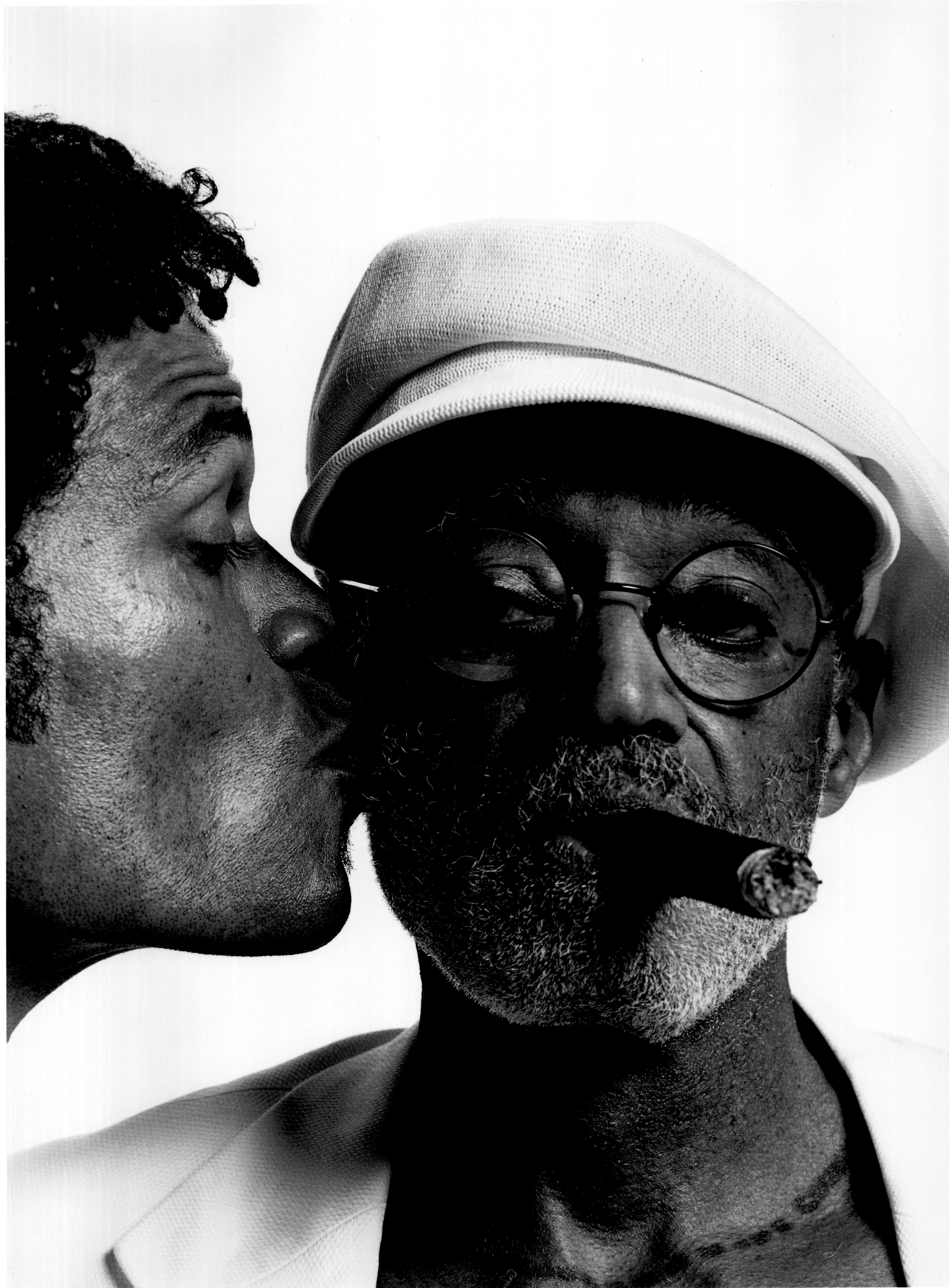

PORTRAITS ON PREVIOUS PAGES

GEORGE W. BUSH

MOS DEF
RENÉE ZELLWEGER

KIEFER SUTHERLAND
JULIAN SCHNABEL

BEN STILLER
ELLEN DEGENERES

LAURA HARRING
JIMMY FALLON

MICHAEL CAINE
RAY LIOTTA

BRIGADIER GENERAL JANIS KARPINSKI
ERICA JONG

JAIME PRESSLY
GAEL GARCIA BERNAL

MARIO & MELVIN VAN PEEBLES

...MMM, SOMETHING FUNNY? (LAUGHS OUT LOUD)... JERRY LEWIS!

CHRISTOPHER WALKEN

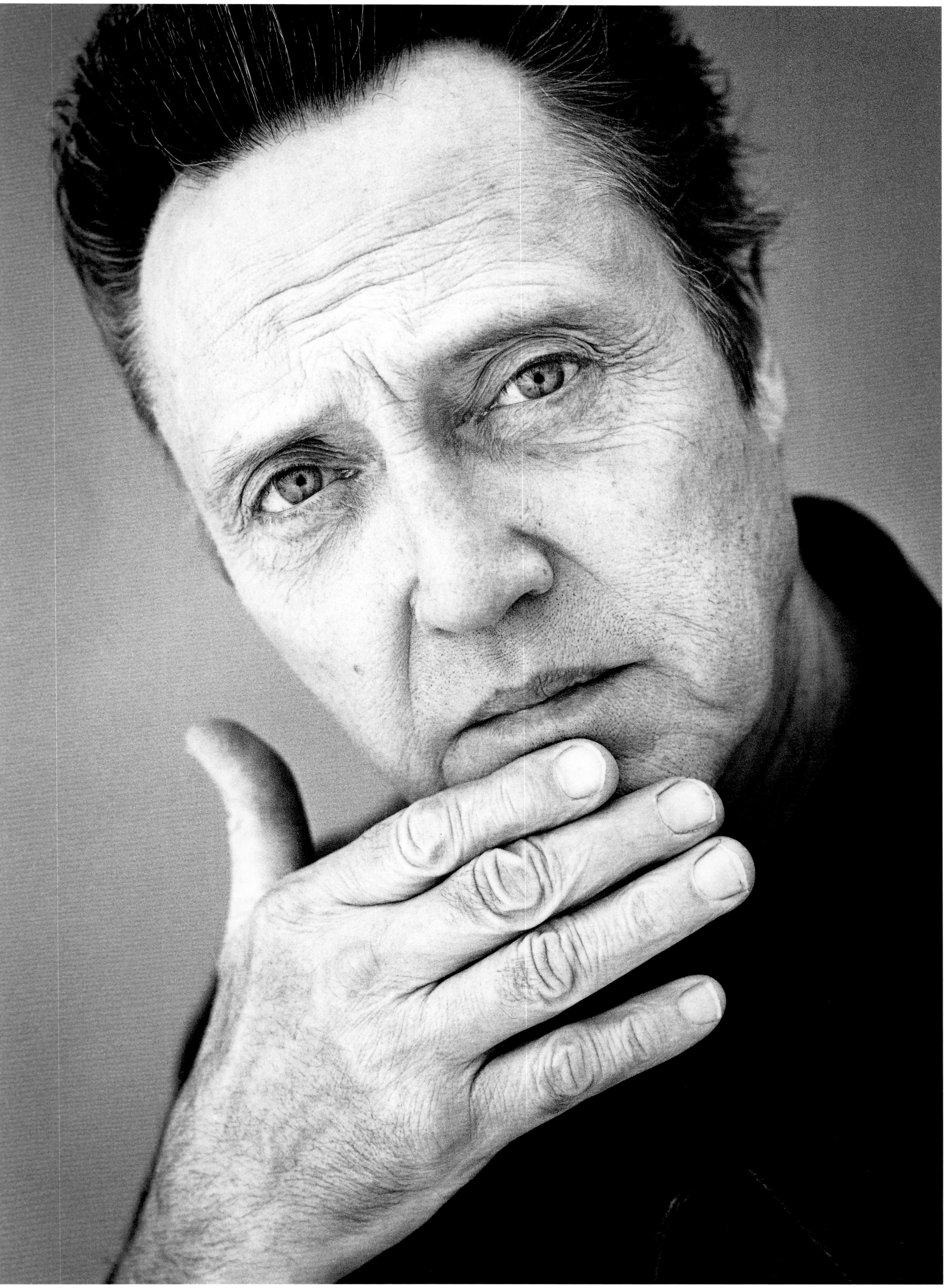

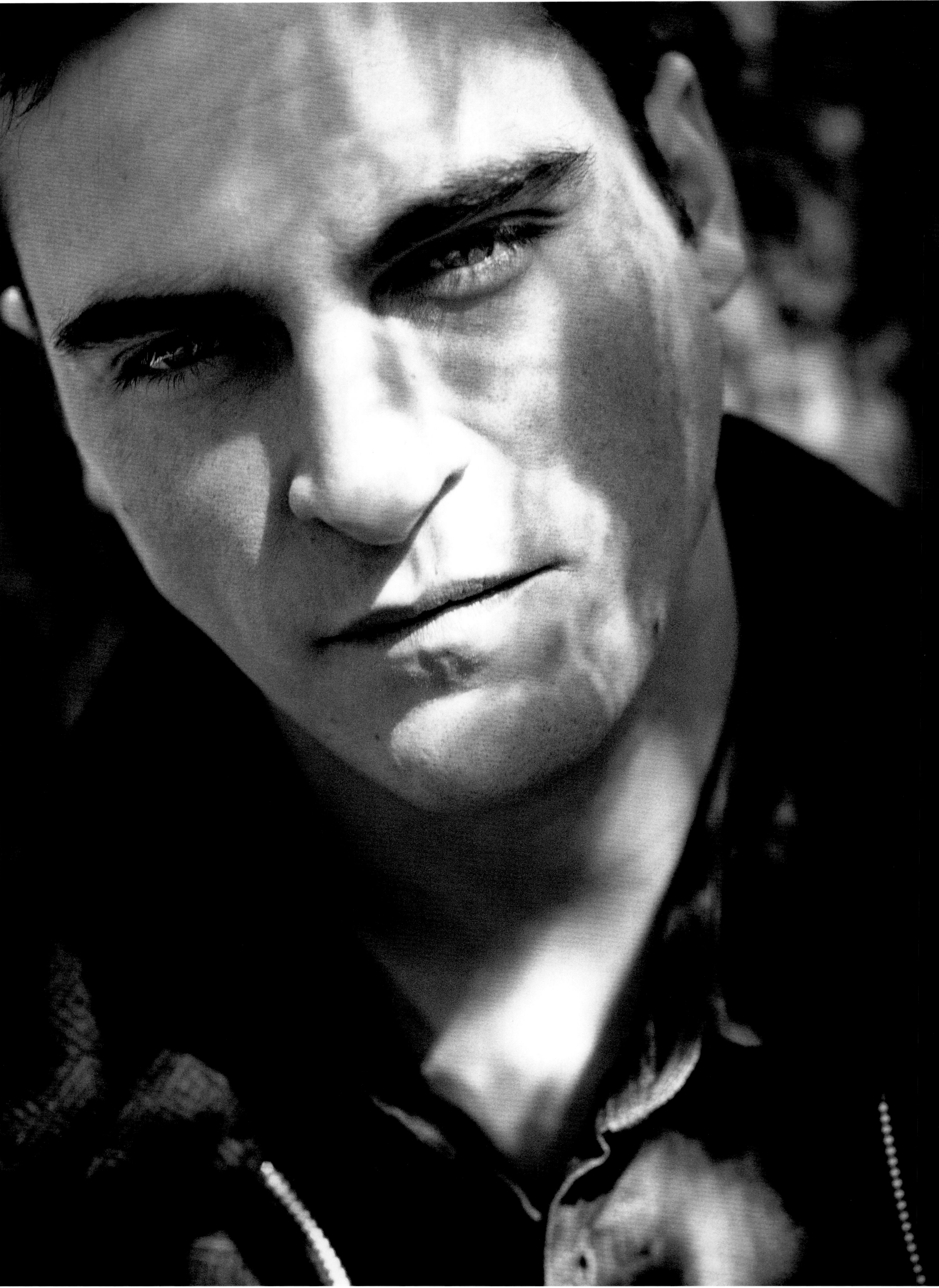

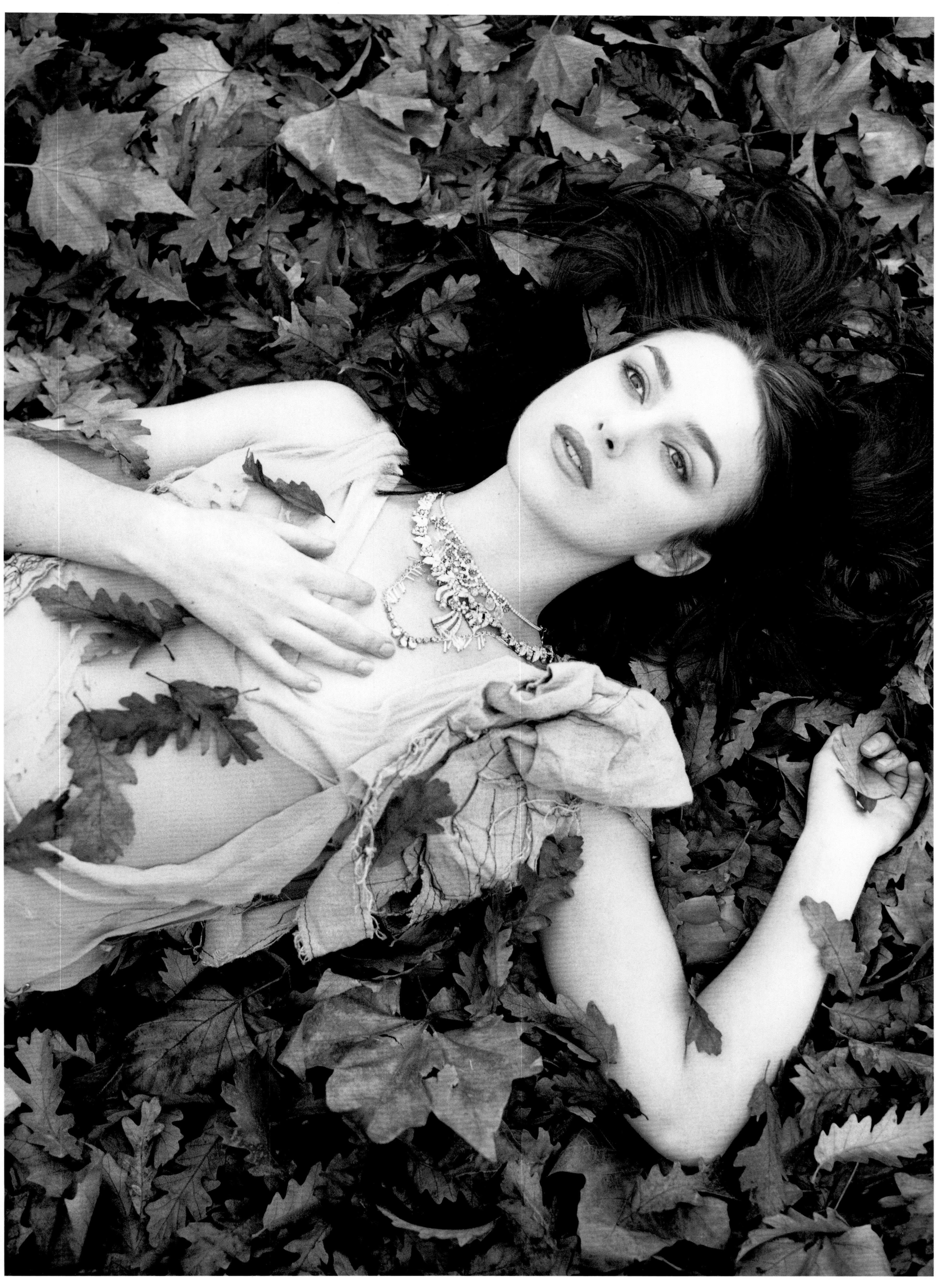

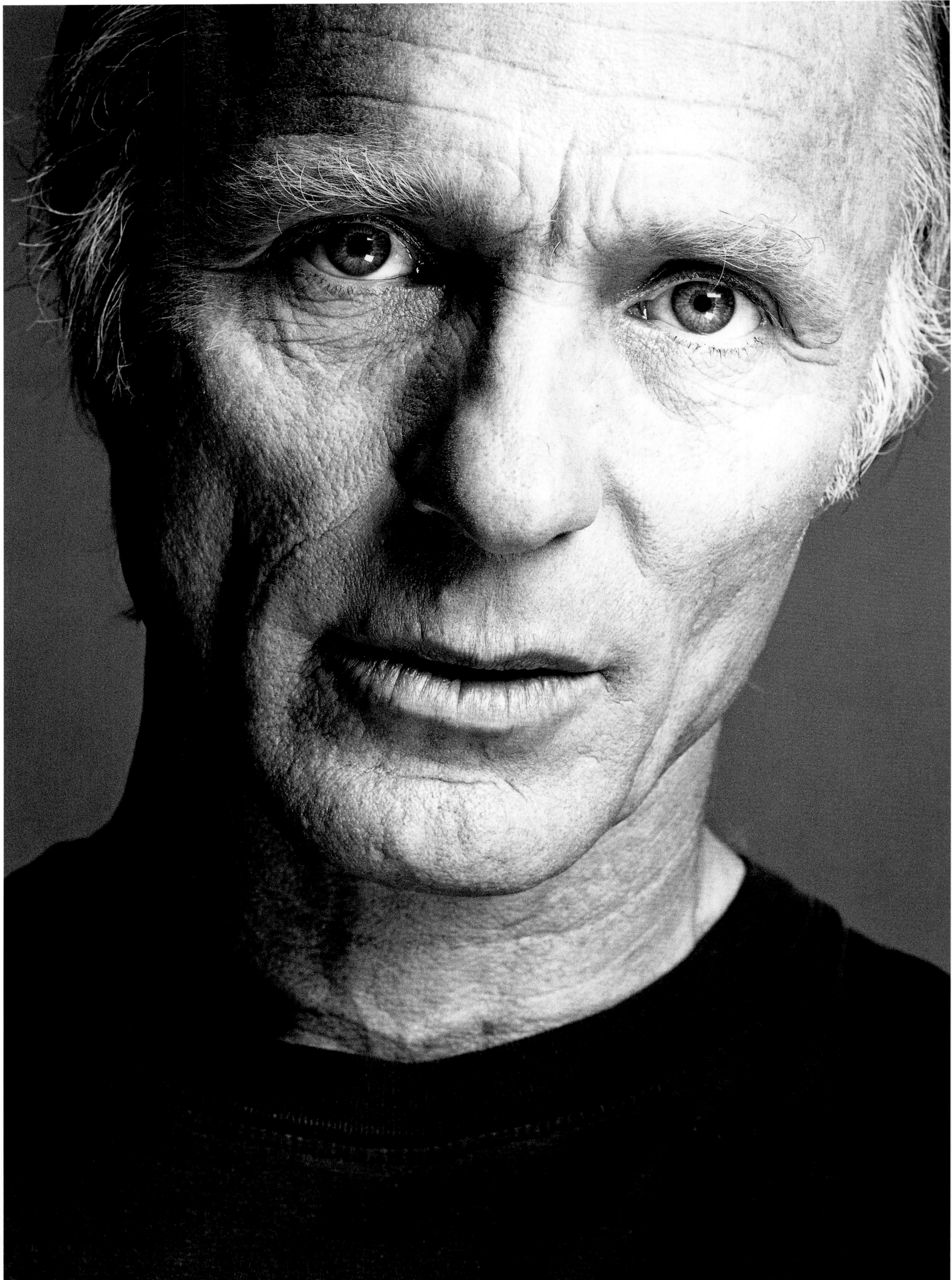

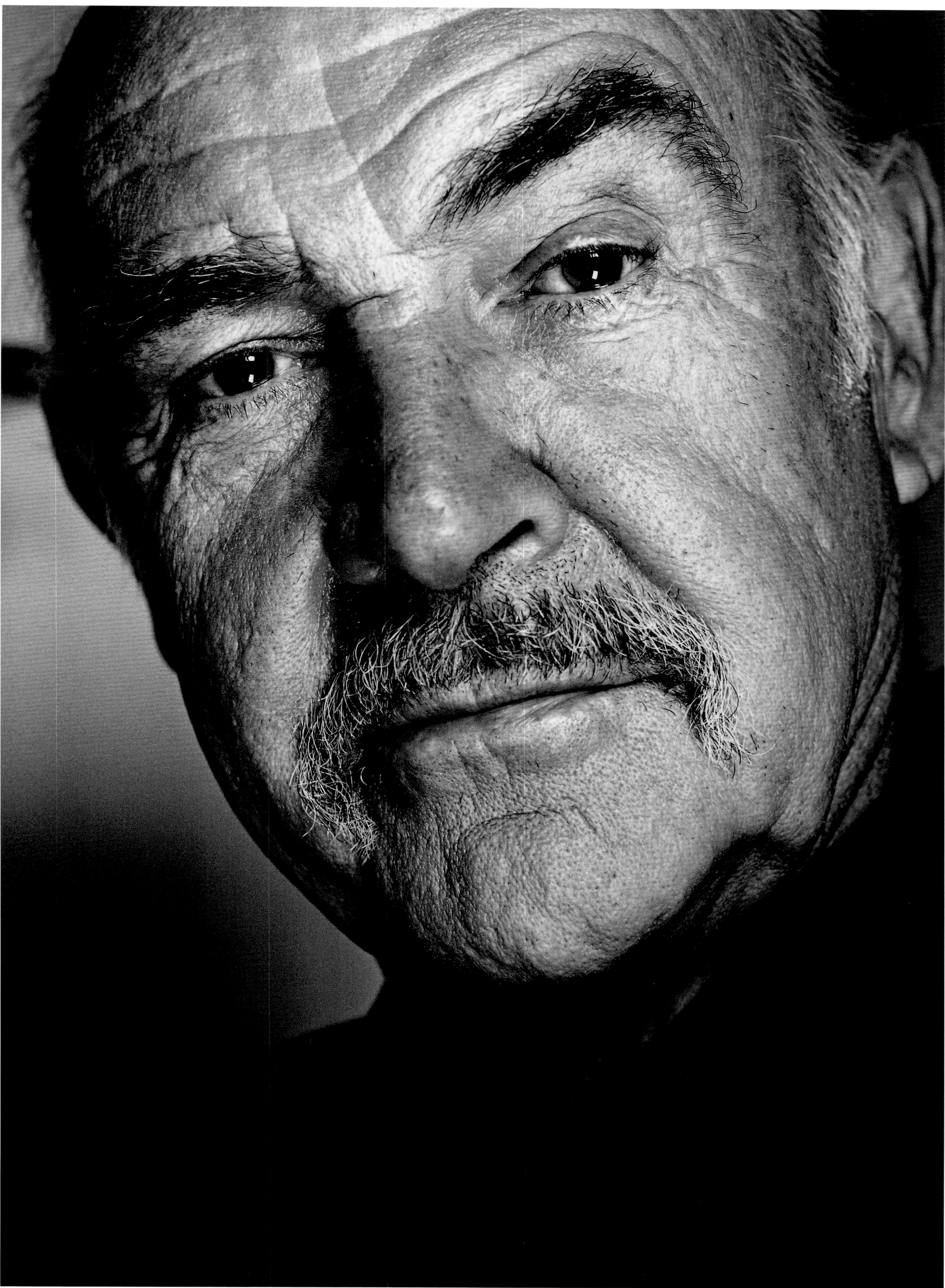

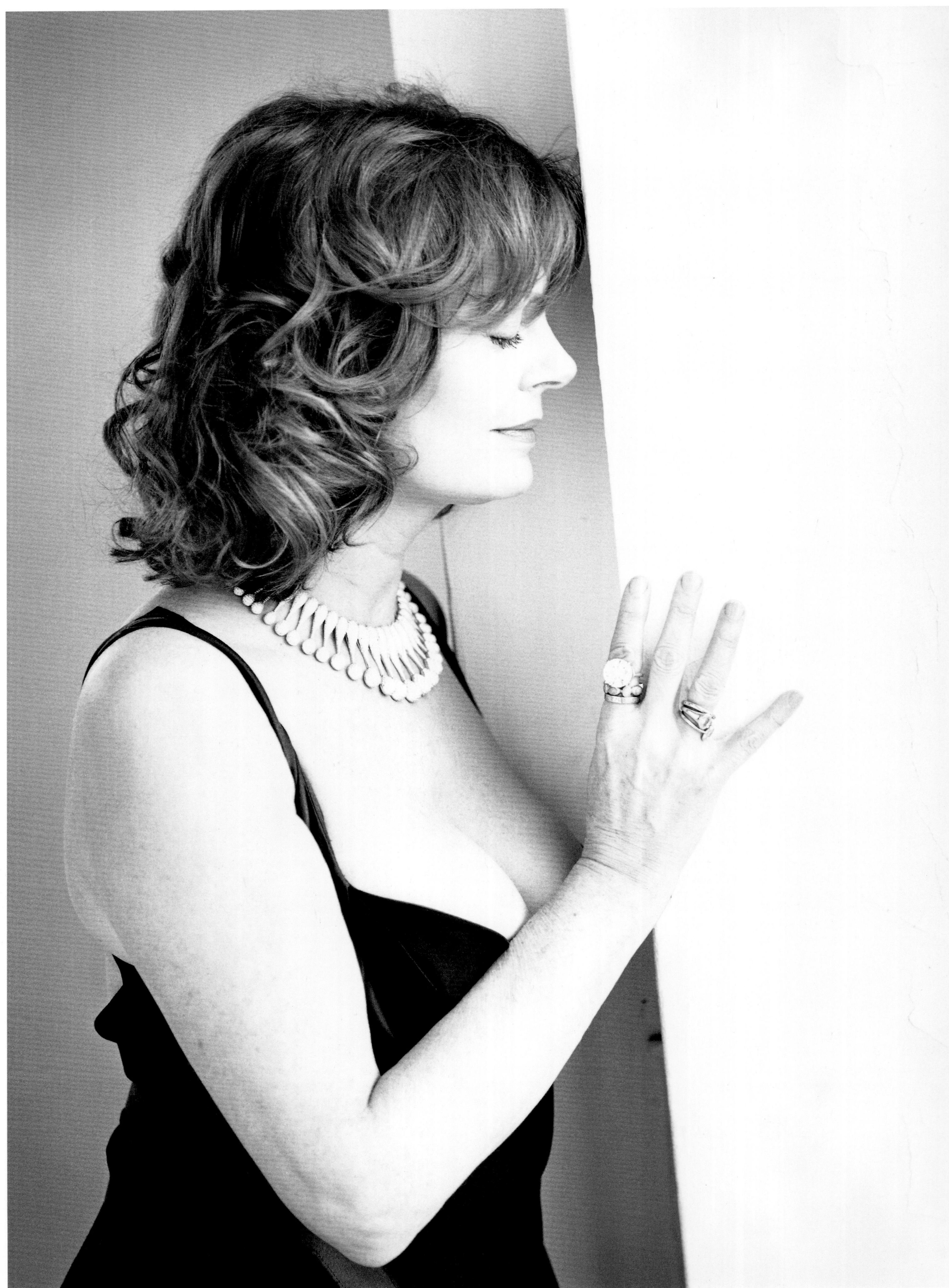

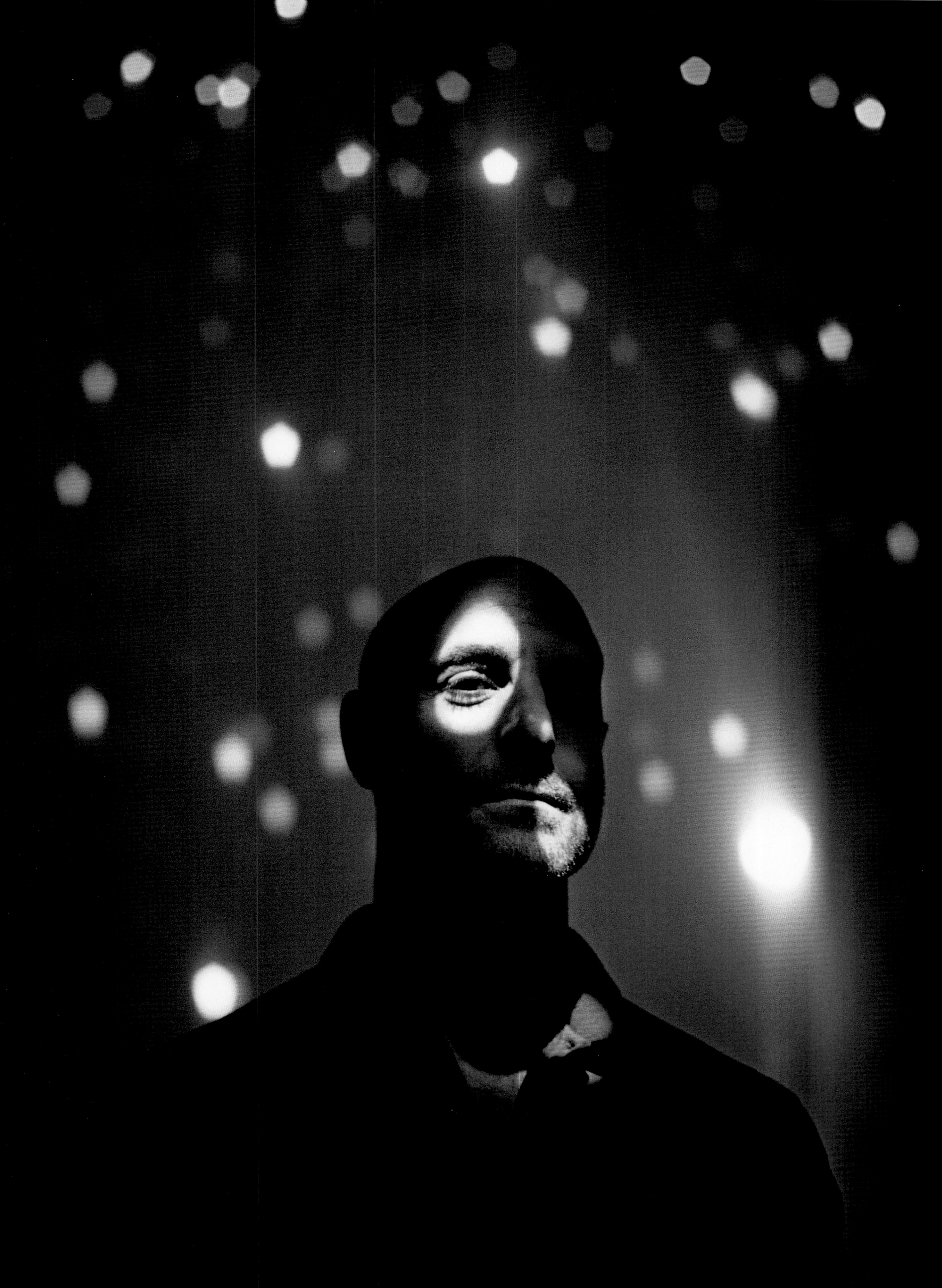

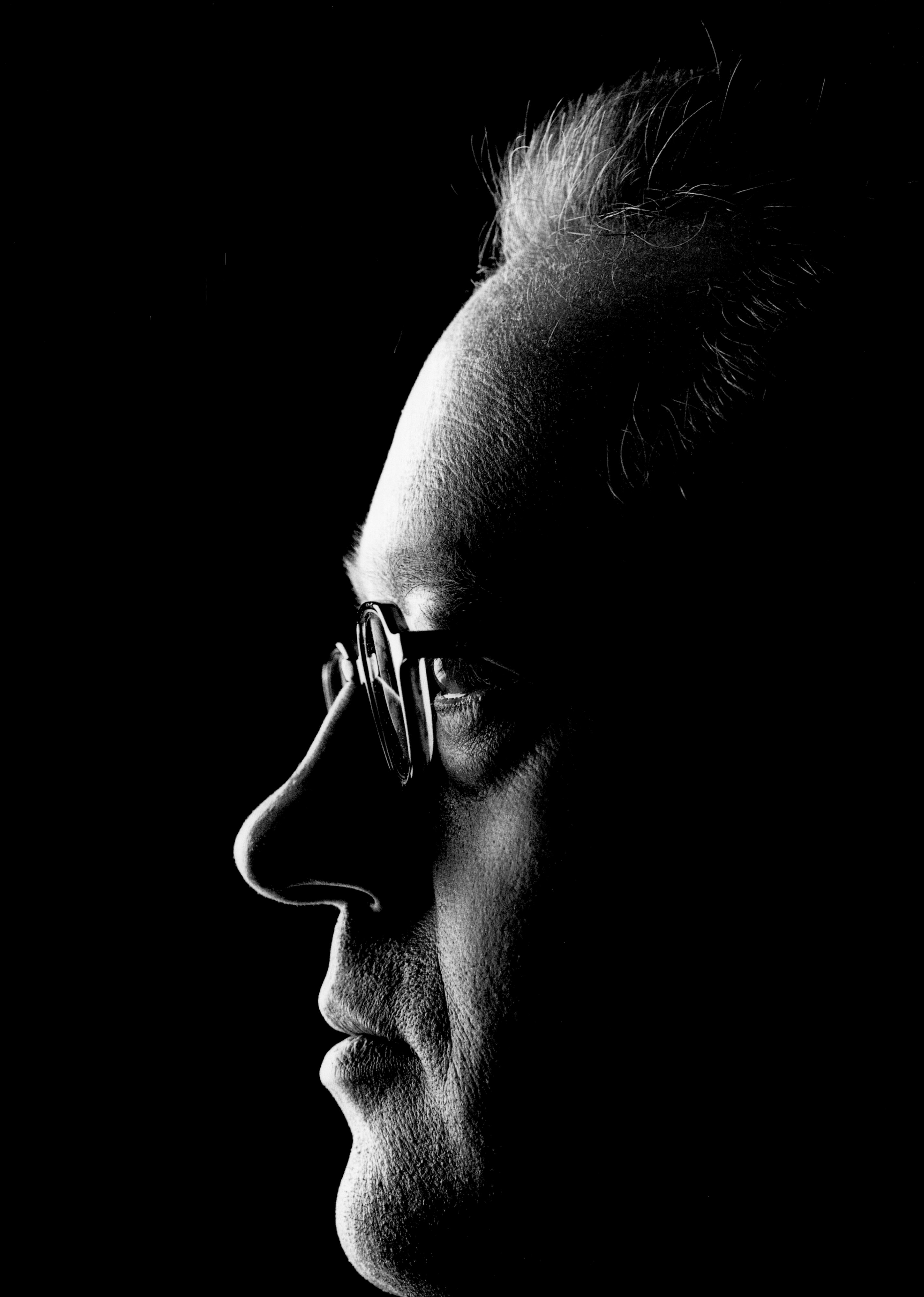

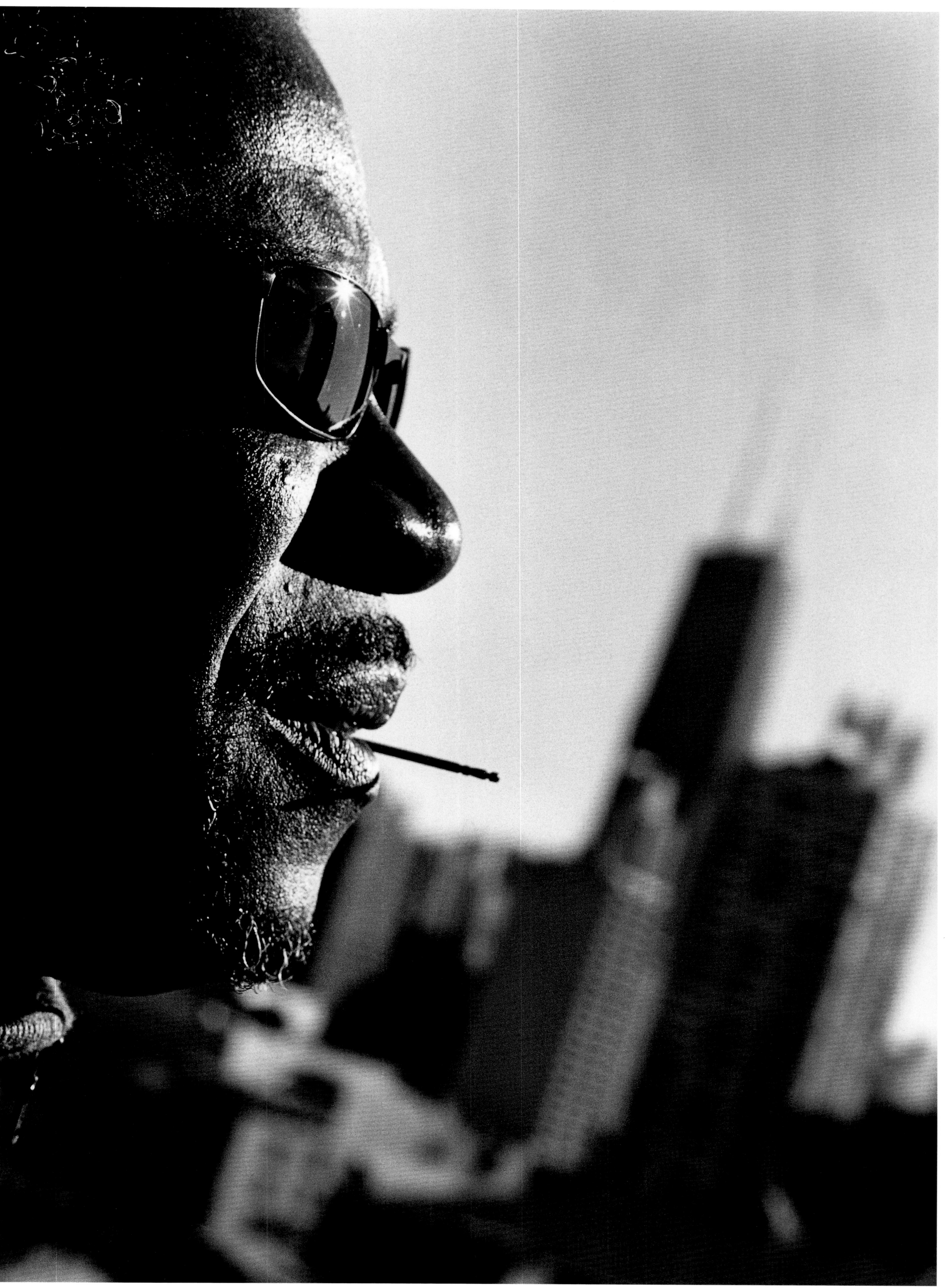

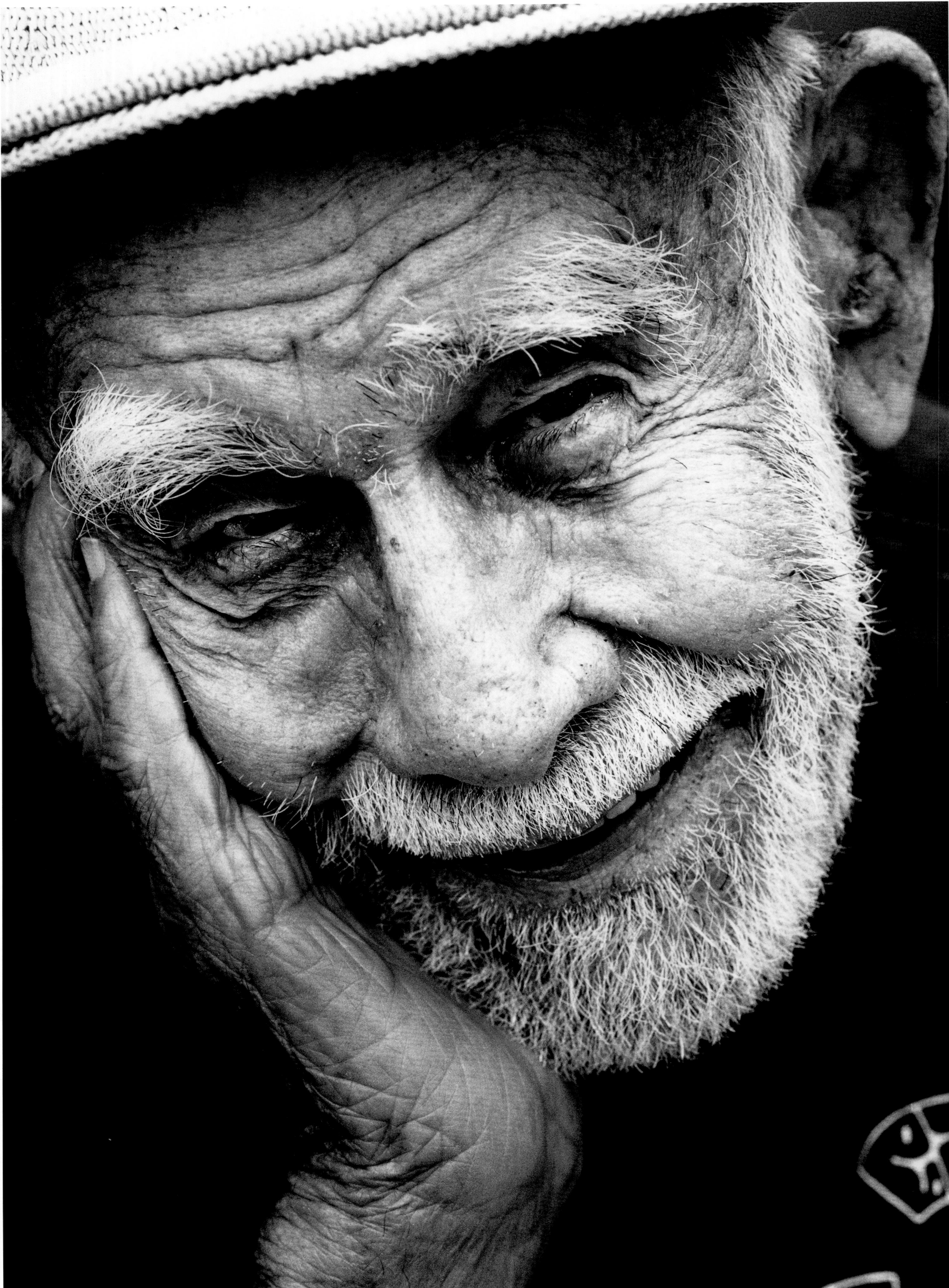

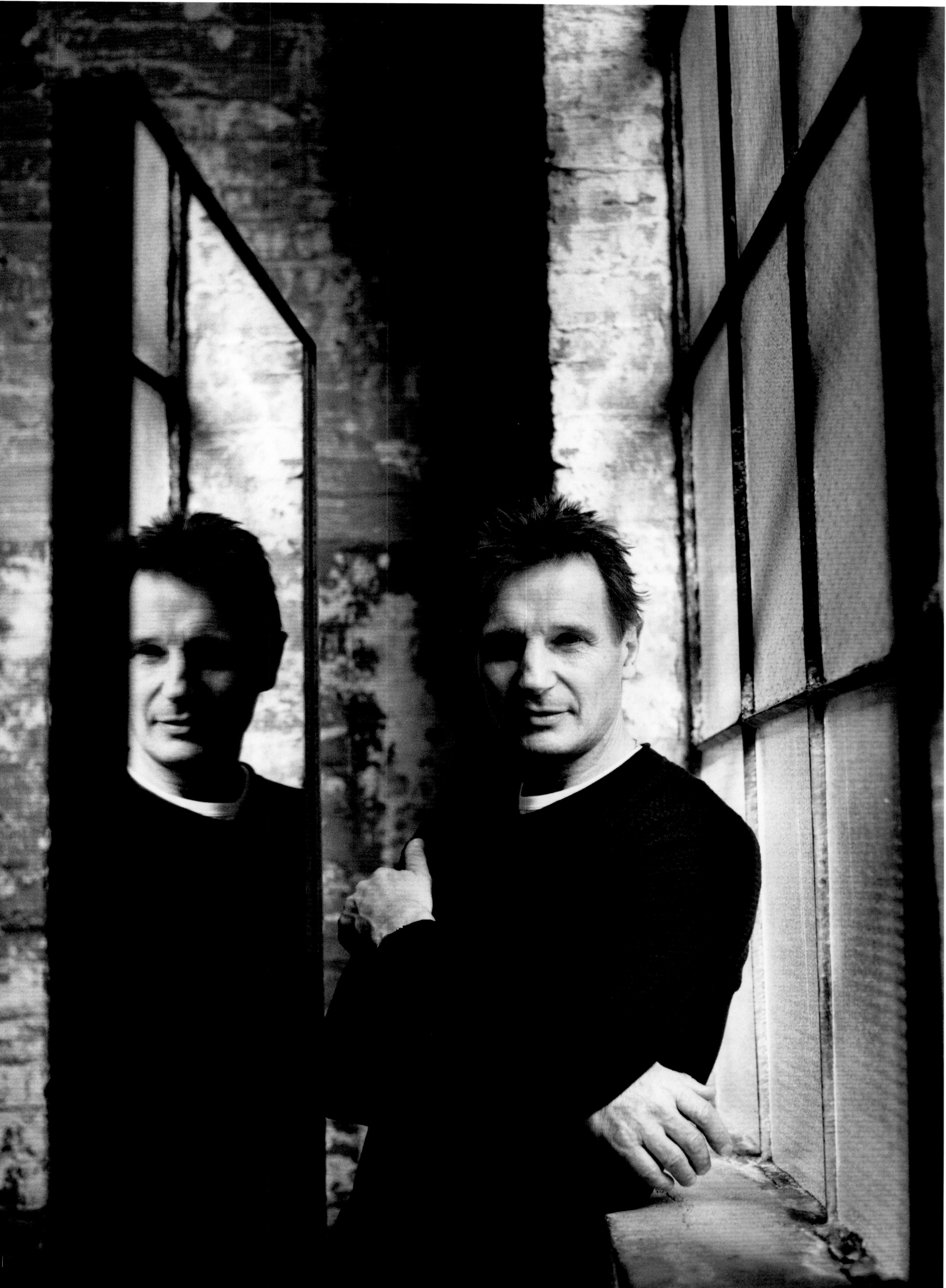

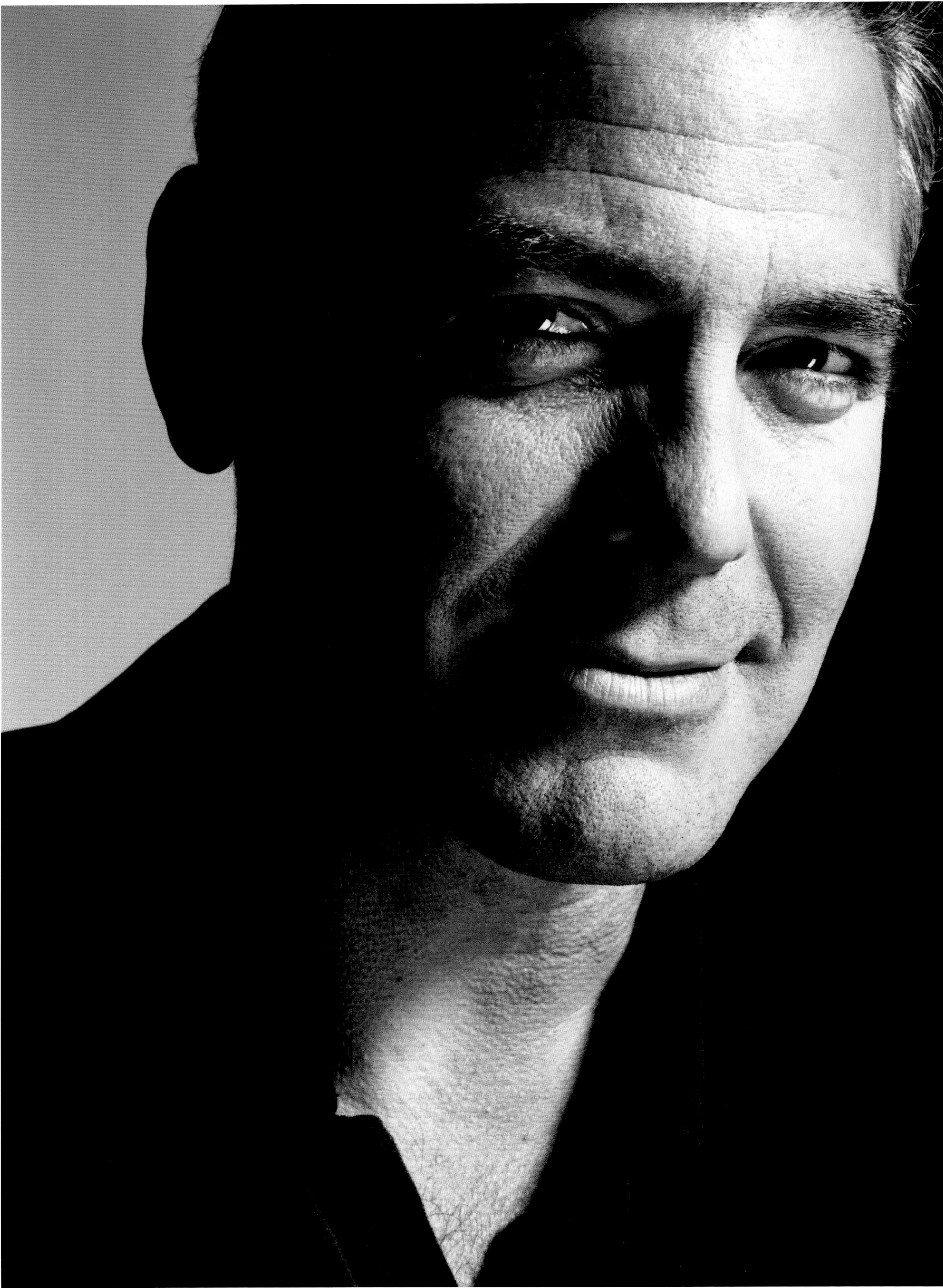

PORTRAITS ON PREVIOUS PAGES

CHRISTOPHER WALKEN

JOAQUIN PHOENIX
KEIRA KNIGHTLEY

ED HARRIS
SEAN CONNERY

SUSAN SARANDON
STANLEY TUCCI

GEOFF KATZ
DUSTY BAKER

JERRY WEXLER
LIAM NEESON

GEORGE CLOONEY

SO WHATEVER WE DO, I DON'T WANT TO DO ANYTHING TO DO WITH CAPOTE.

PHILIP SEYMOUR HOFFMAN'S RESPONSE TO MY IDEA OF PAYING HOMAGE TO THE FAMOUS IRVING PENN SHOT OF TRUMAN CAPOTE.

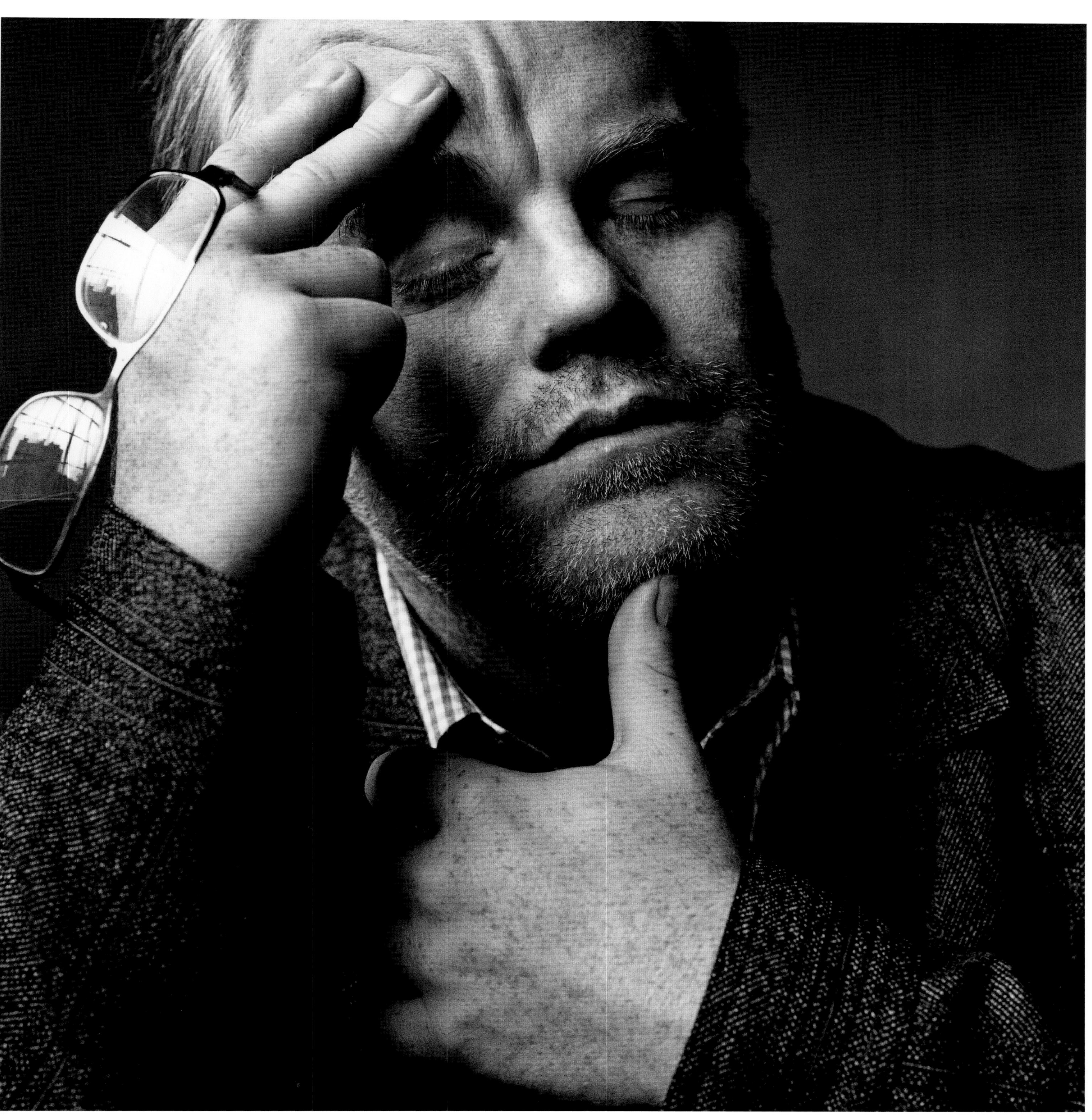

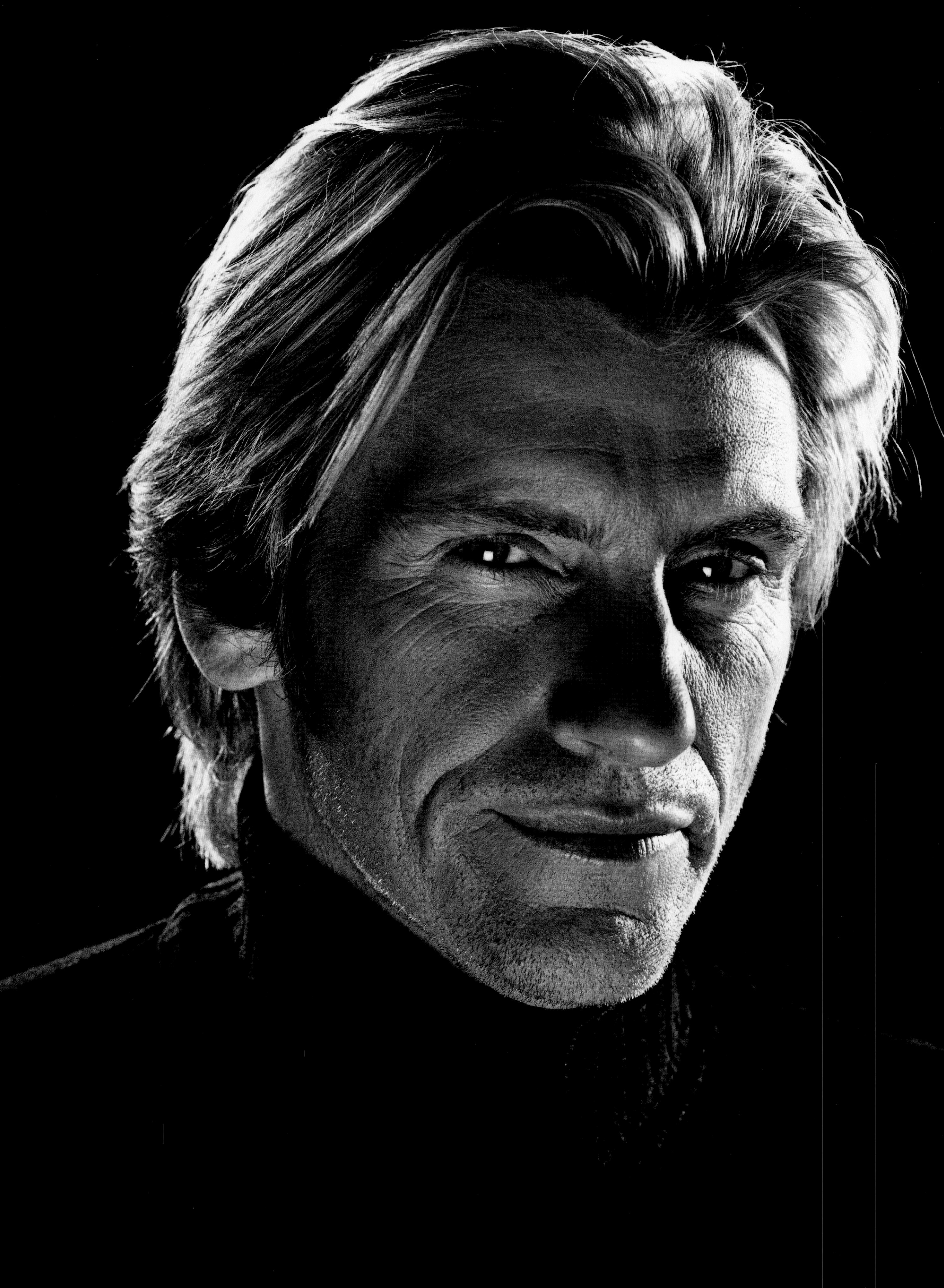

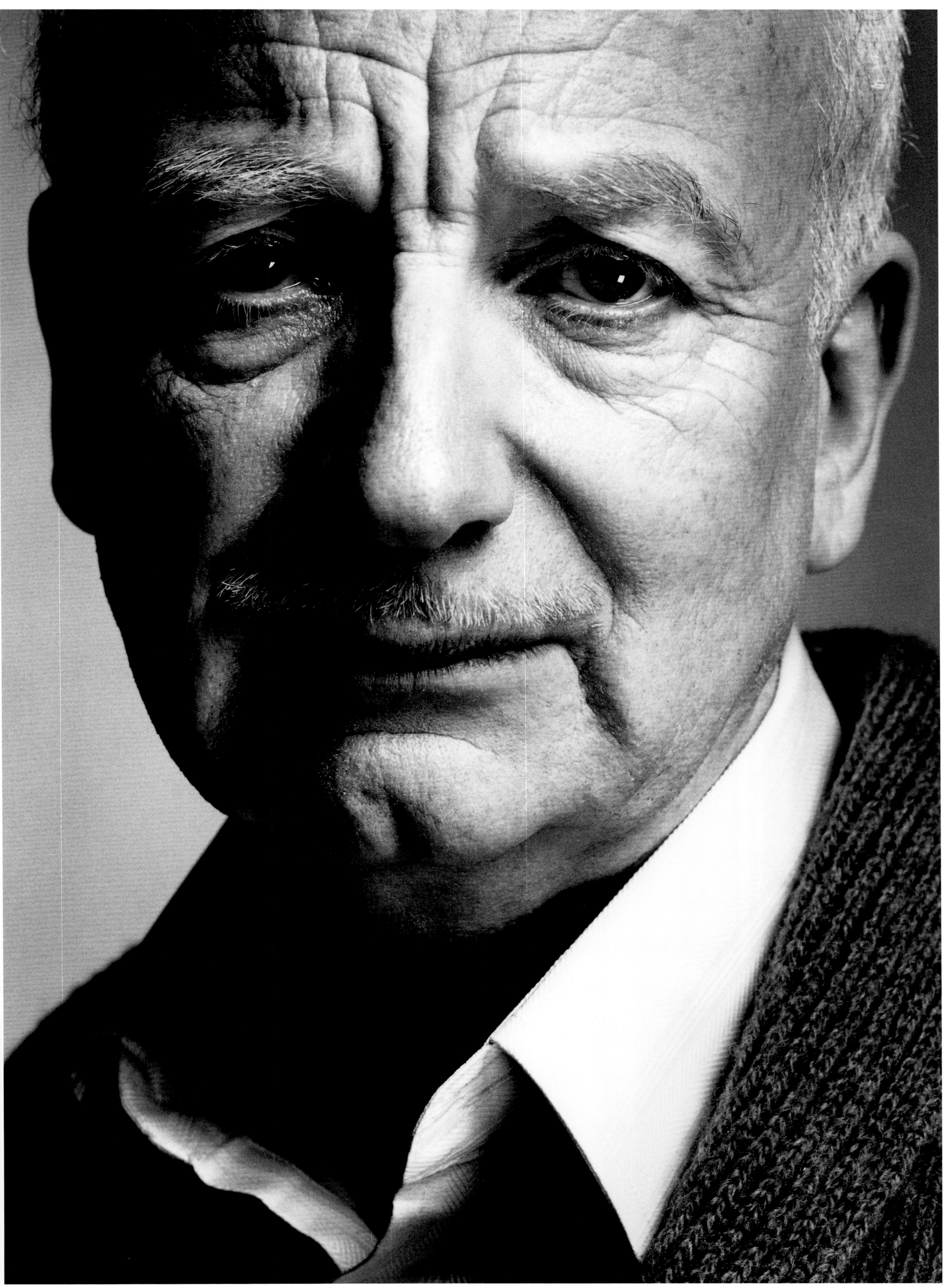

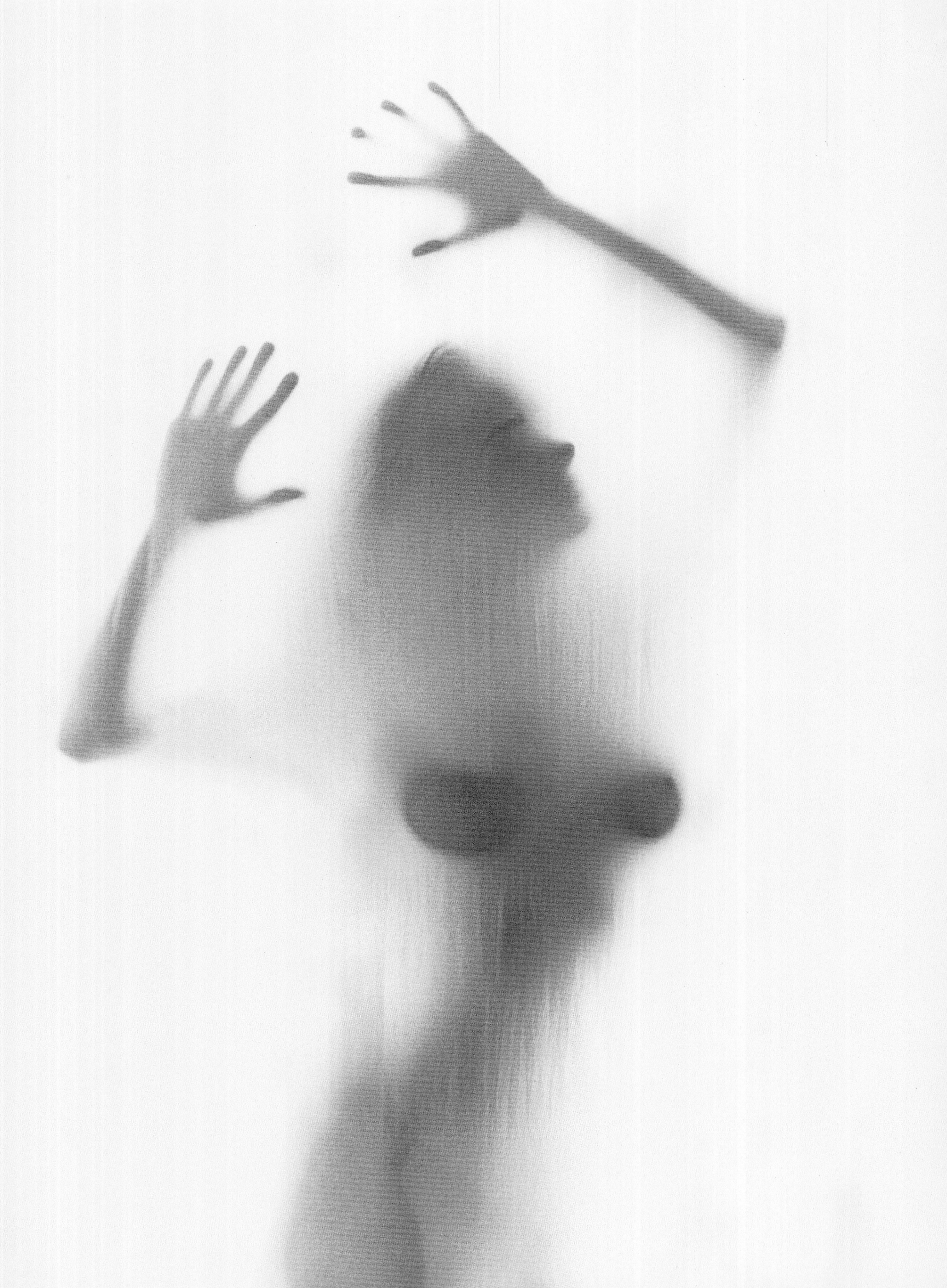

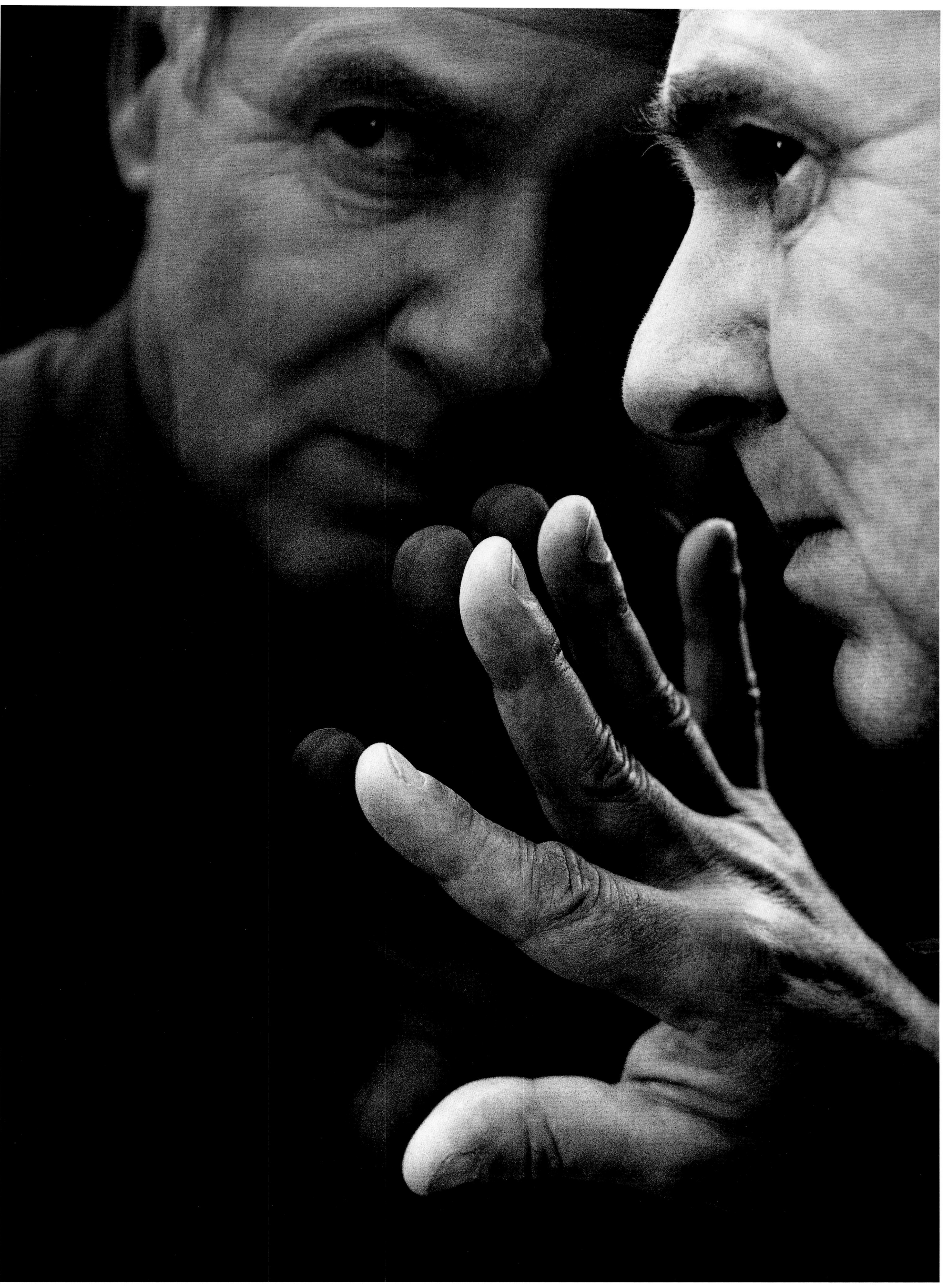

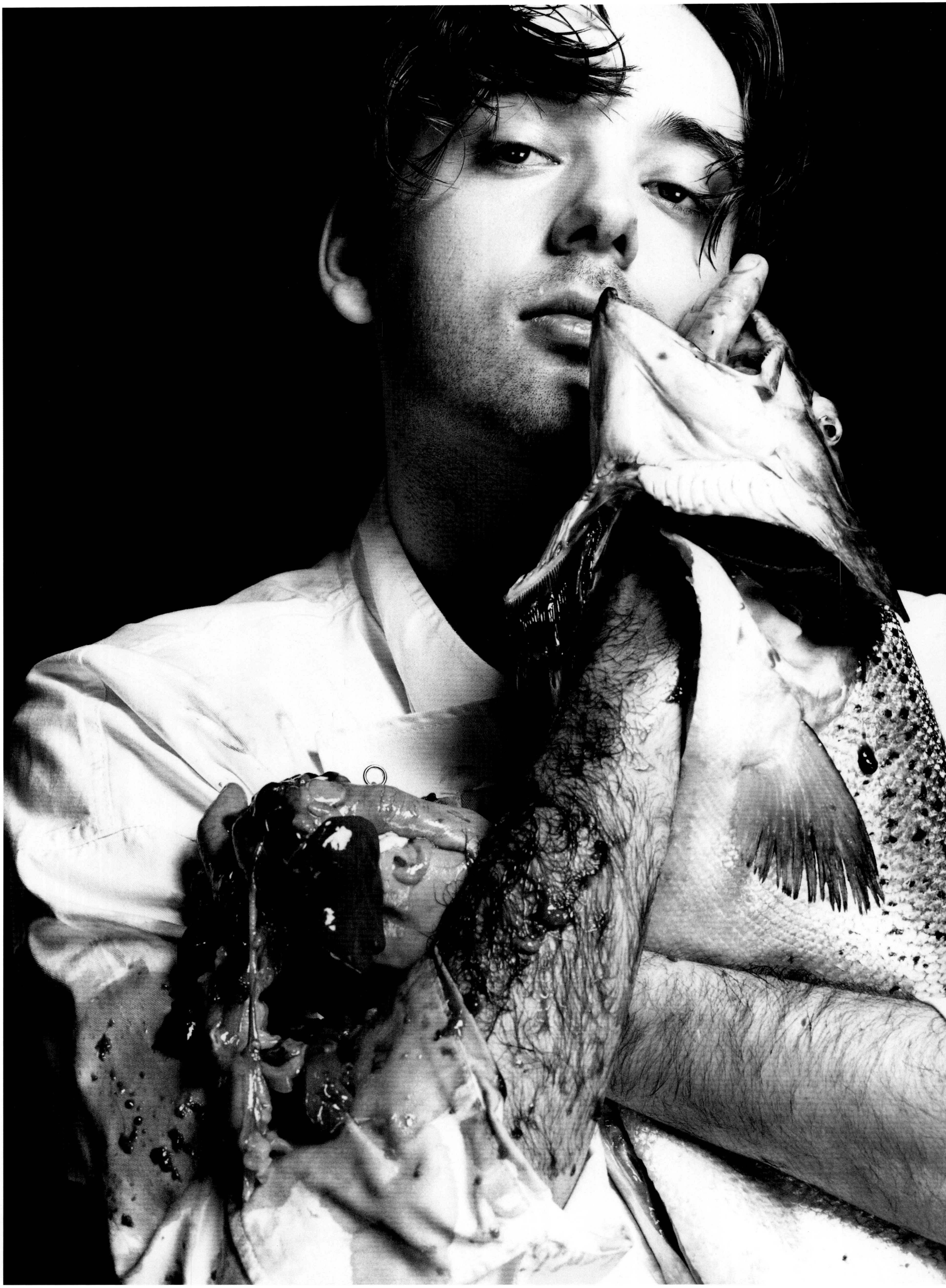

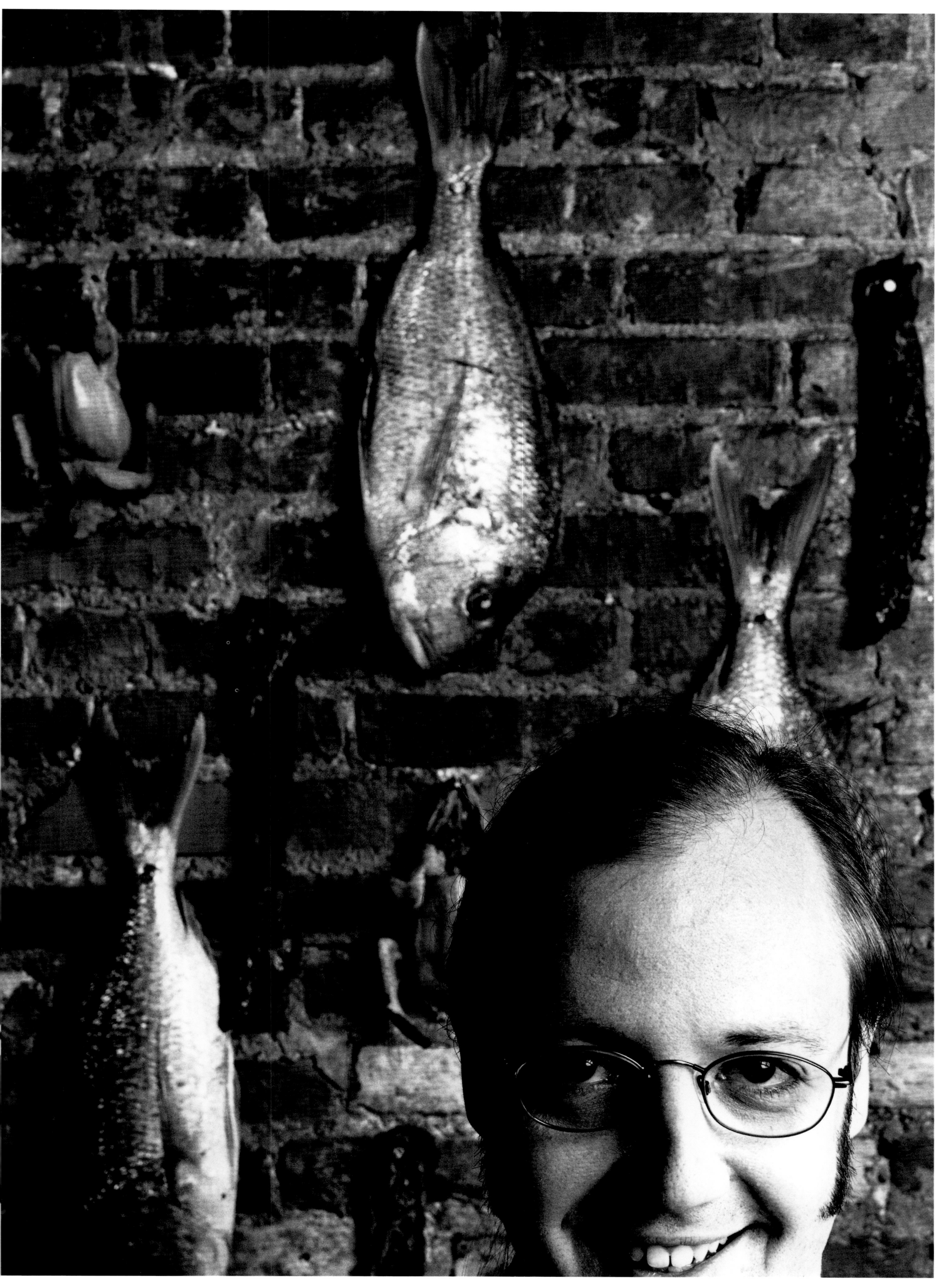

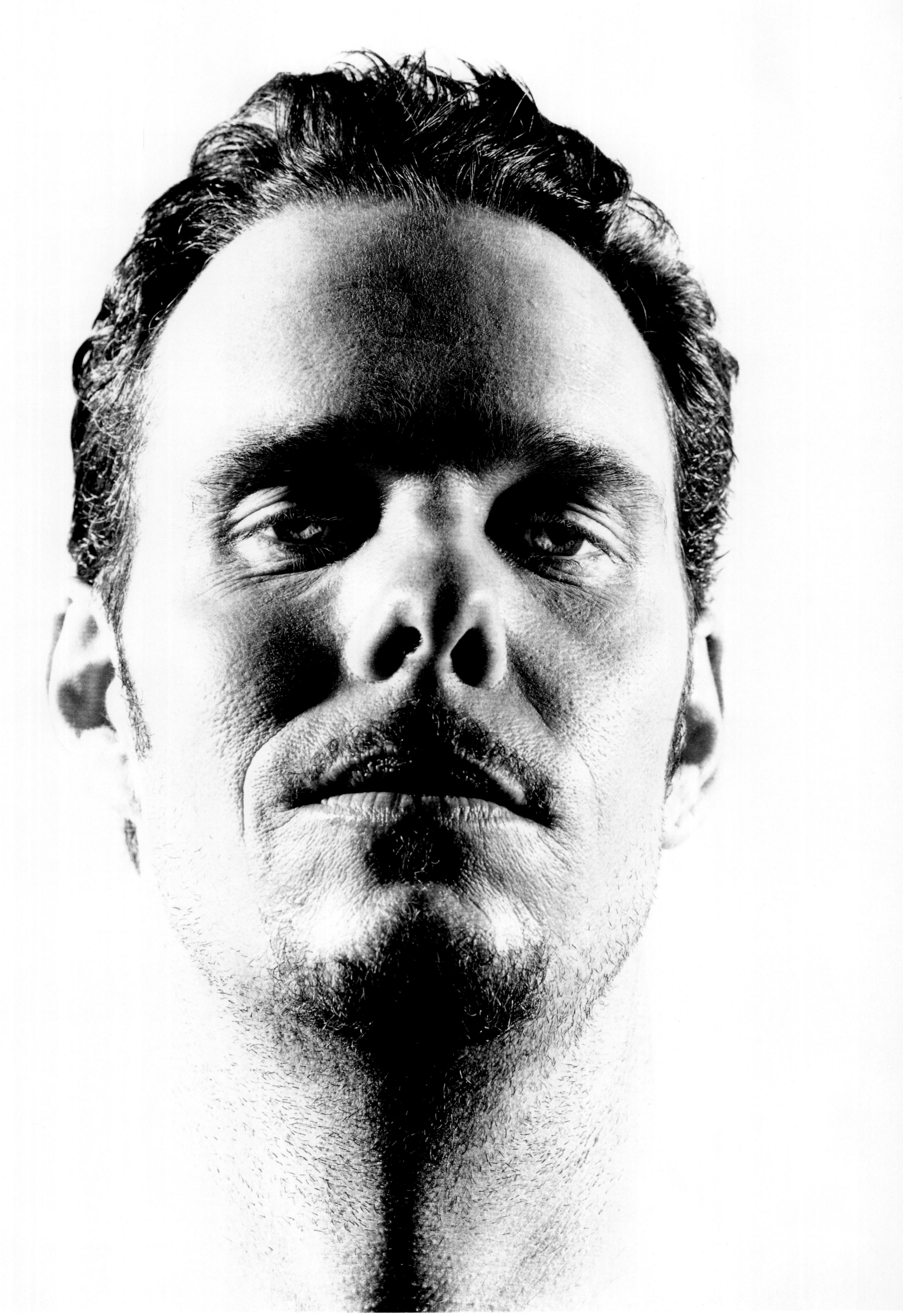

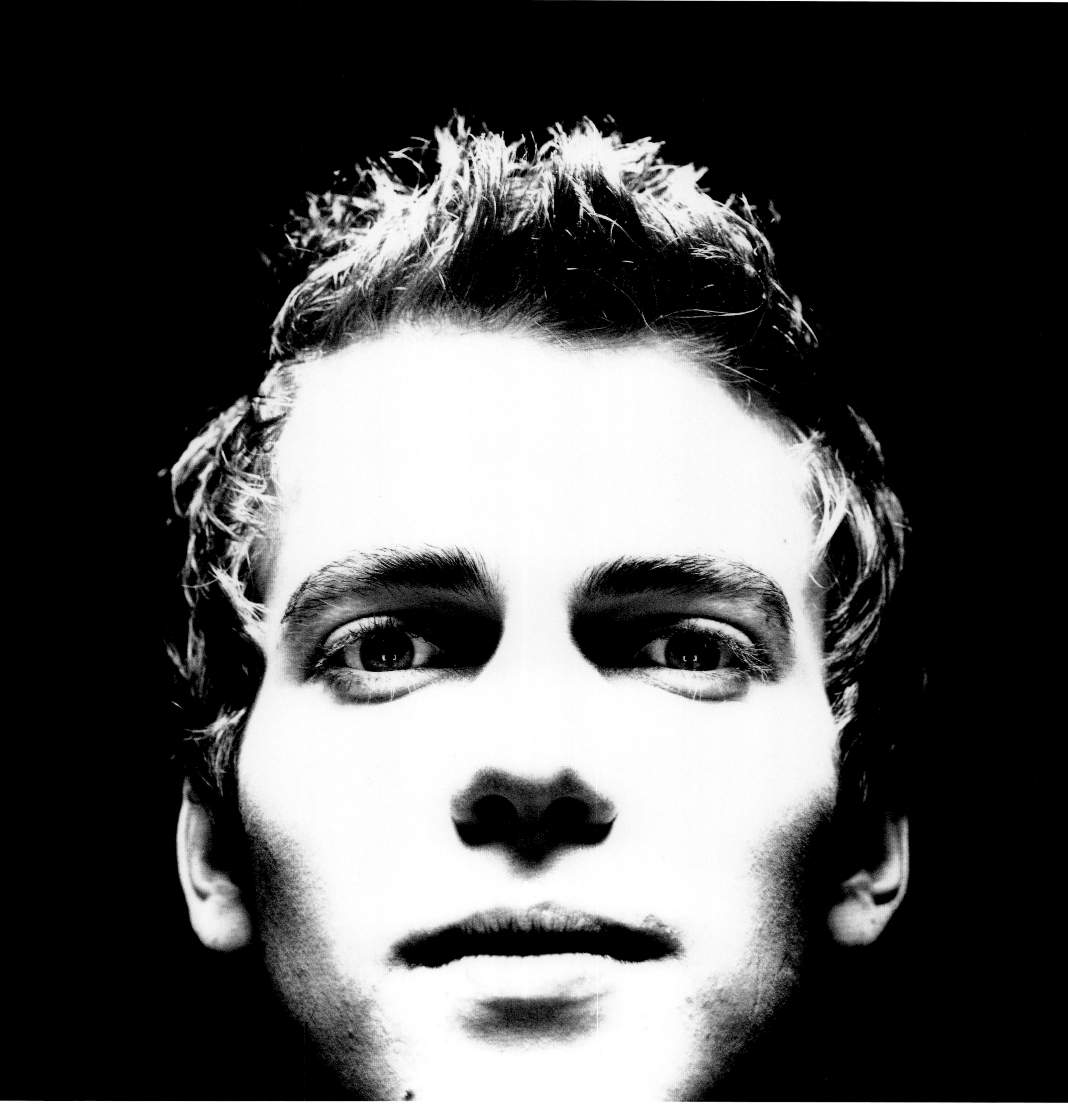

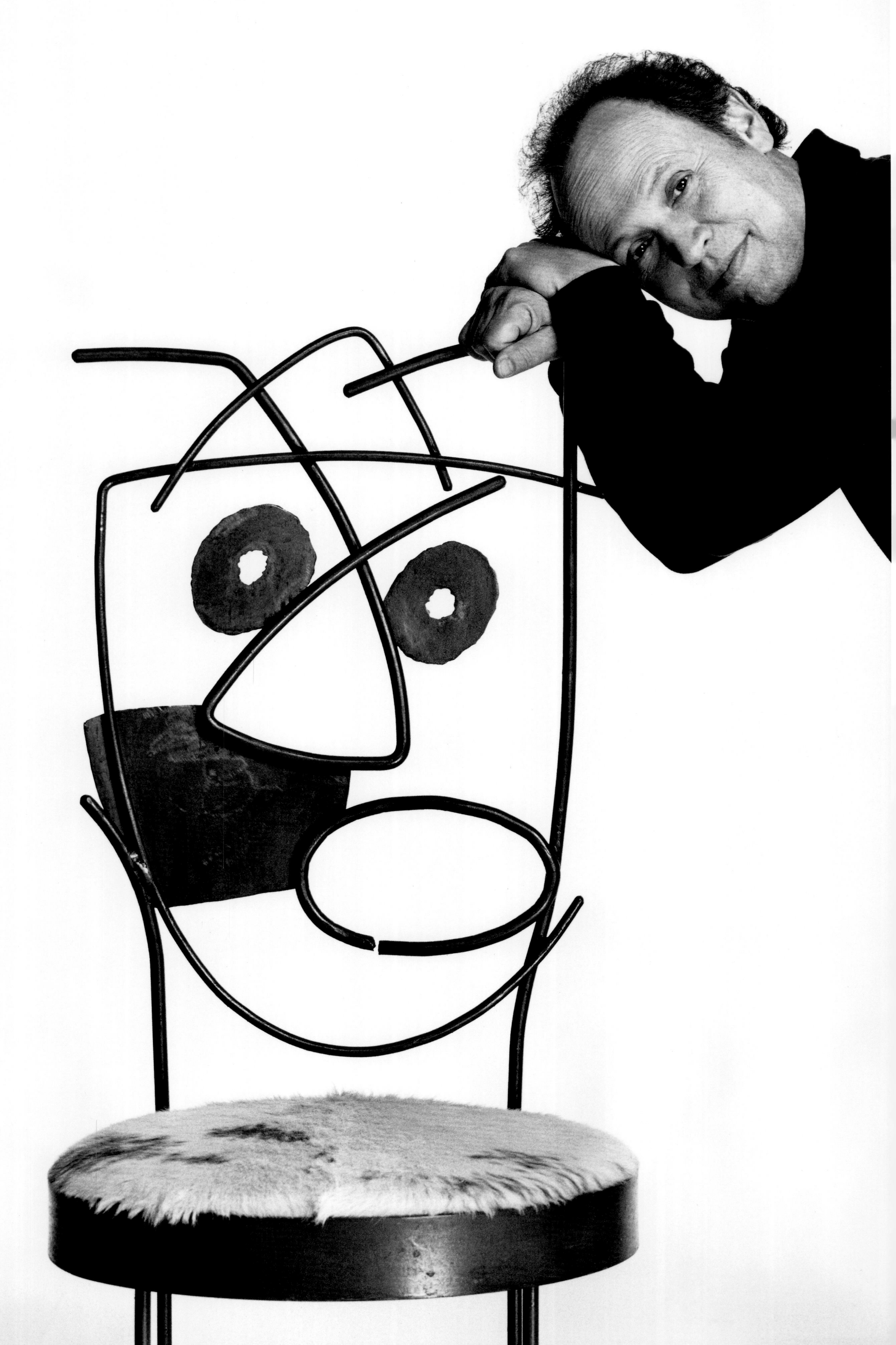

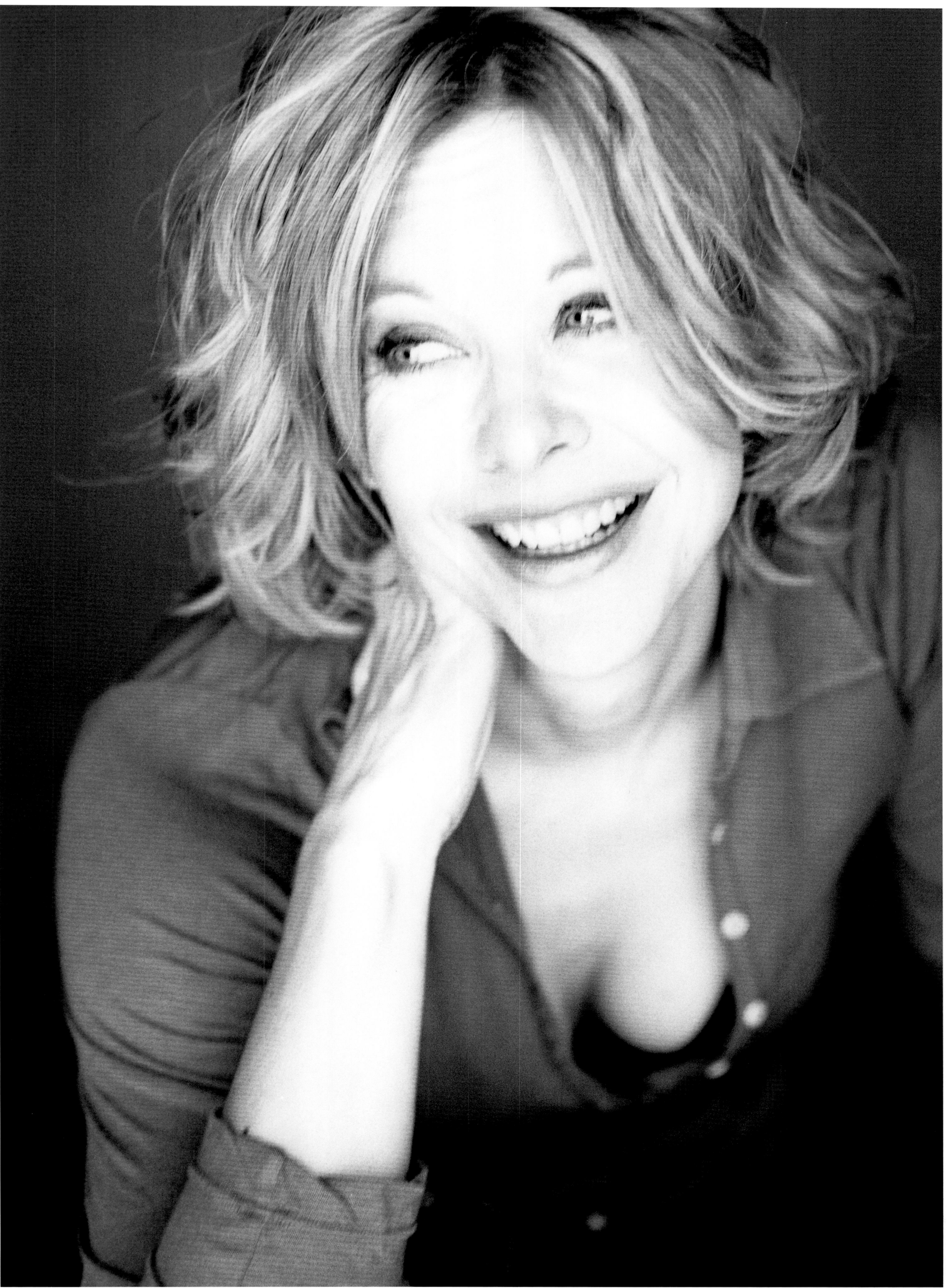

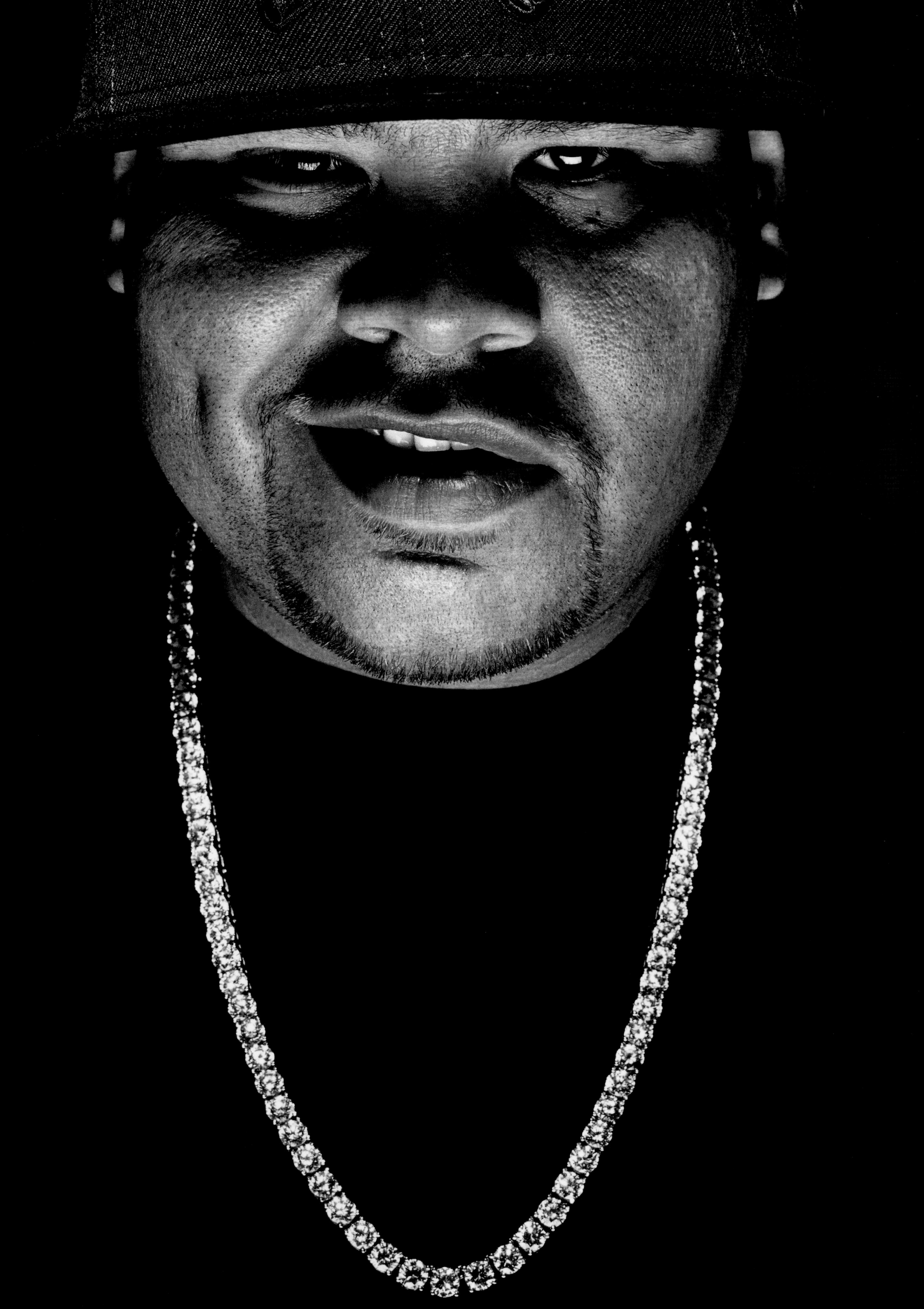

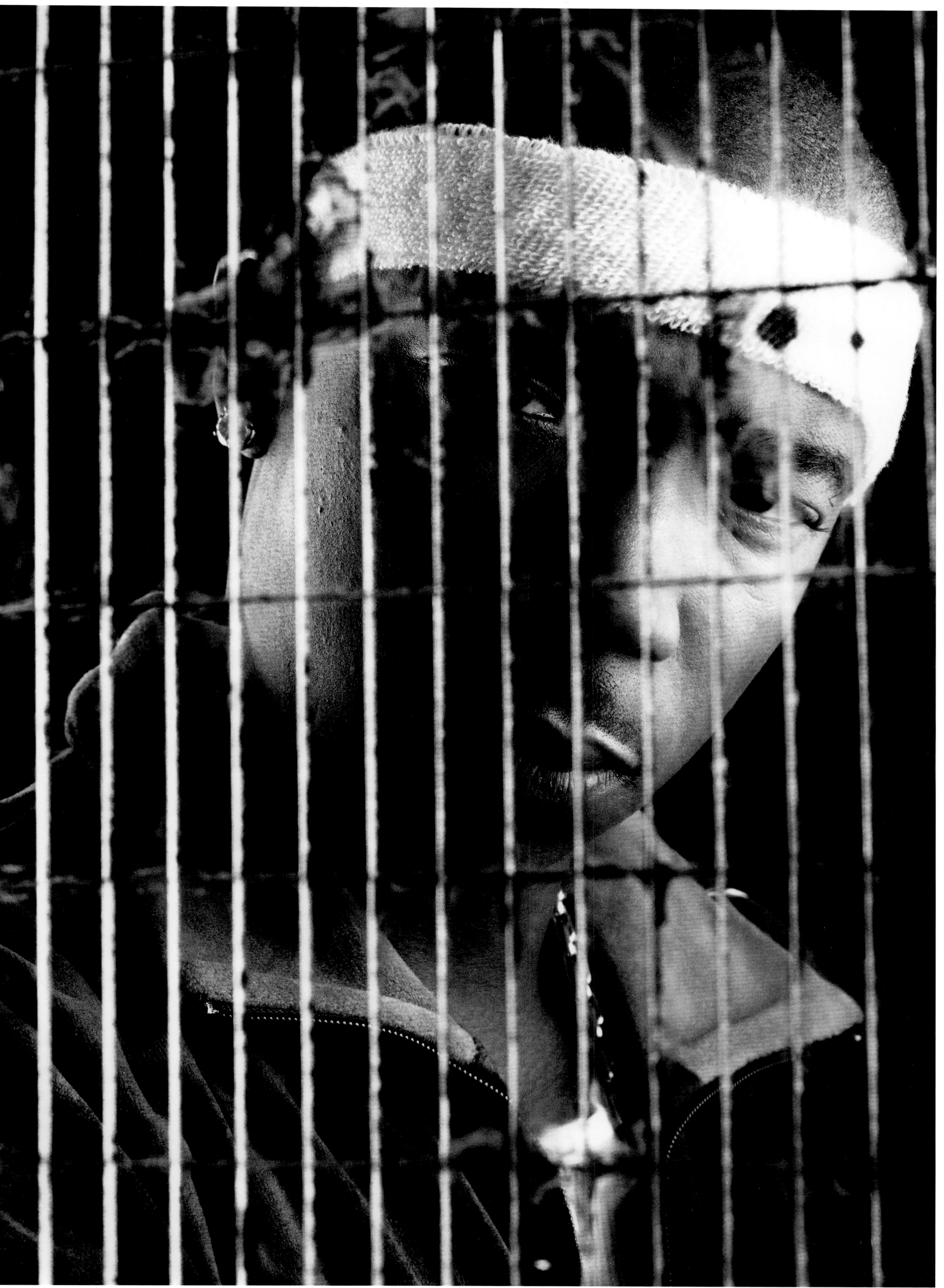

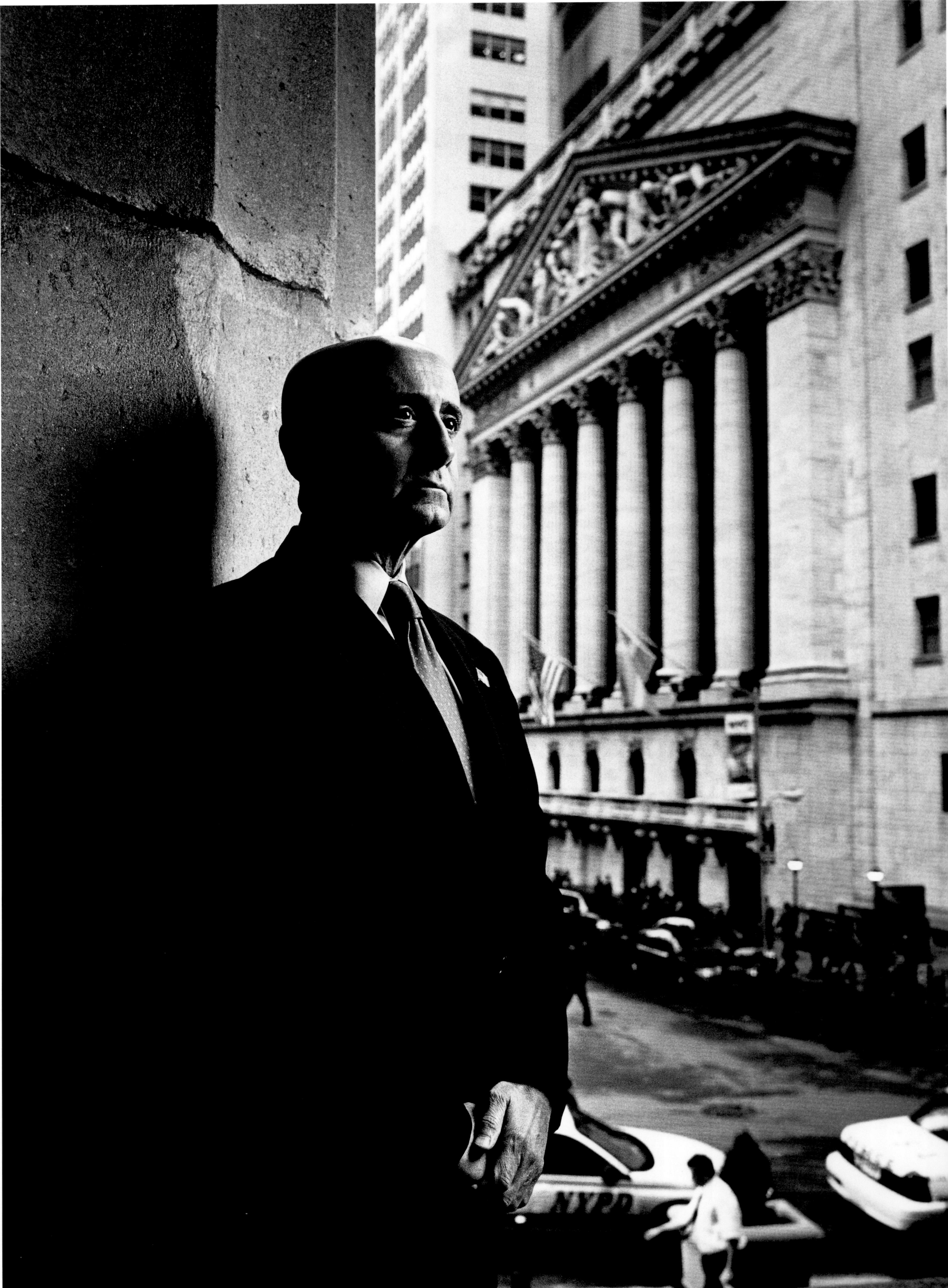
NYPD

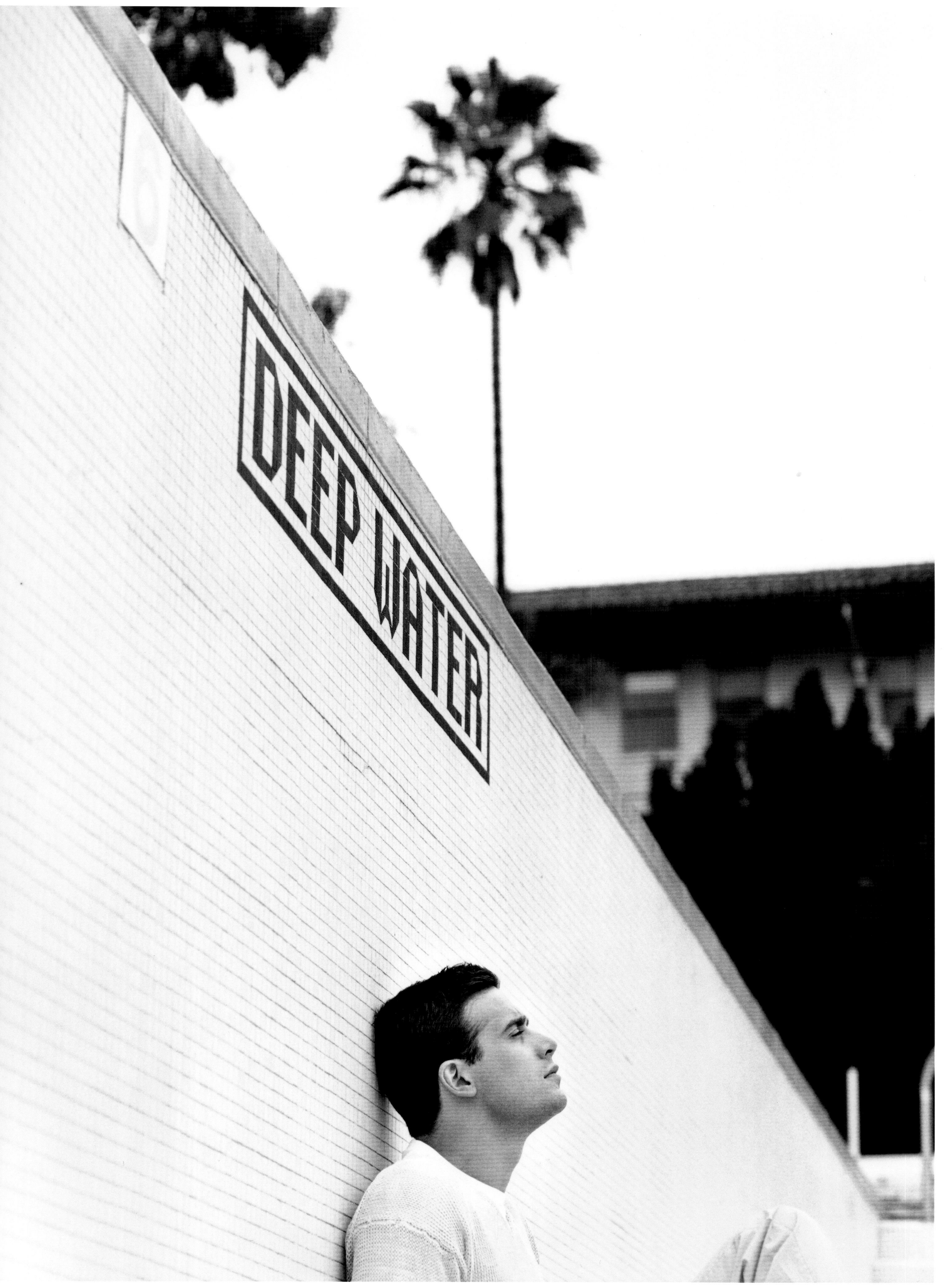
DEEP WATER

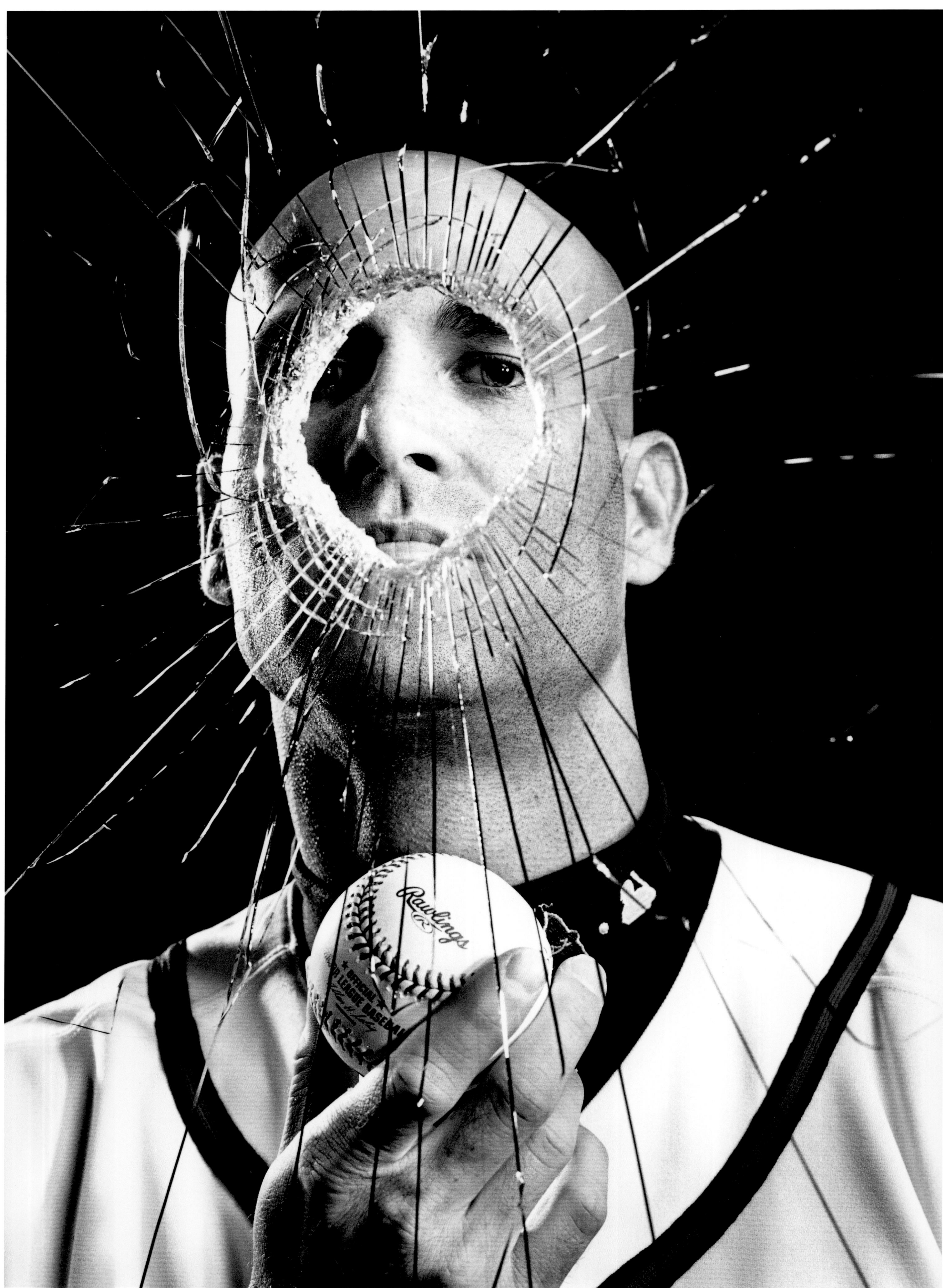
Rawlings
OFFICIAL

PORTRAITS ON PREVIOUS PAGES

PHILIP SEYMOUR HOFFMANN

DENIS LEARY
IAN MCDIARMID

AMANDA MARCUM
TOM WILKINSON

PAUL LIEBRANDT
WYLIE DUFRESNE

KEVIN DILLON
HAYDEN CHRISTENSEN

BILLY CRYSTAL
MEG RYAN

FAT JOE
JA RULE

DICK GRASSO
FREDDIE PRINZE JR.

TIM HUDSON

NO NO NO!
TO STAY OUT HERE
FOR AS LONG AS
FIVE MINUTES
WOULD BE TOO
DANGEROUS...
EVEN FOR YOU!

SECURITY ADVISOR TO THE QUEEN, ON THE SAFETY OF THE CHOSEN LOCATION
IN AMMAN, JORDAN WHERE WE INTENDED TO PHOTOGRAPH HER ROYAL HIGHNESS.
A WEEK LATER 3 HOTELS THERE WERE BOMBED BY TERRORISTS.

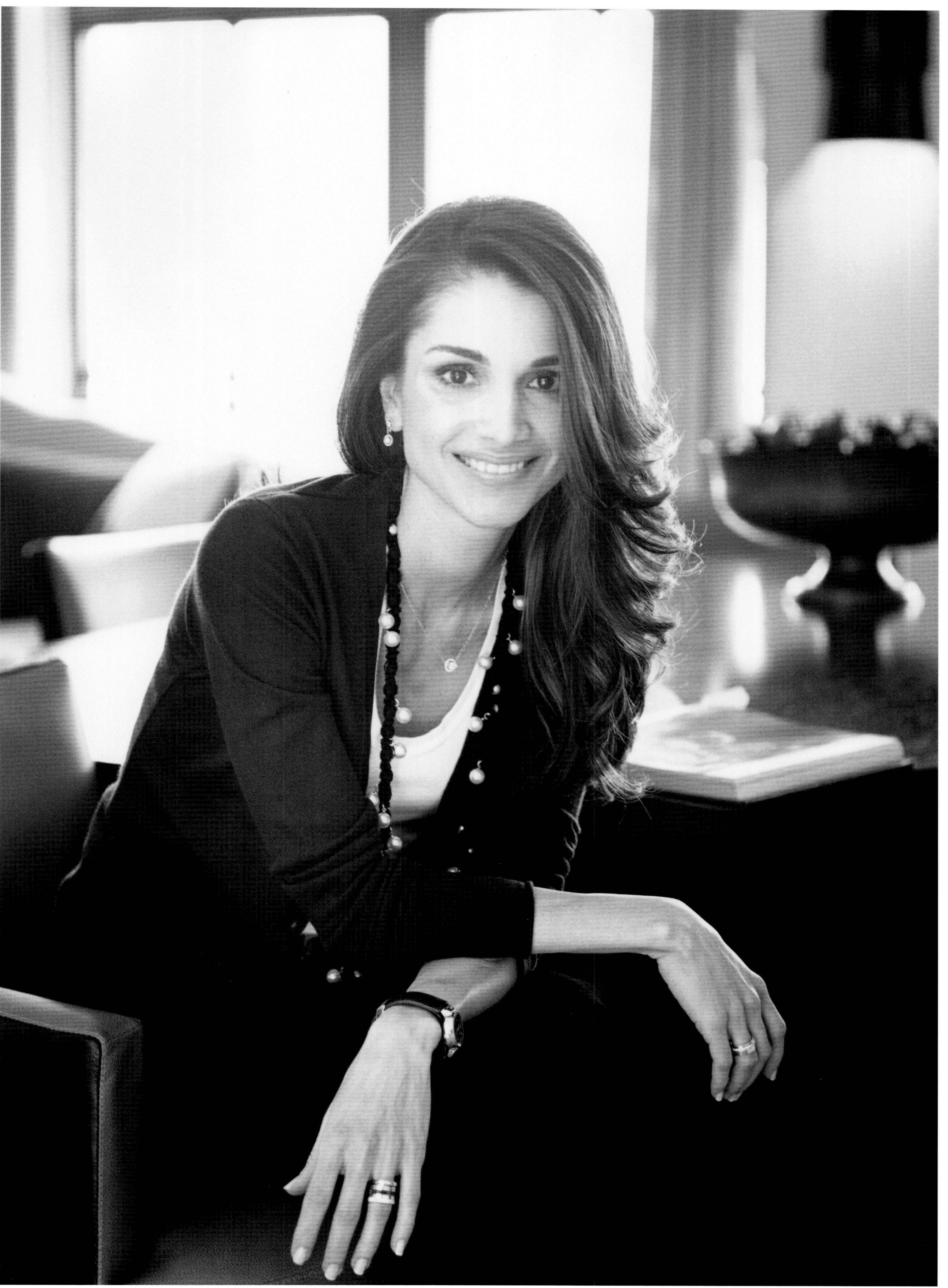

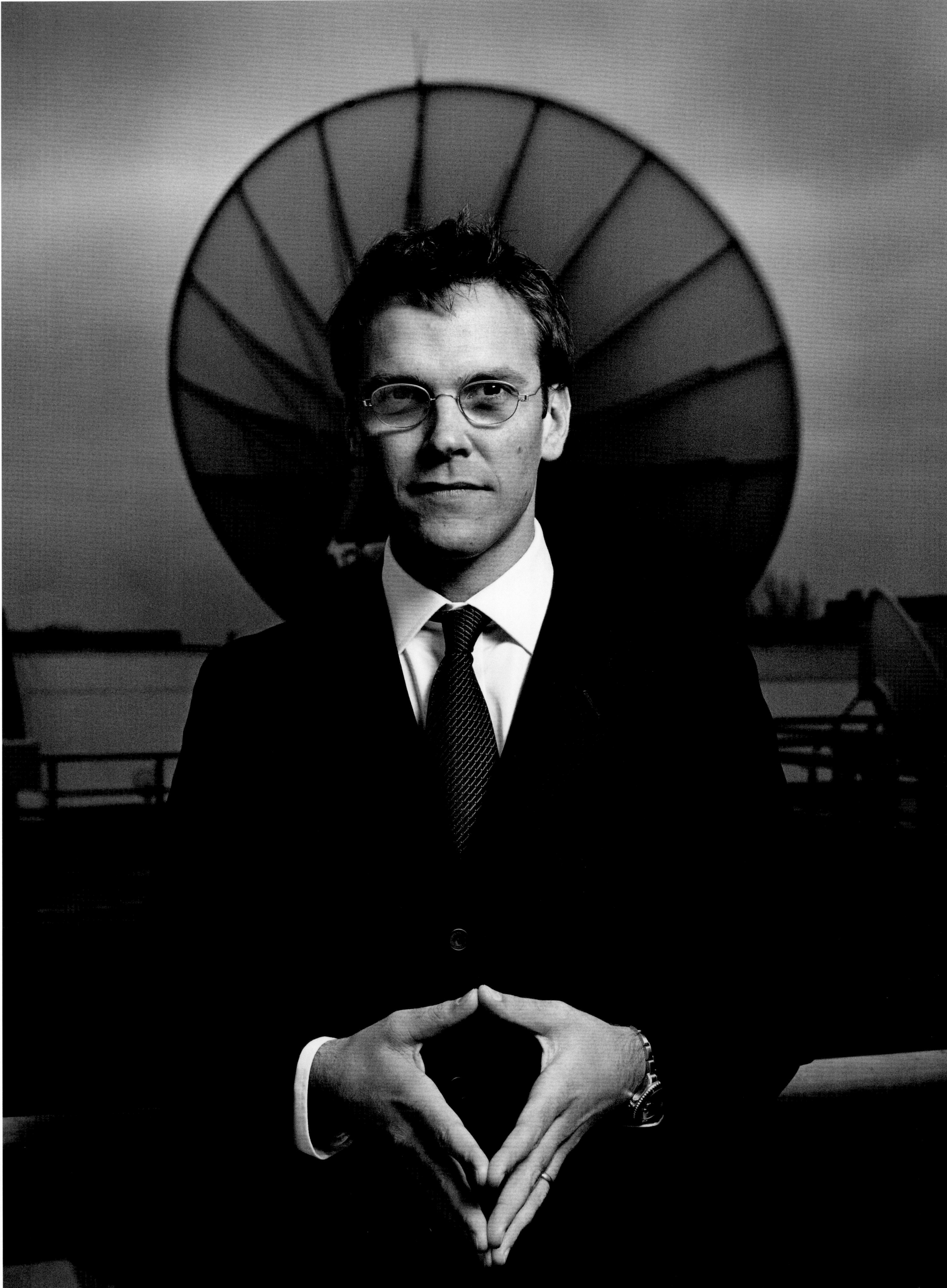

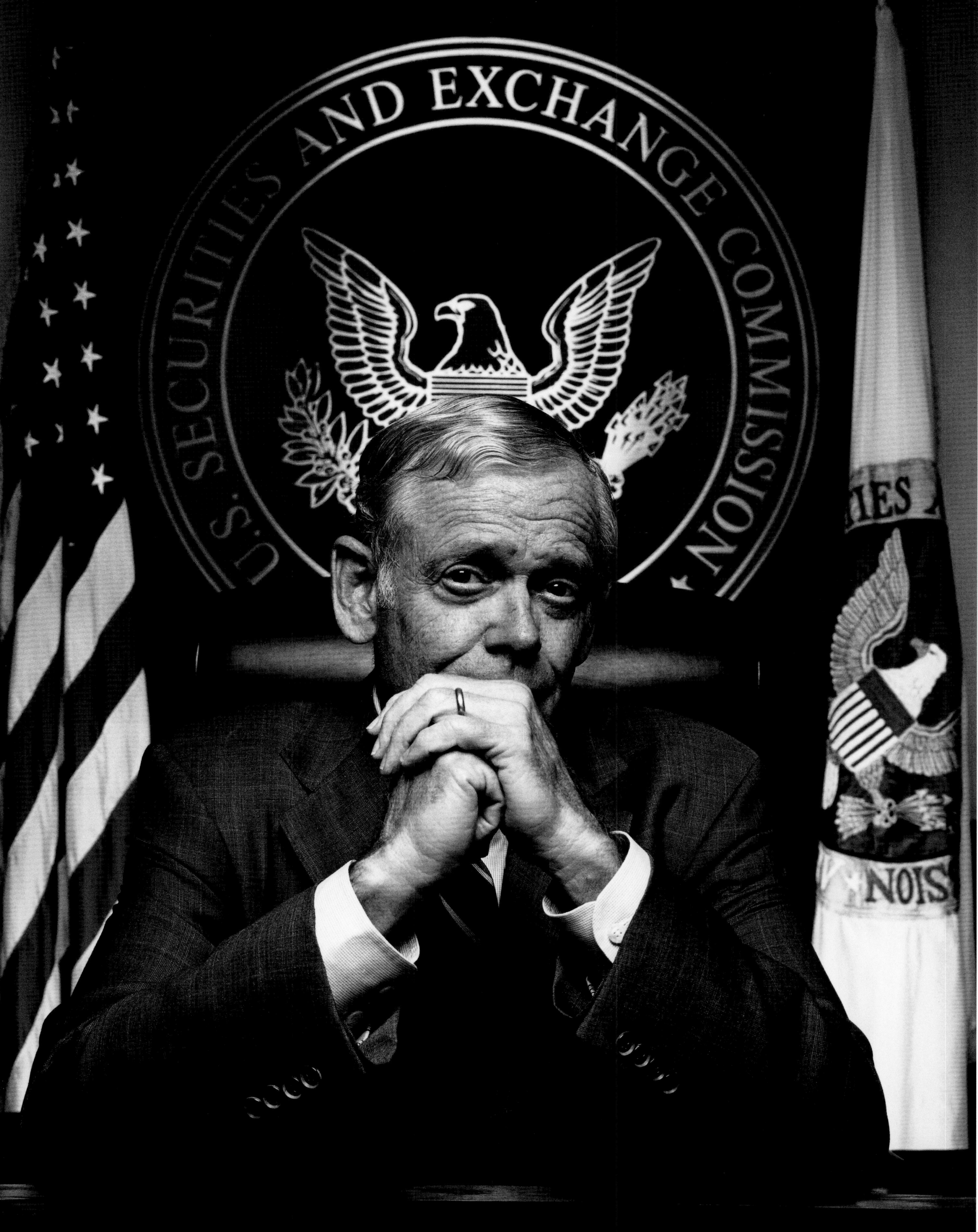
U.S. SECURITIES AND EXCHANGE COMMISSION

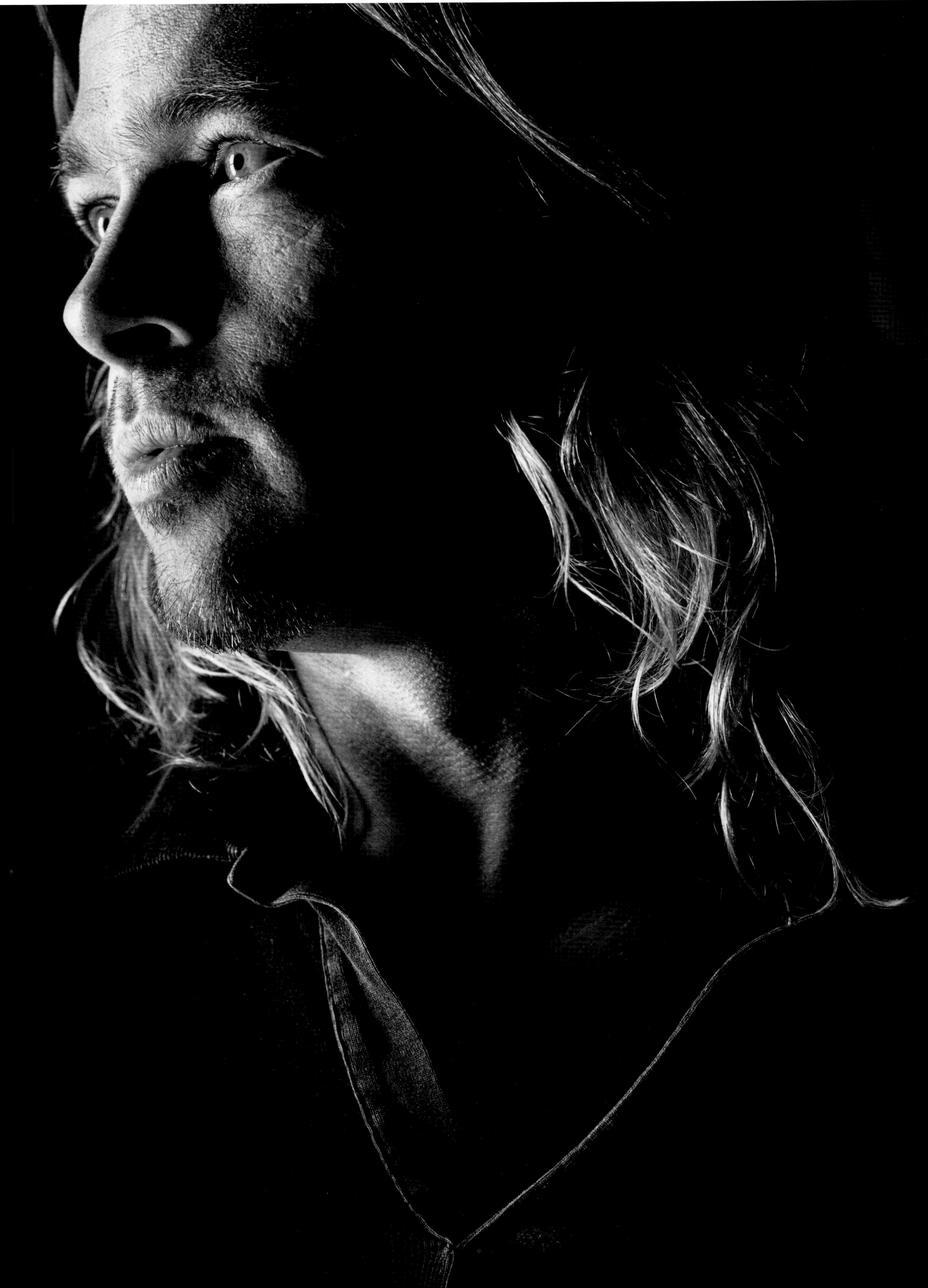

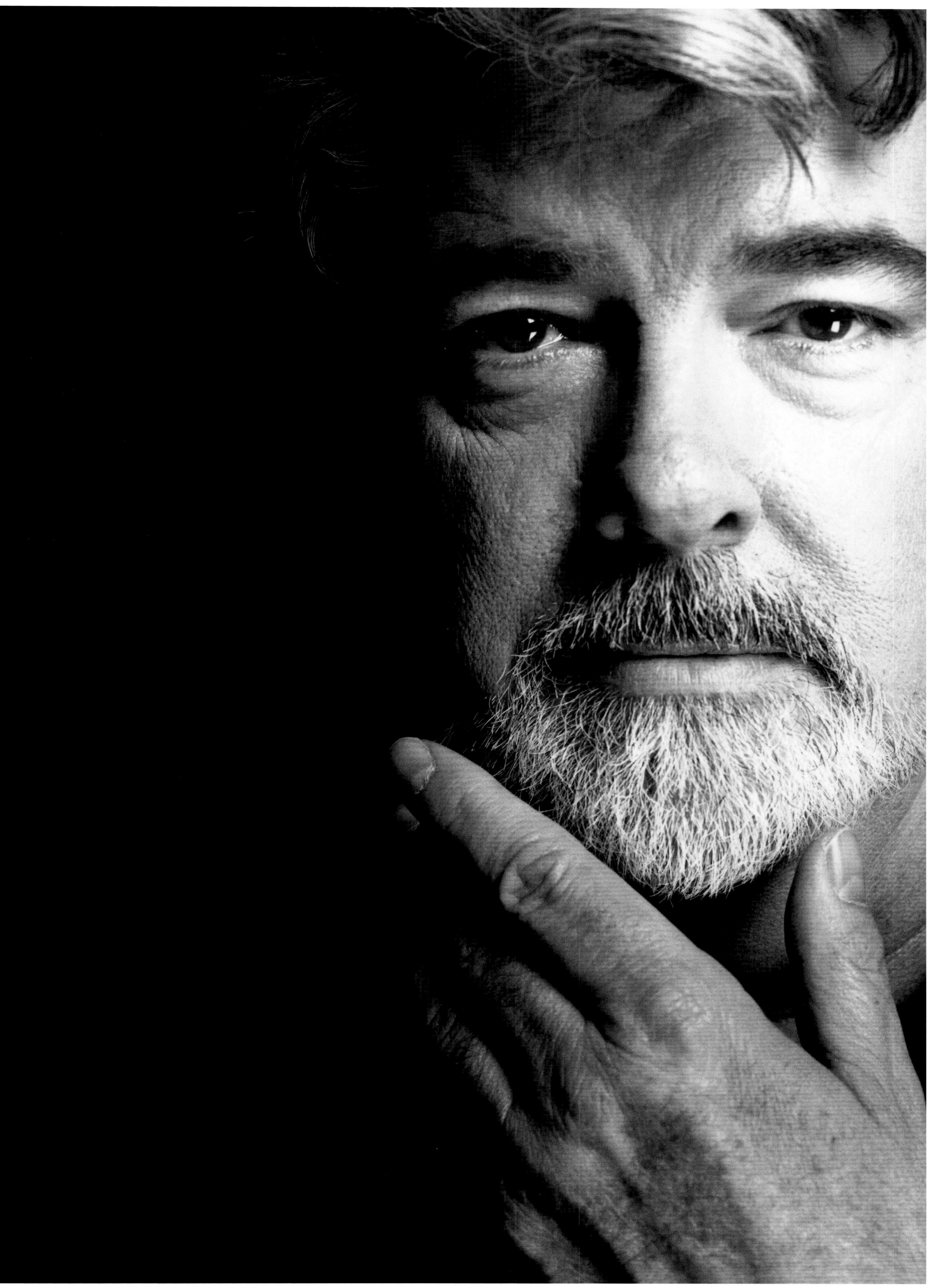

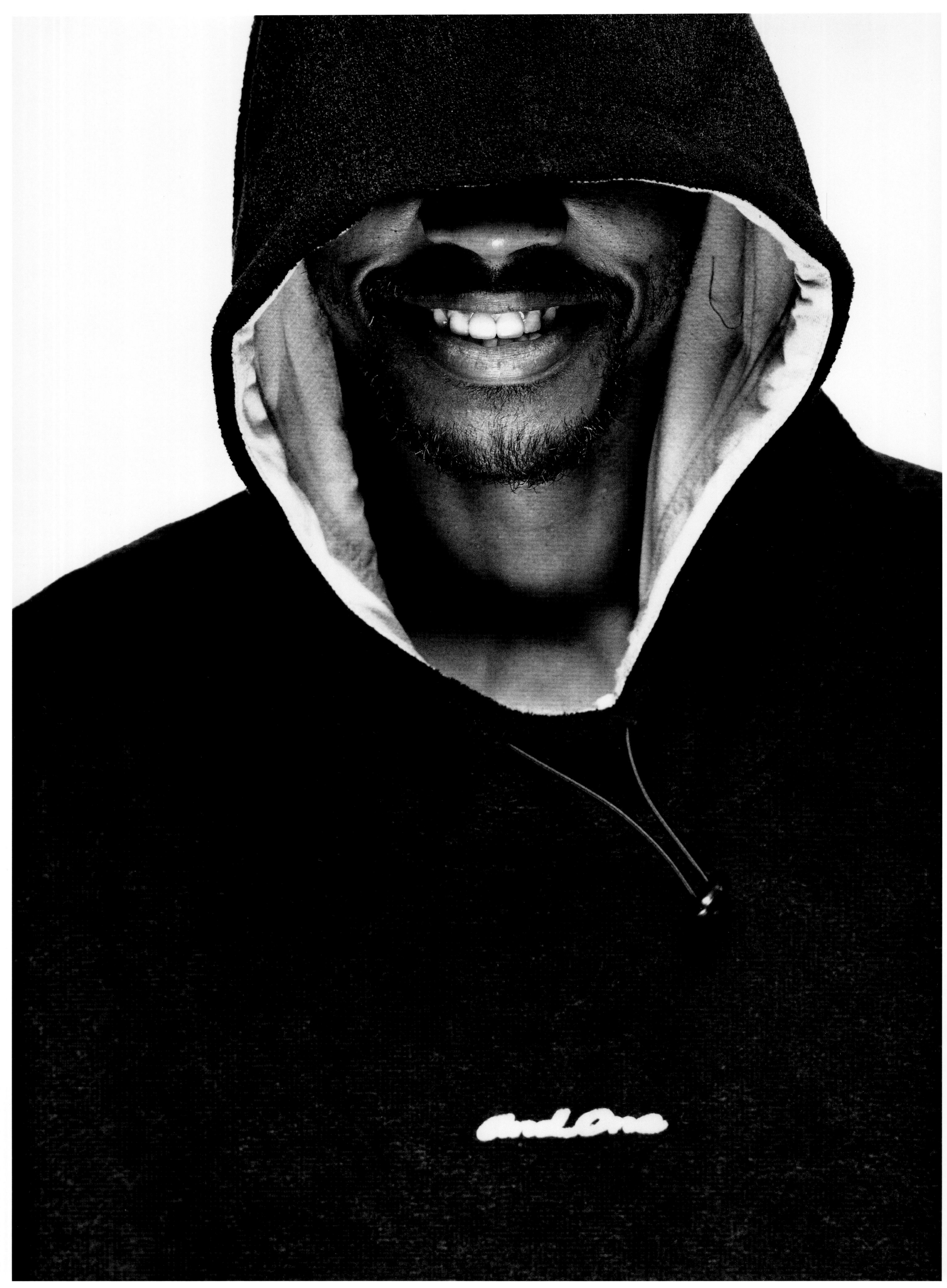
And One

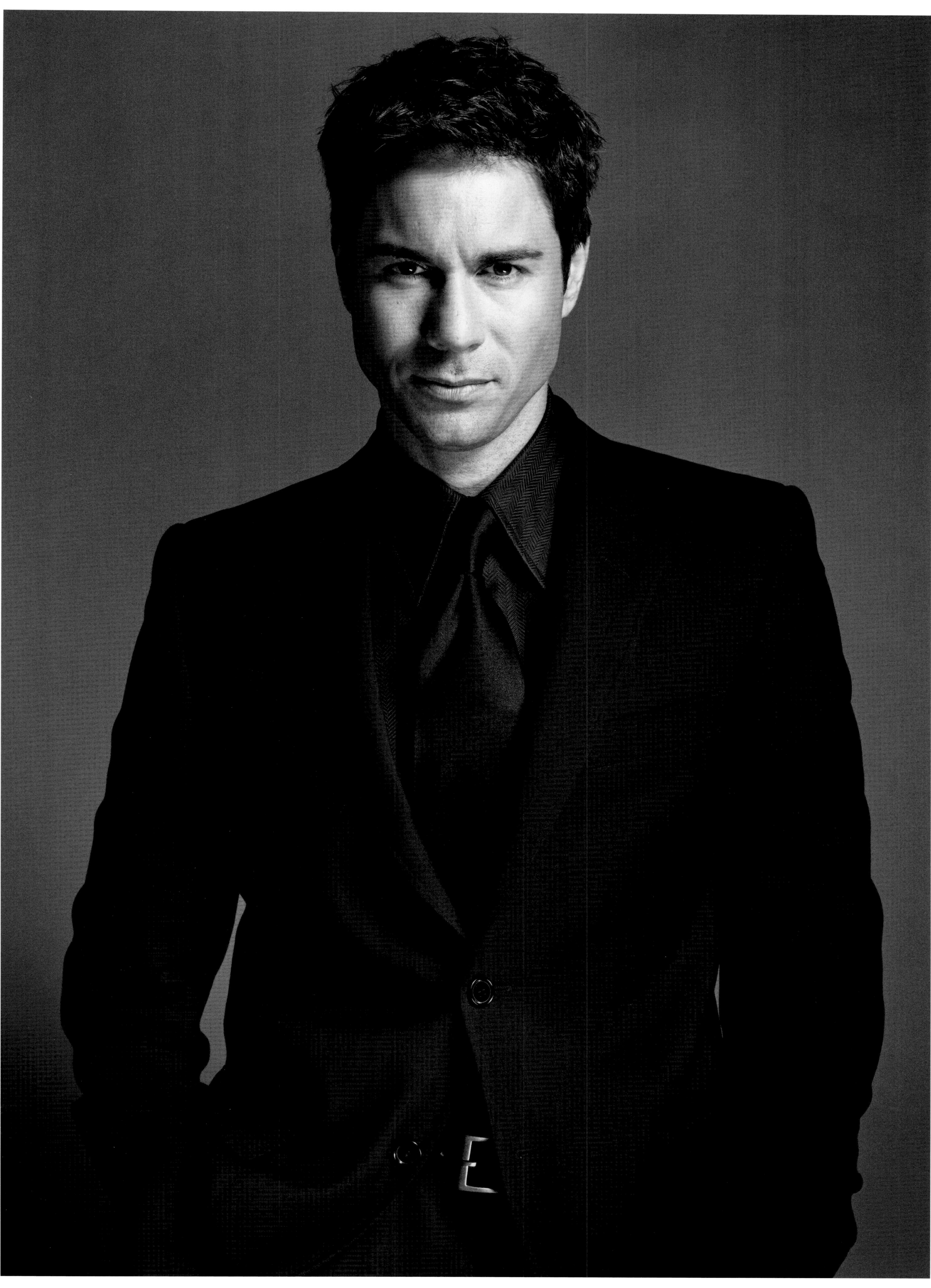

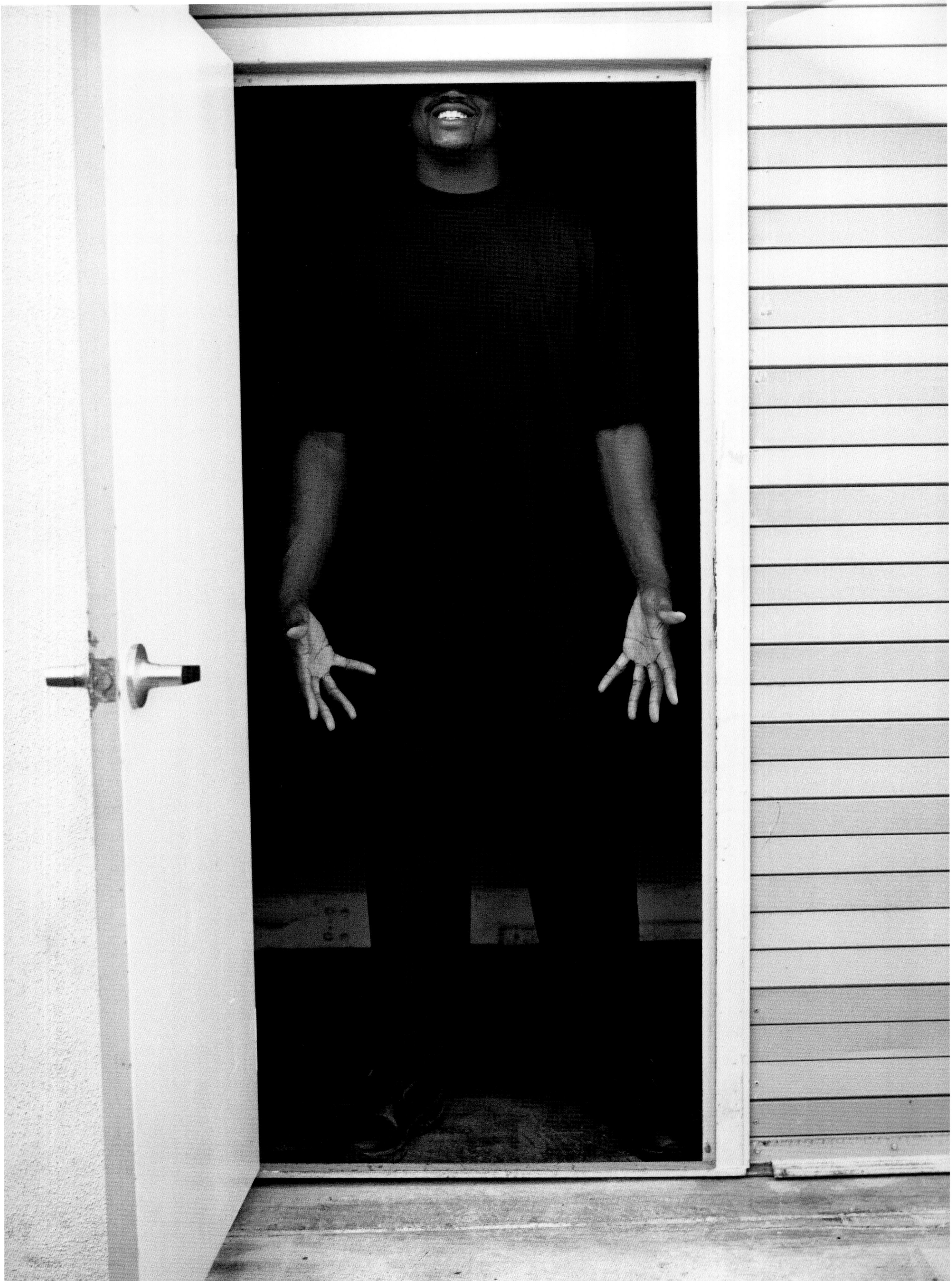

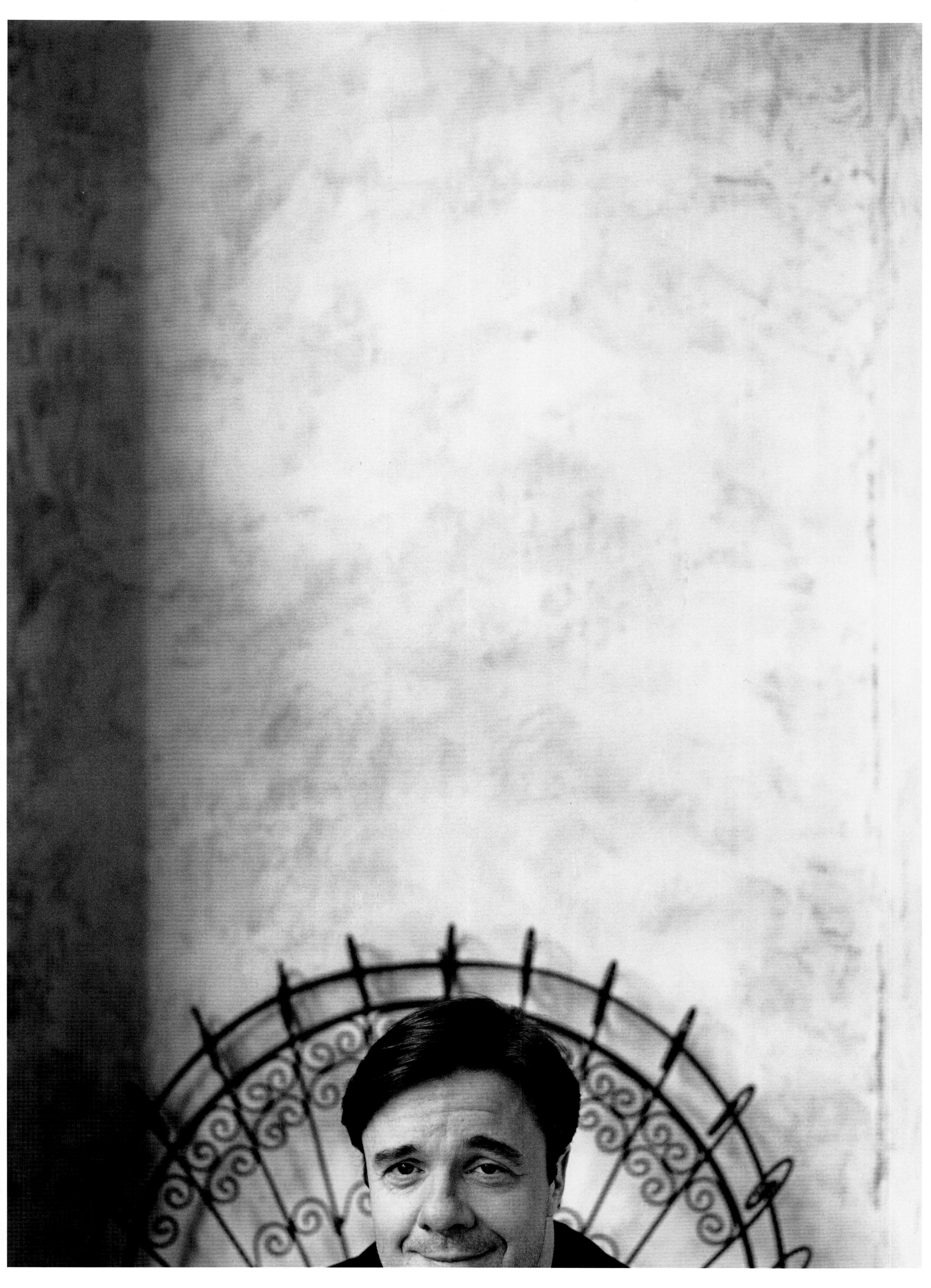

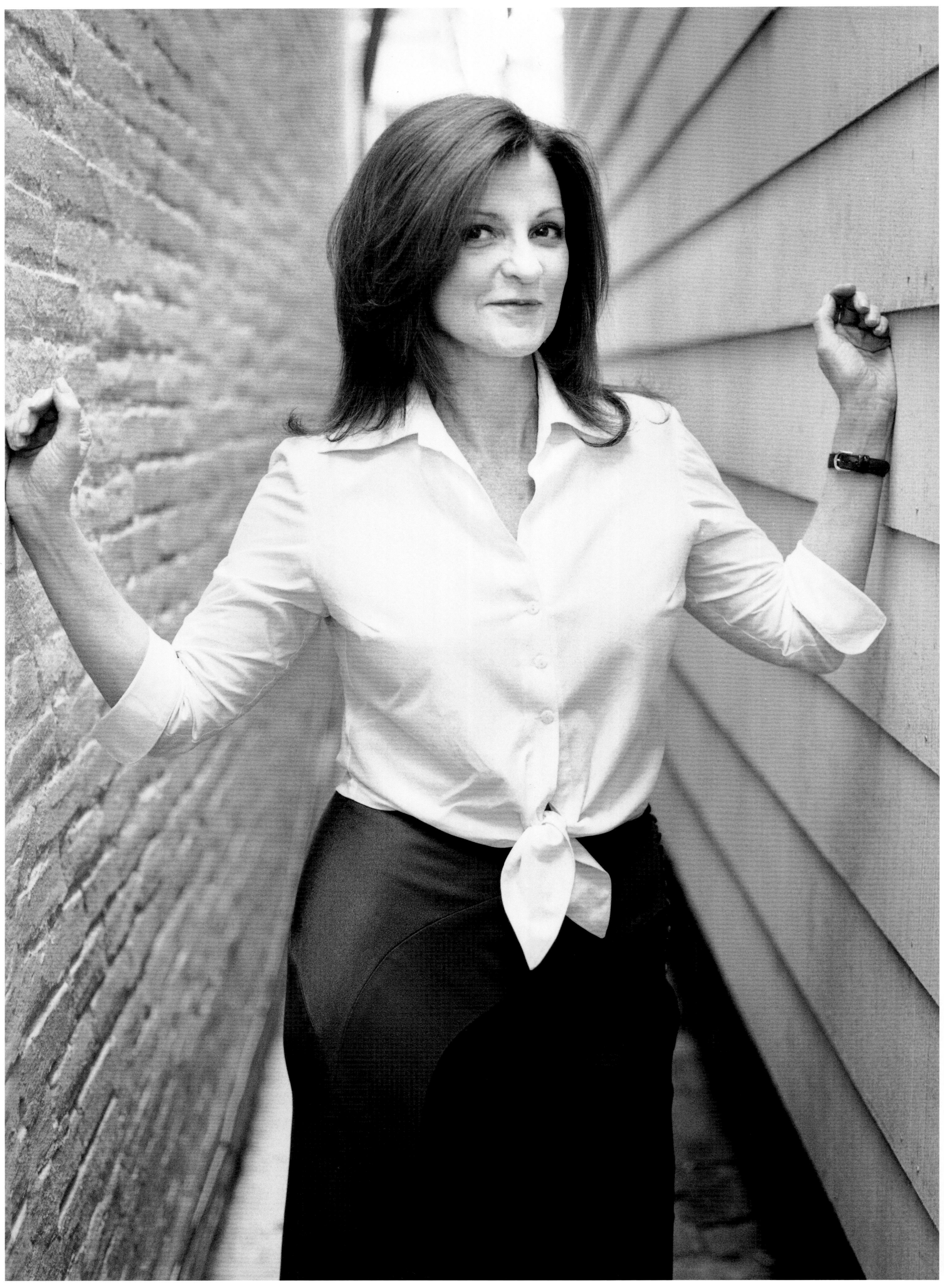

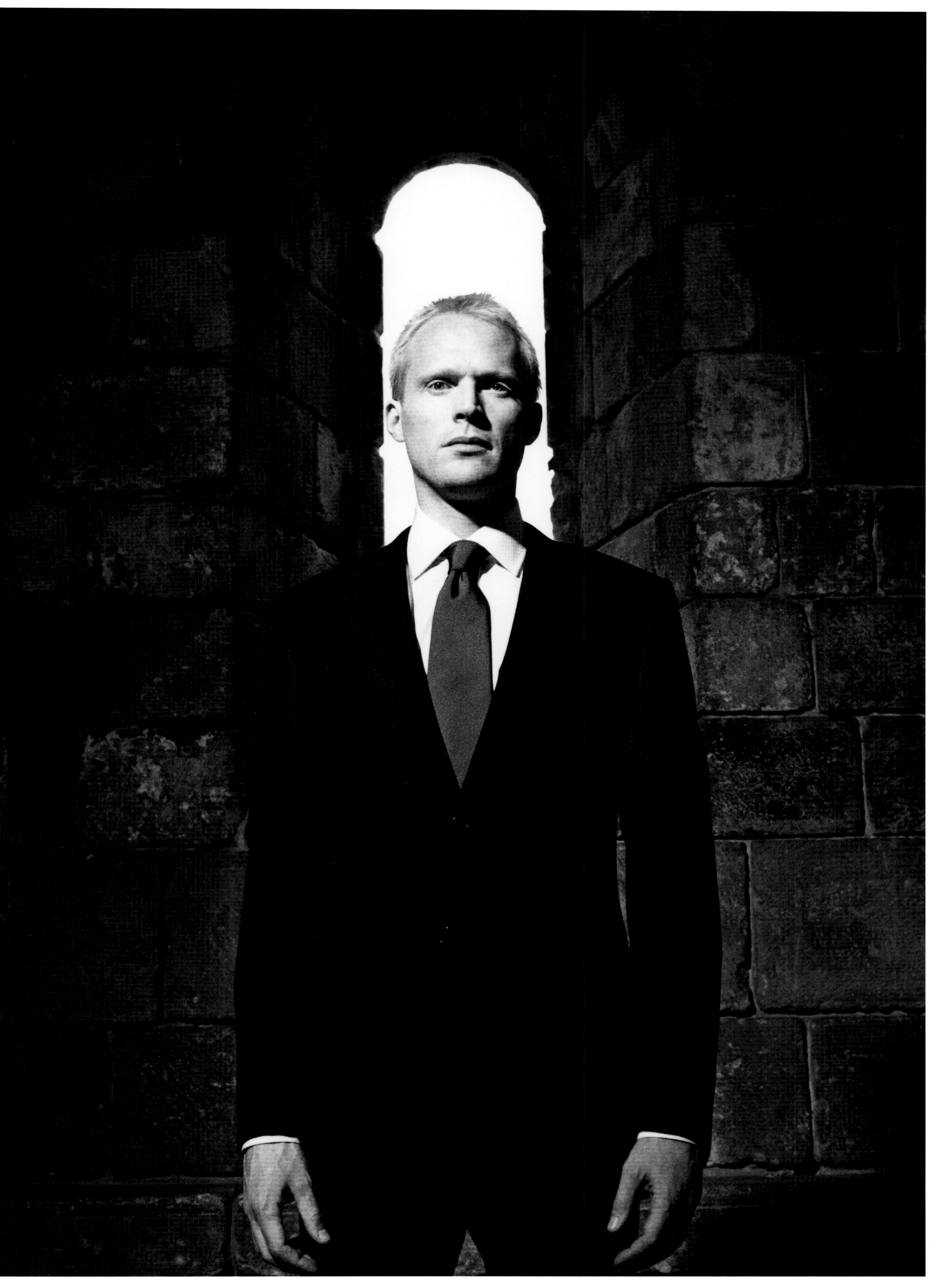

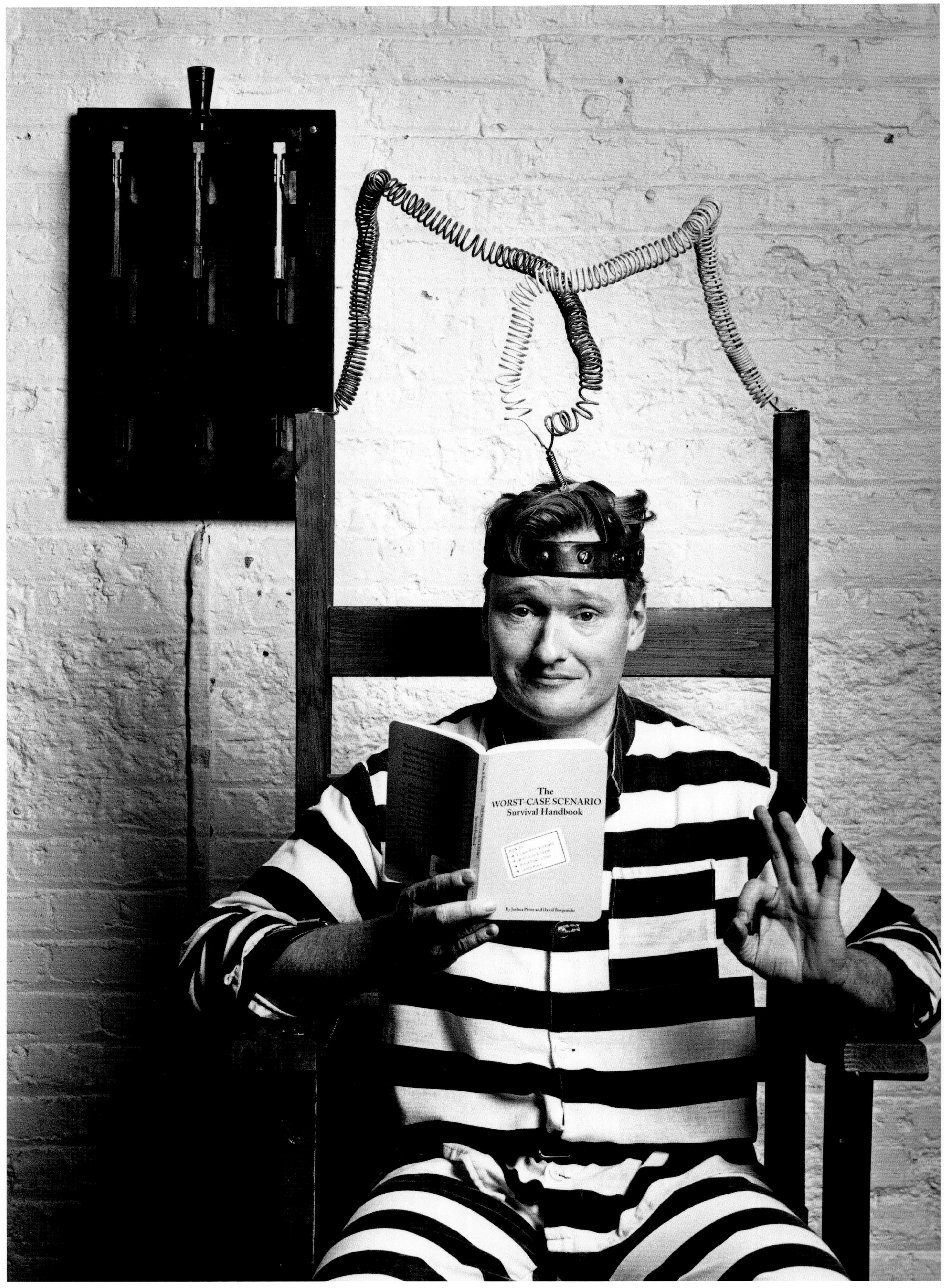

The
WORST-CASE SCENARIO
Survival Handbook
By Joshua Piven and David Borgenicht

PORTRAITS ON PREVIOUS PAGES

QUEEN RANIA OF JORDAN

JAMES MURDOCH
WILLIAM DONALDSON

BRAD PITT
GEORGE LUCAS

LATRELL SPREWELL
ERIC MCCORMACK

SHAQUILLE O'NEAL
NATHAN LANE

MAUREEN DOWD
PAUL BETTANY

CONAN O'BRIEN

WELL, THAT'S WHAT SORTS OUT THE MEN FROM THE BOYS ISN'T IT— THE WAY YOU HAVE TO TURN IT ON WHEN IT'S NEEDED IN THE RING.

LENNOX LEWIS' COMMENTS ABOUT THE FEROCITY WITH WHICH HE ENDS A TRAINING ROUND, LEAVING A FRIEND AND SPARRING PARTNER COVERED IN BLOOD.

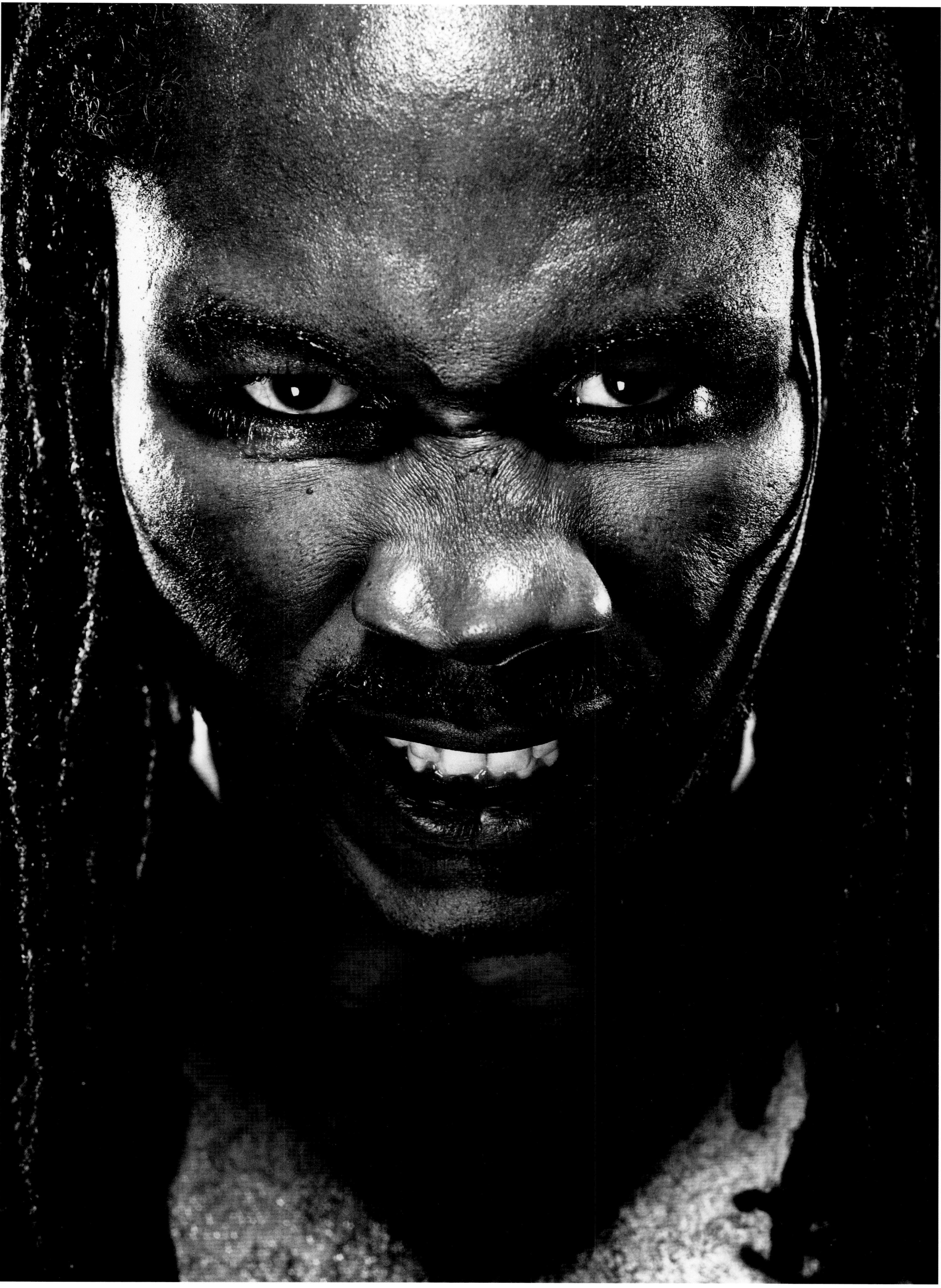

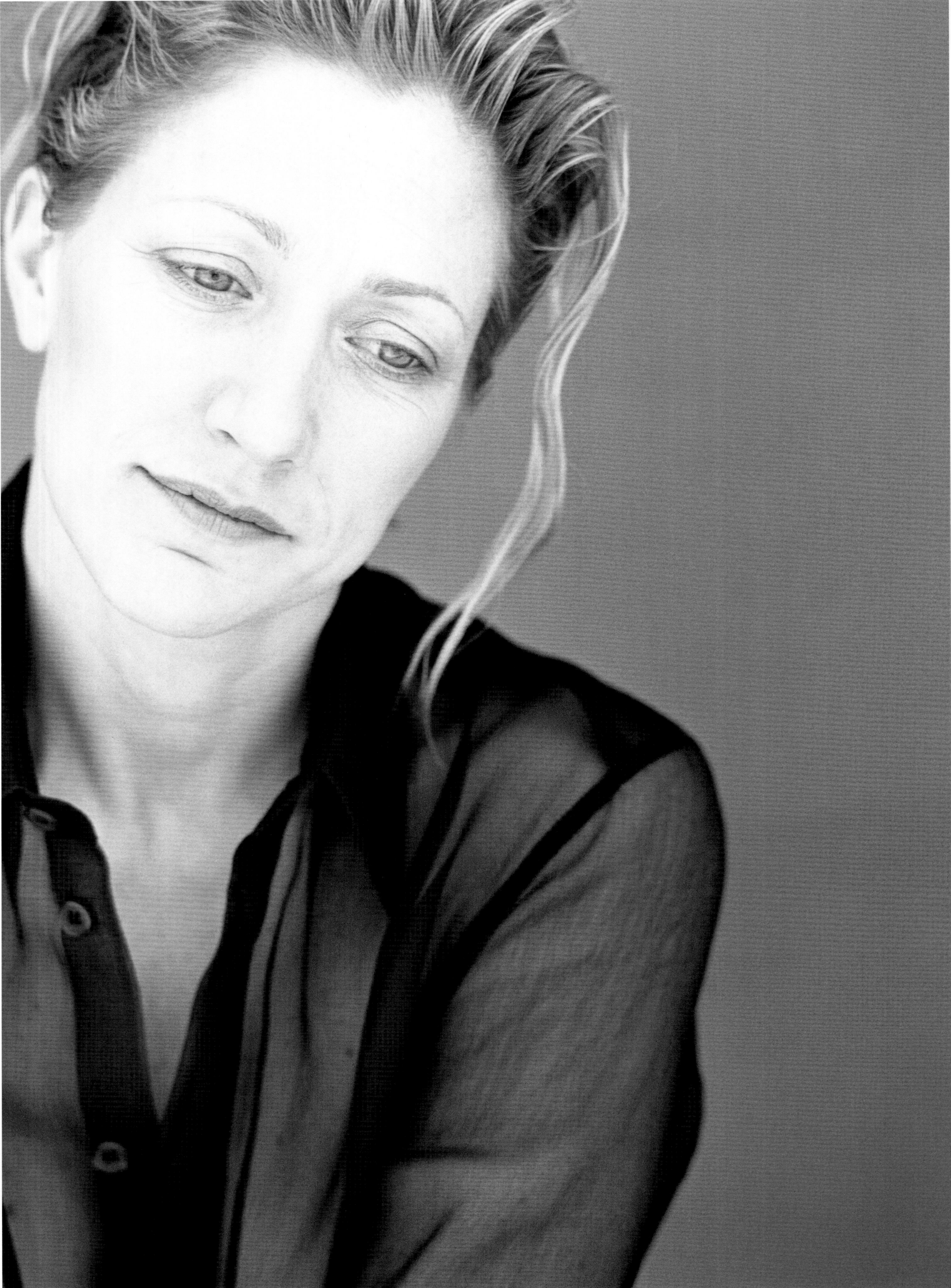

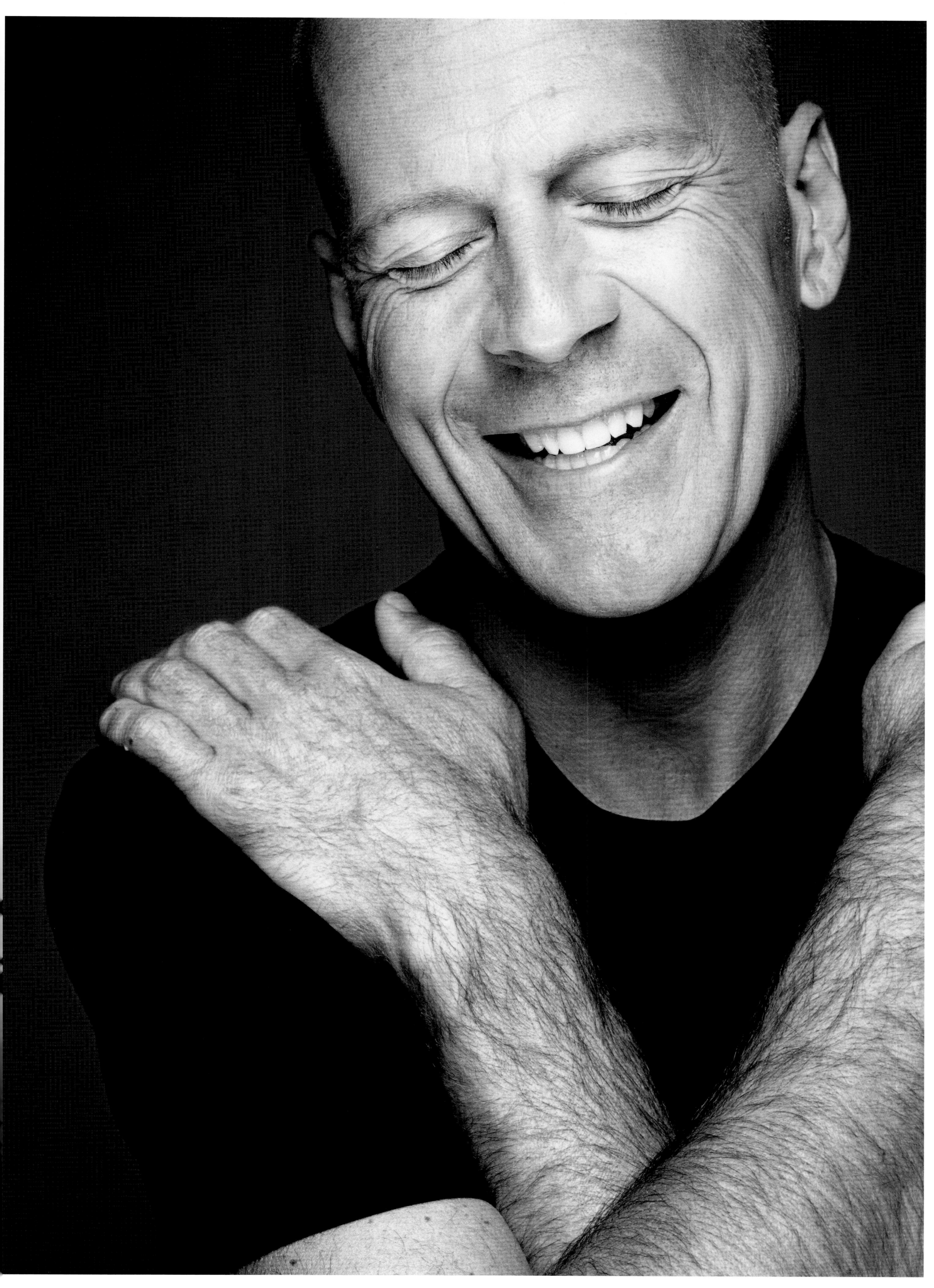

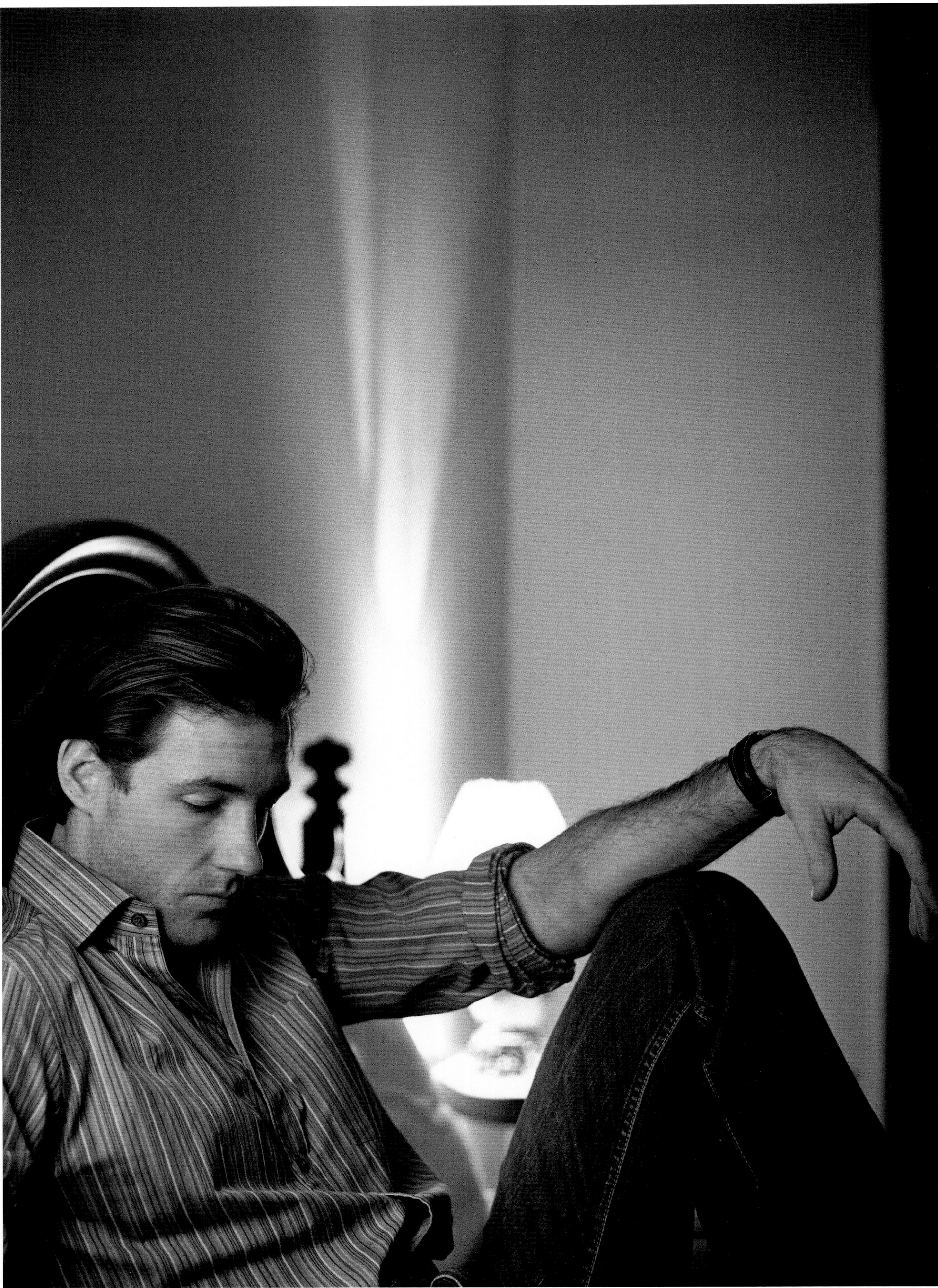

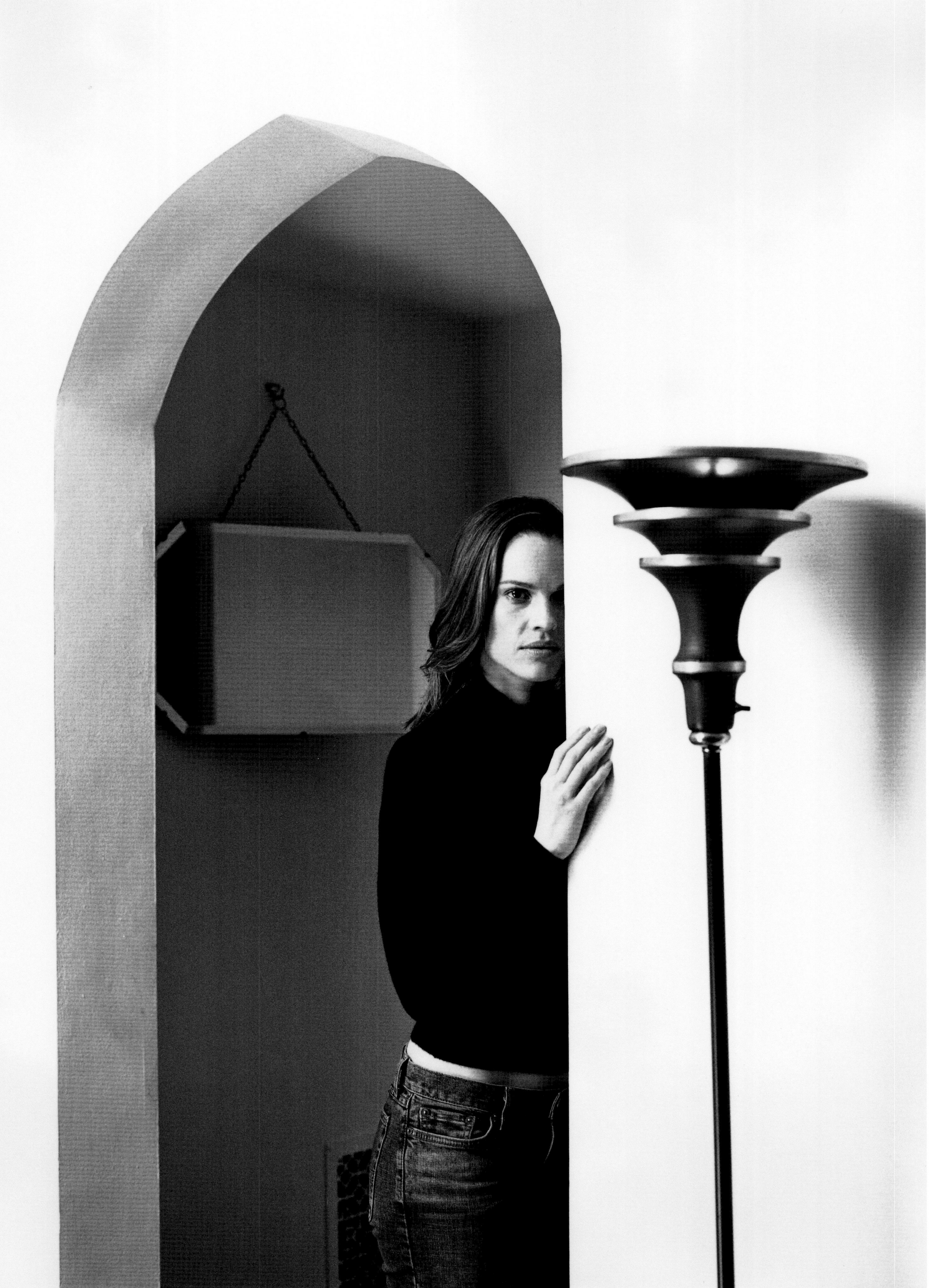

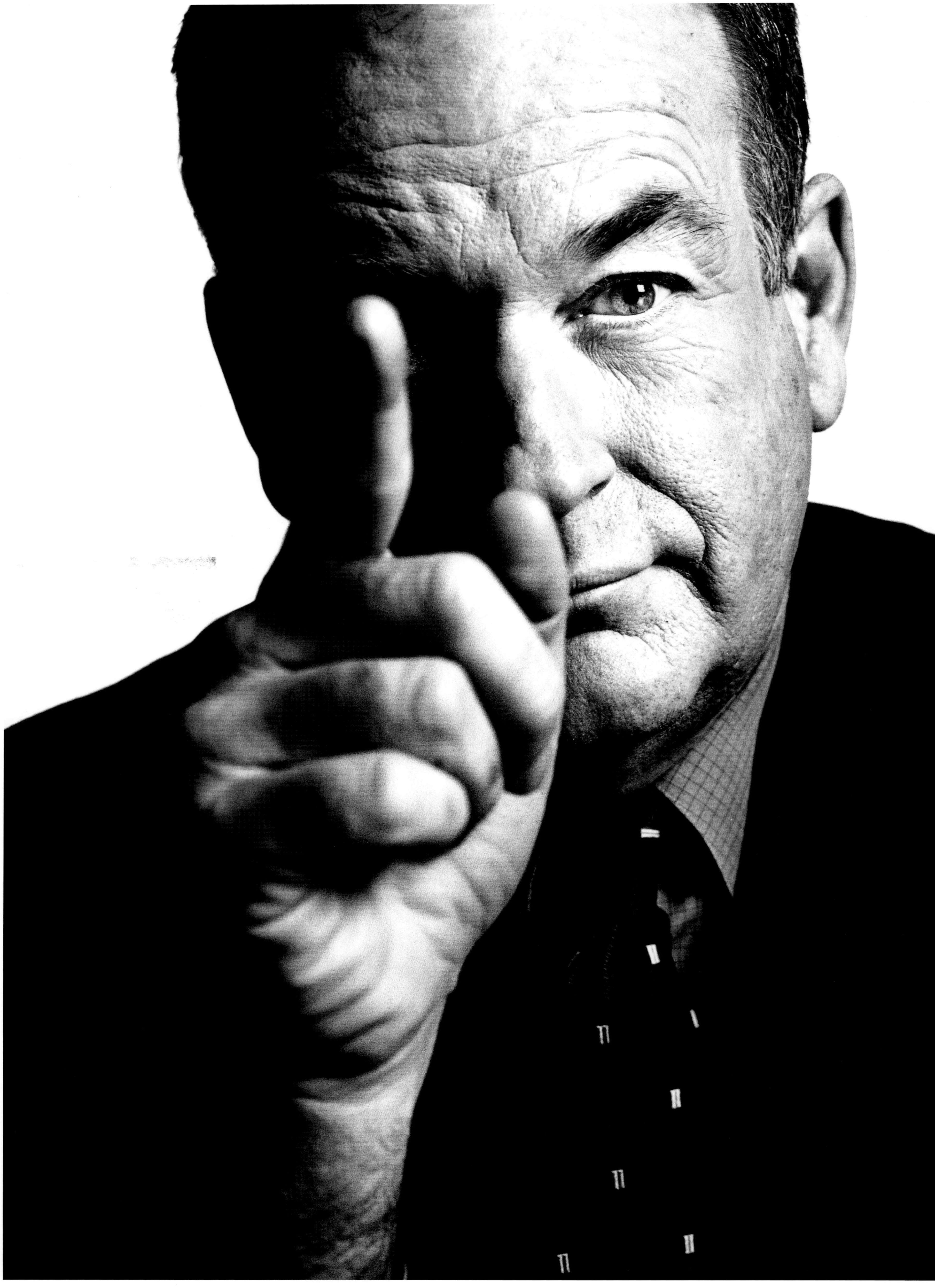

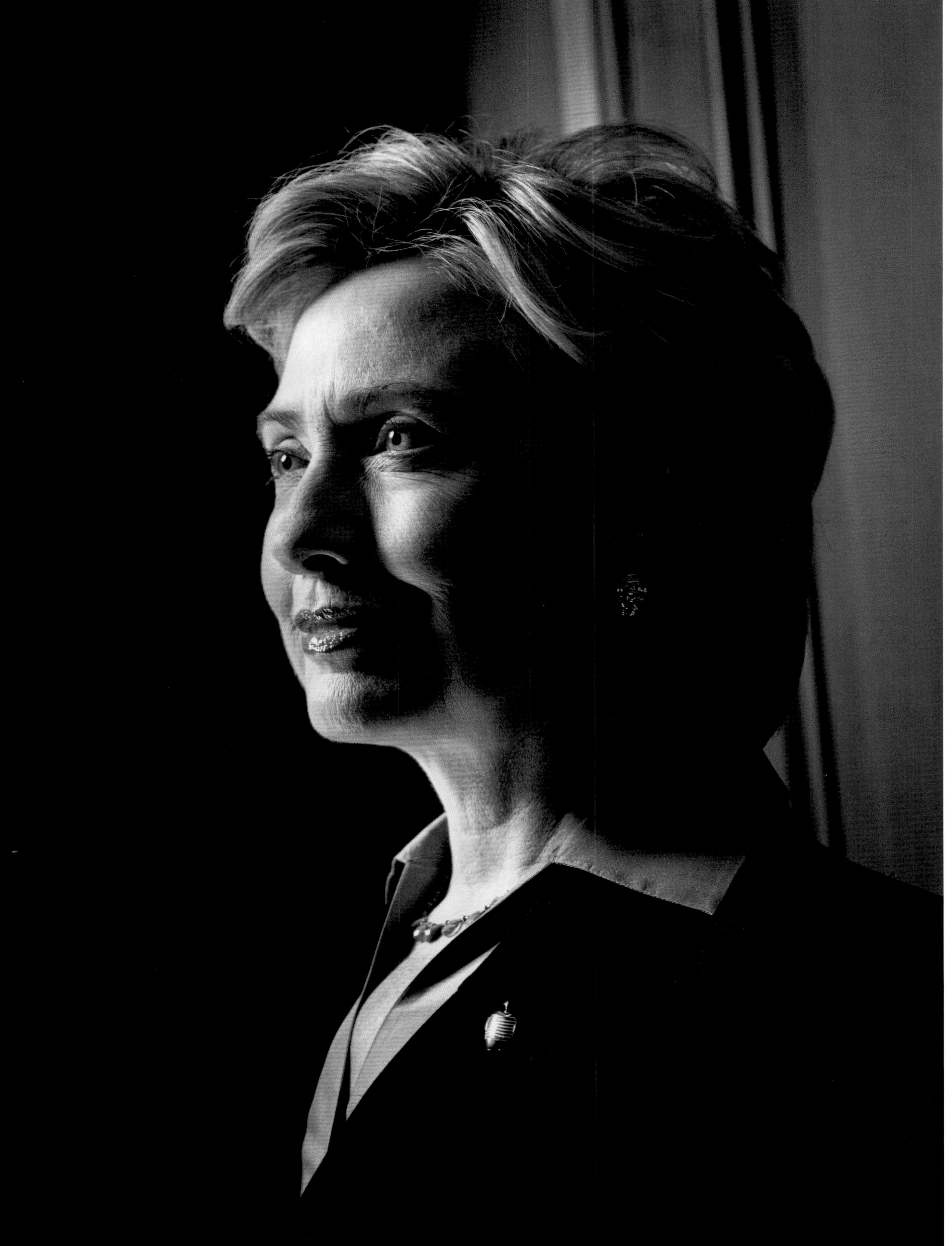

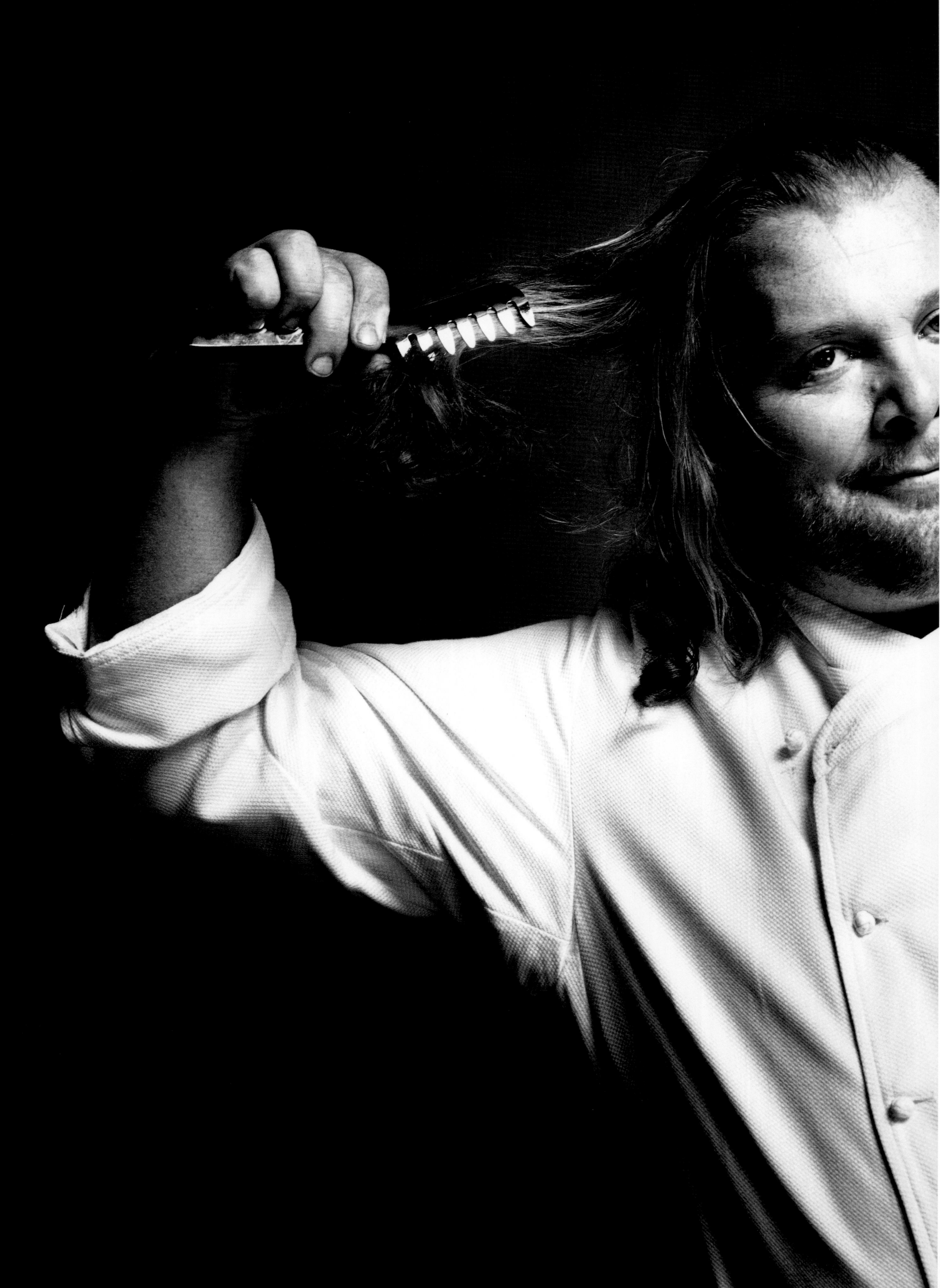

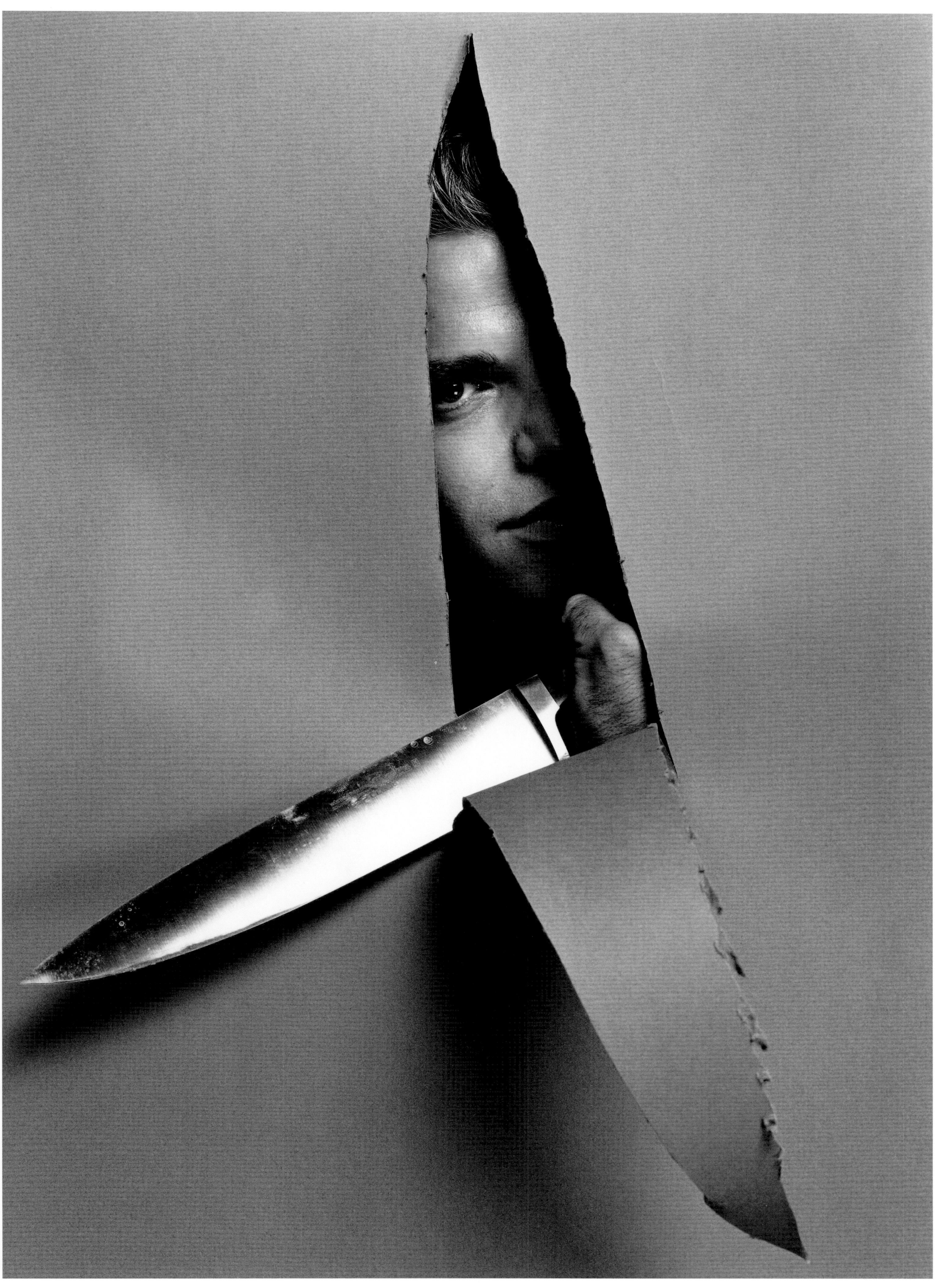

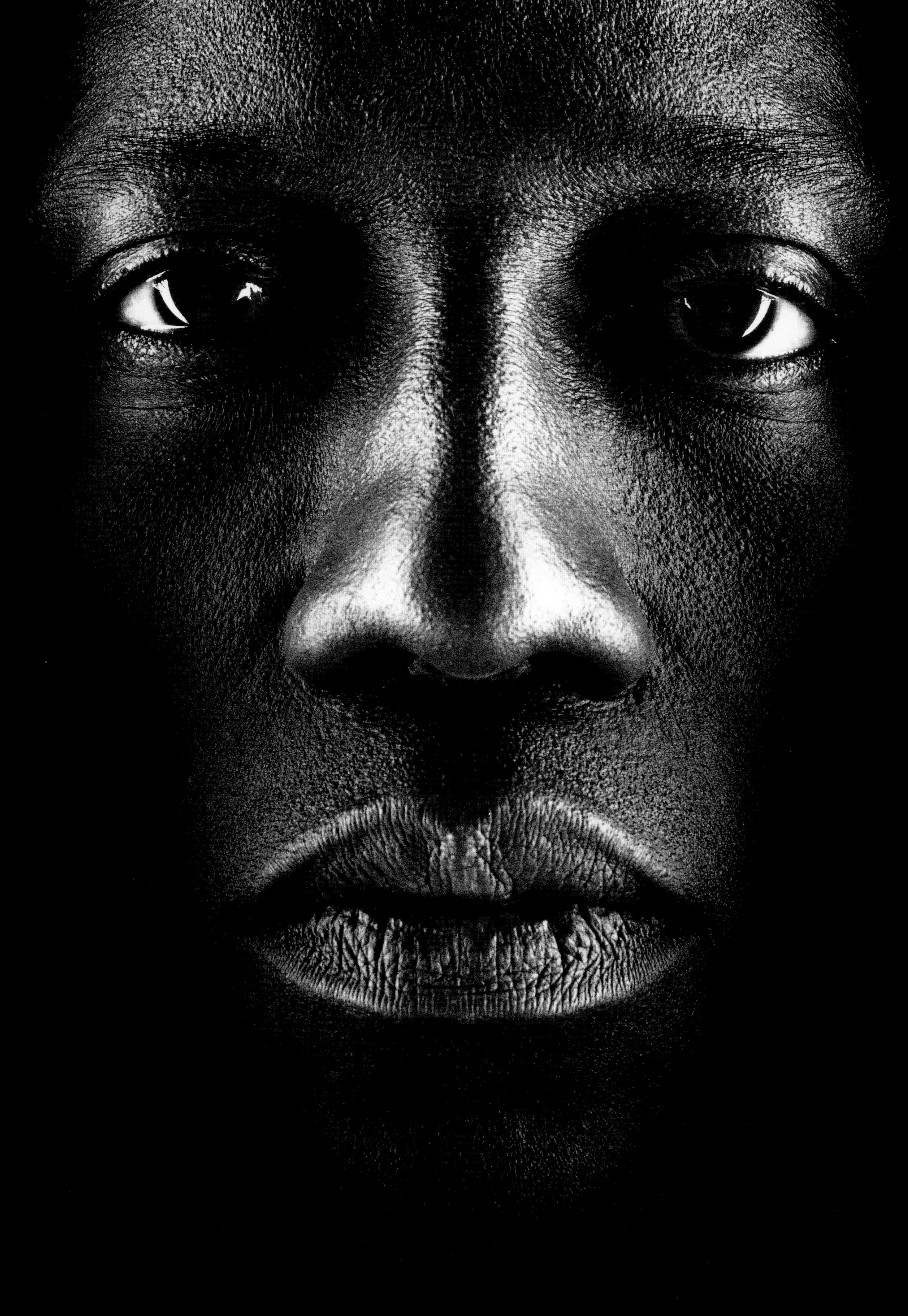

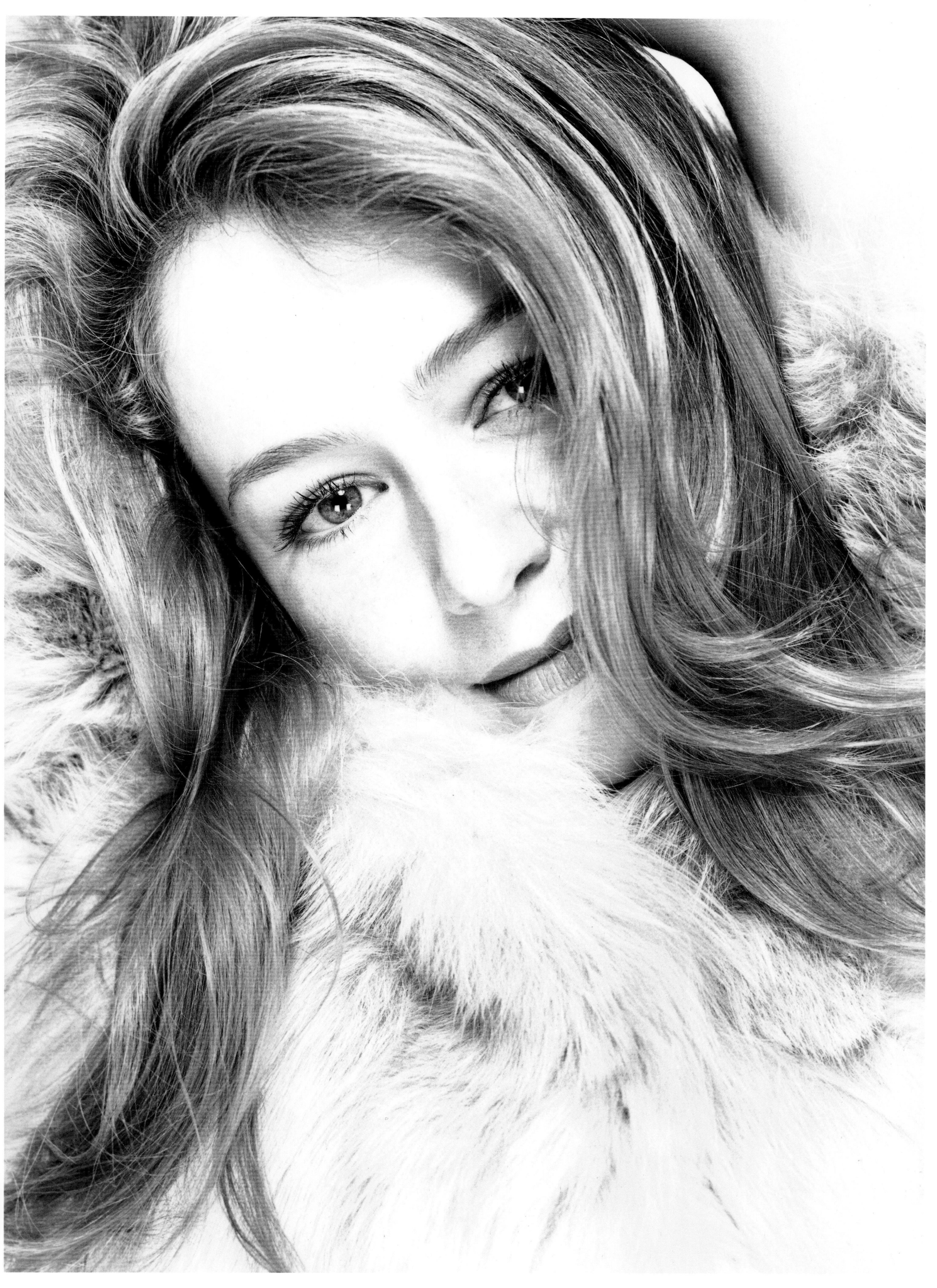

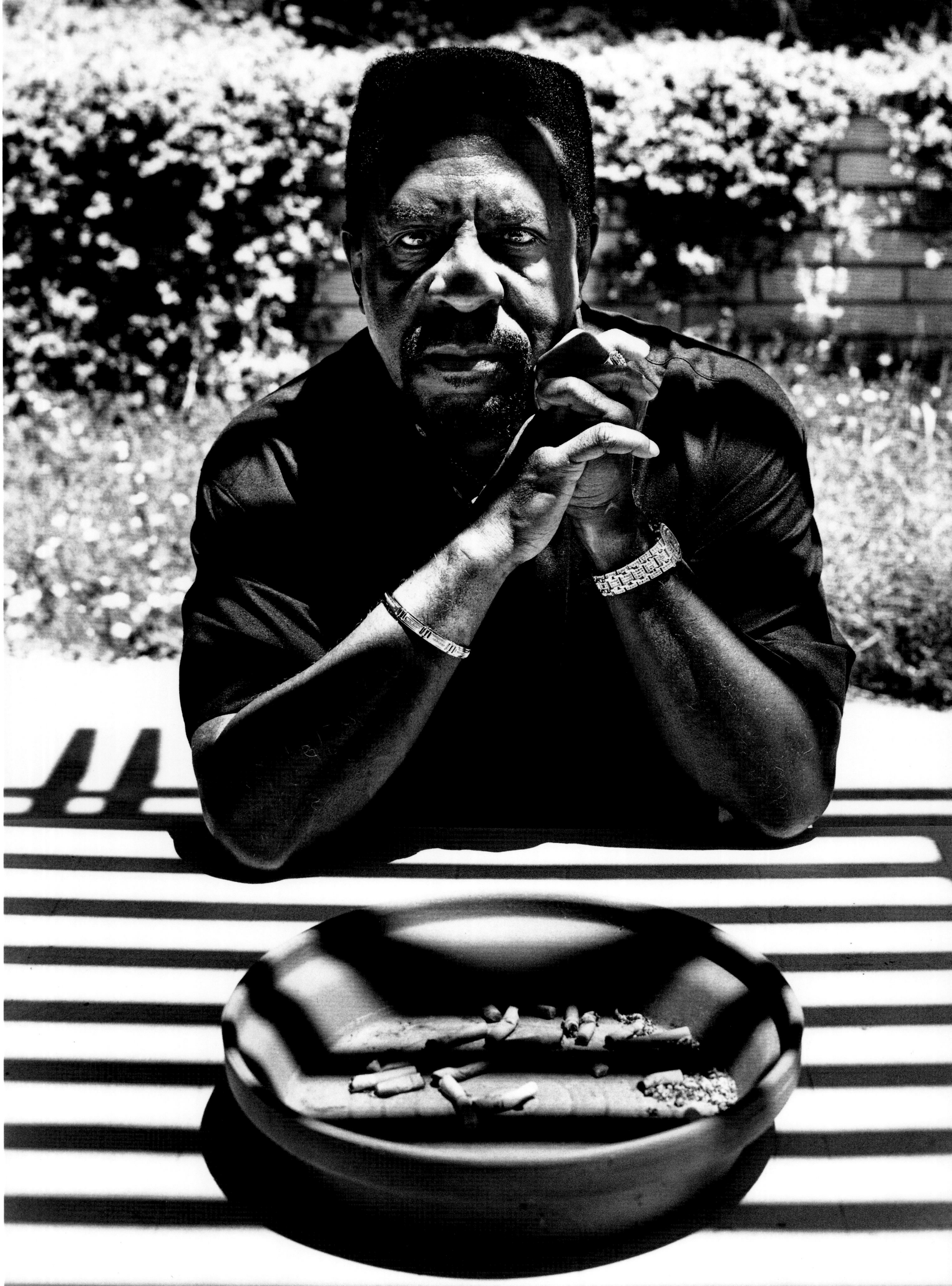

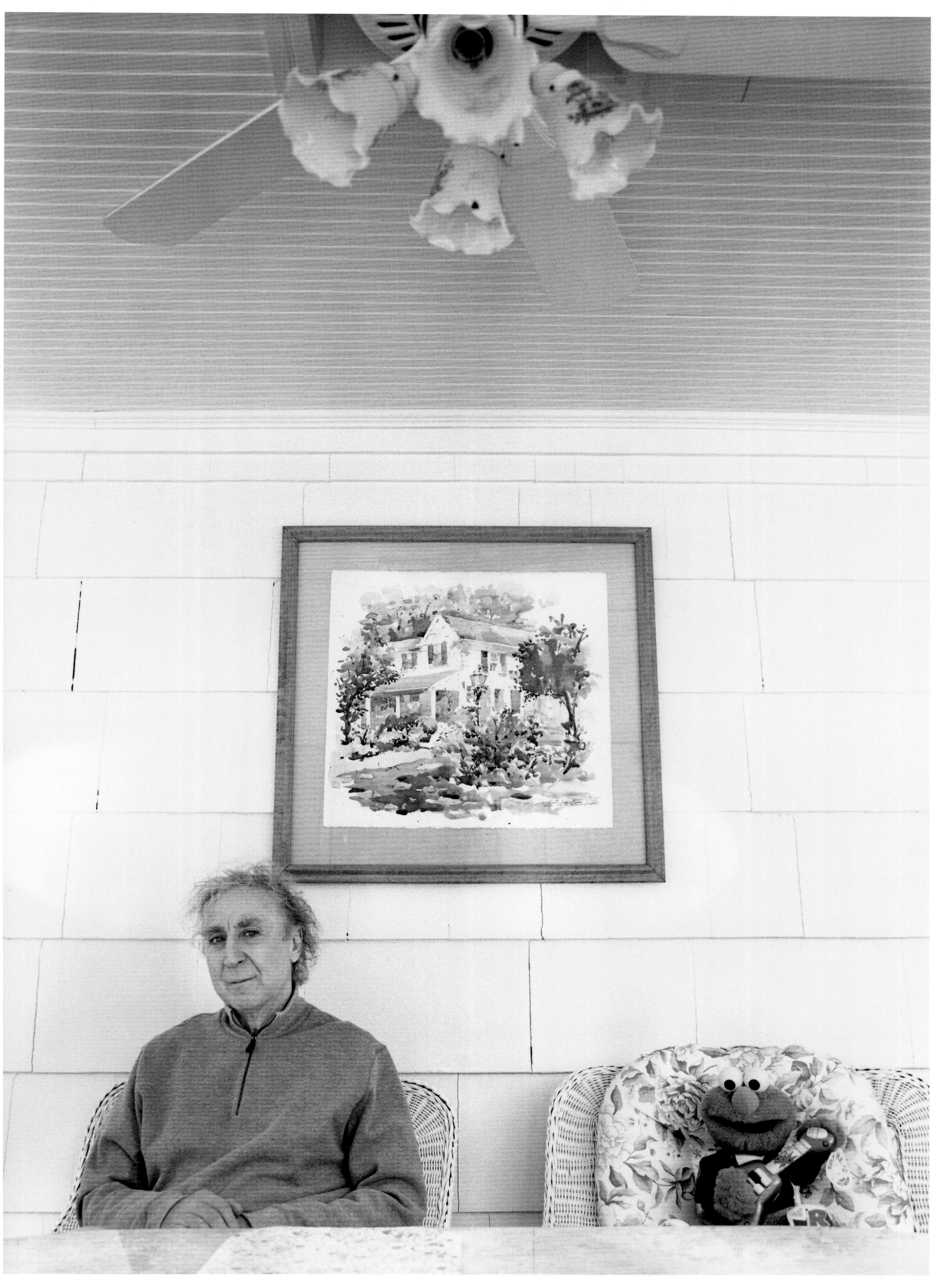

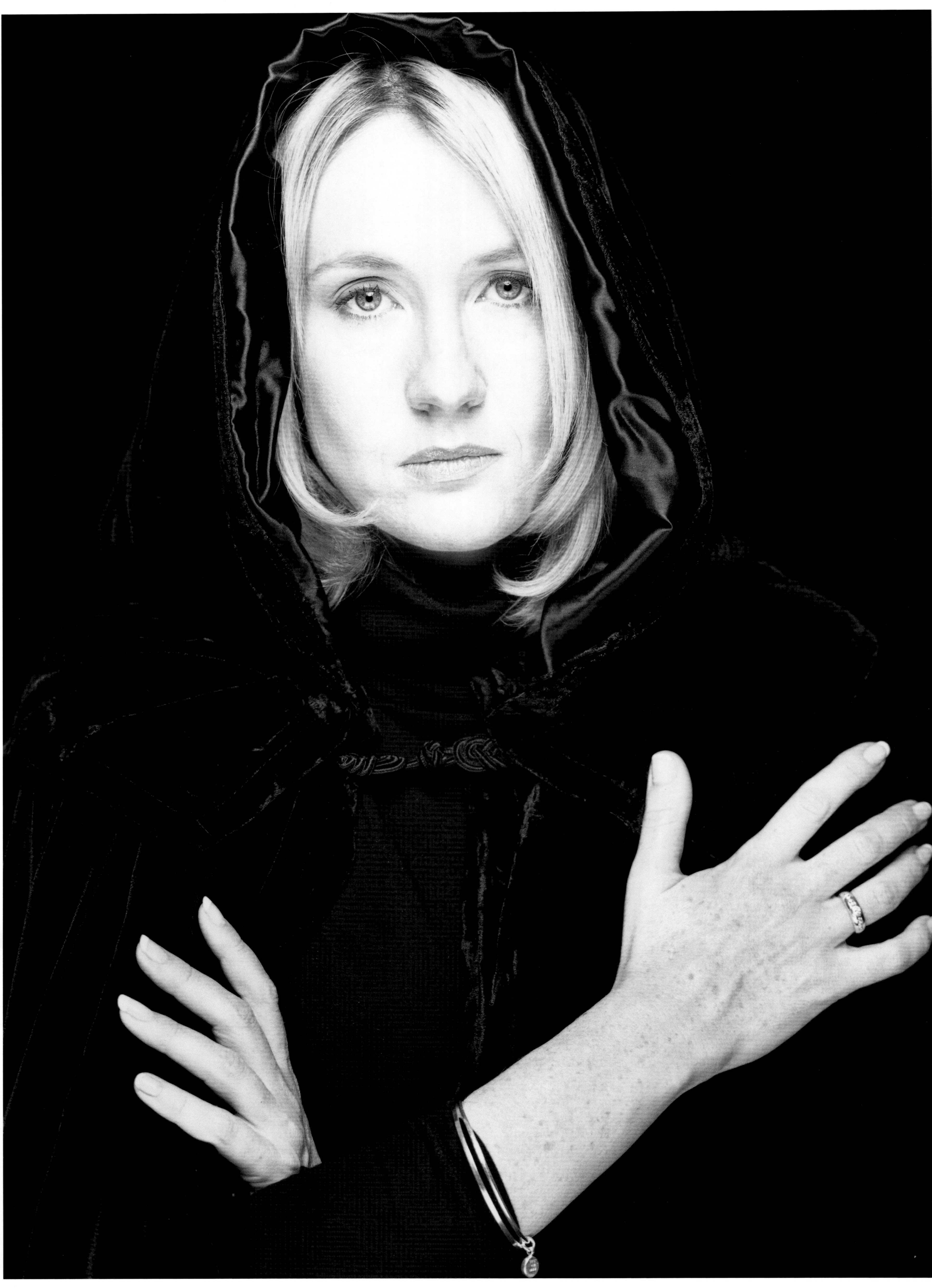

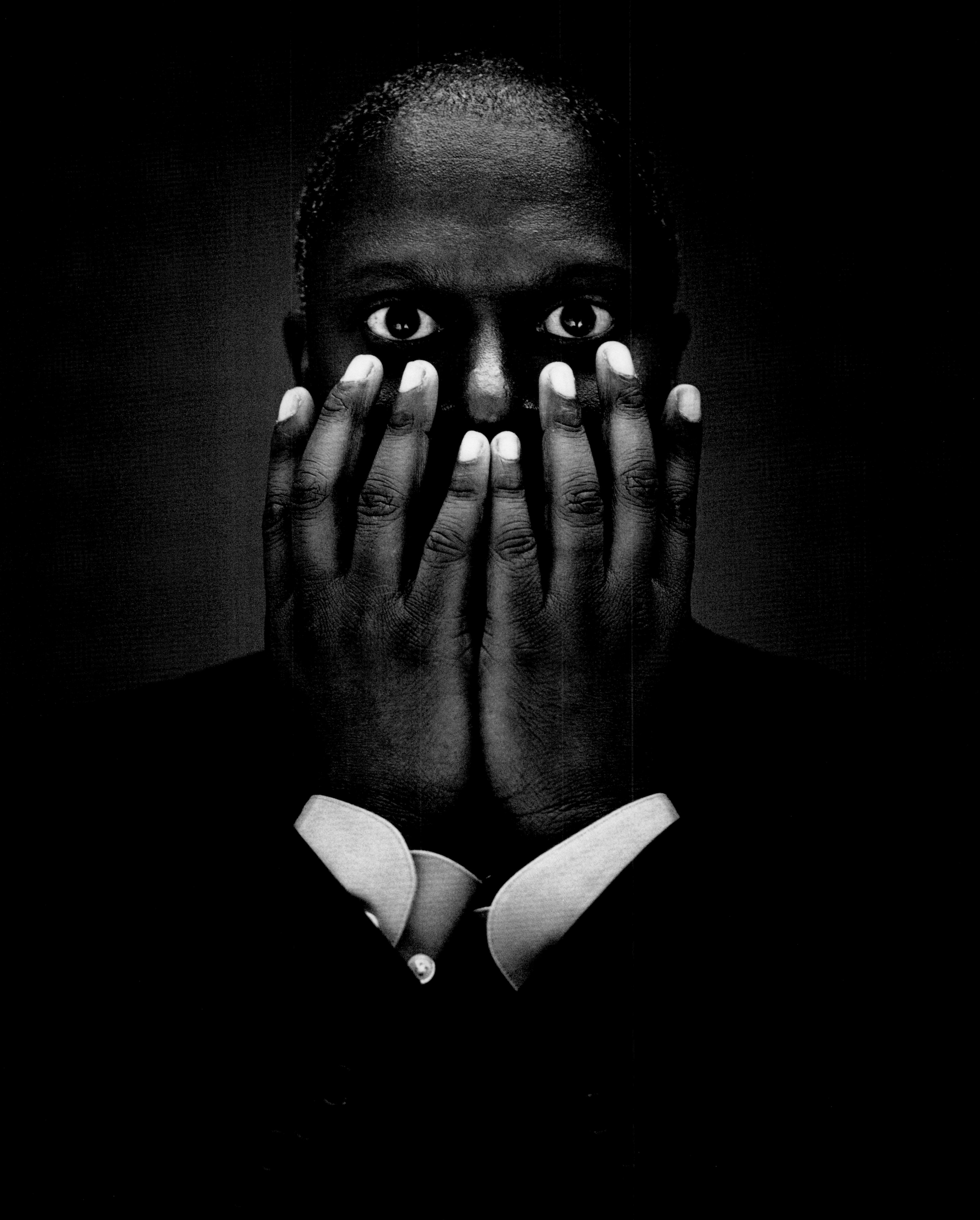

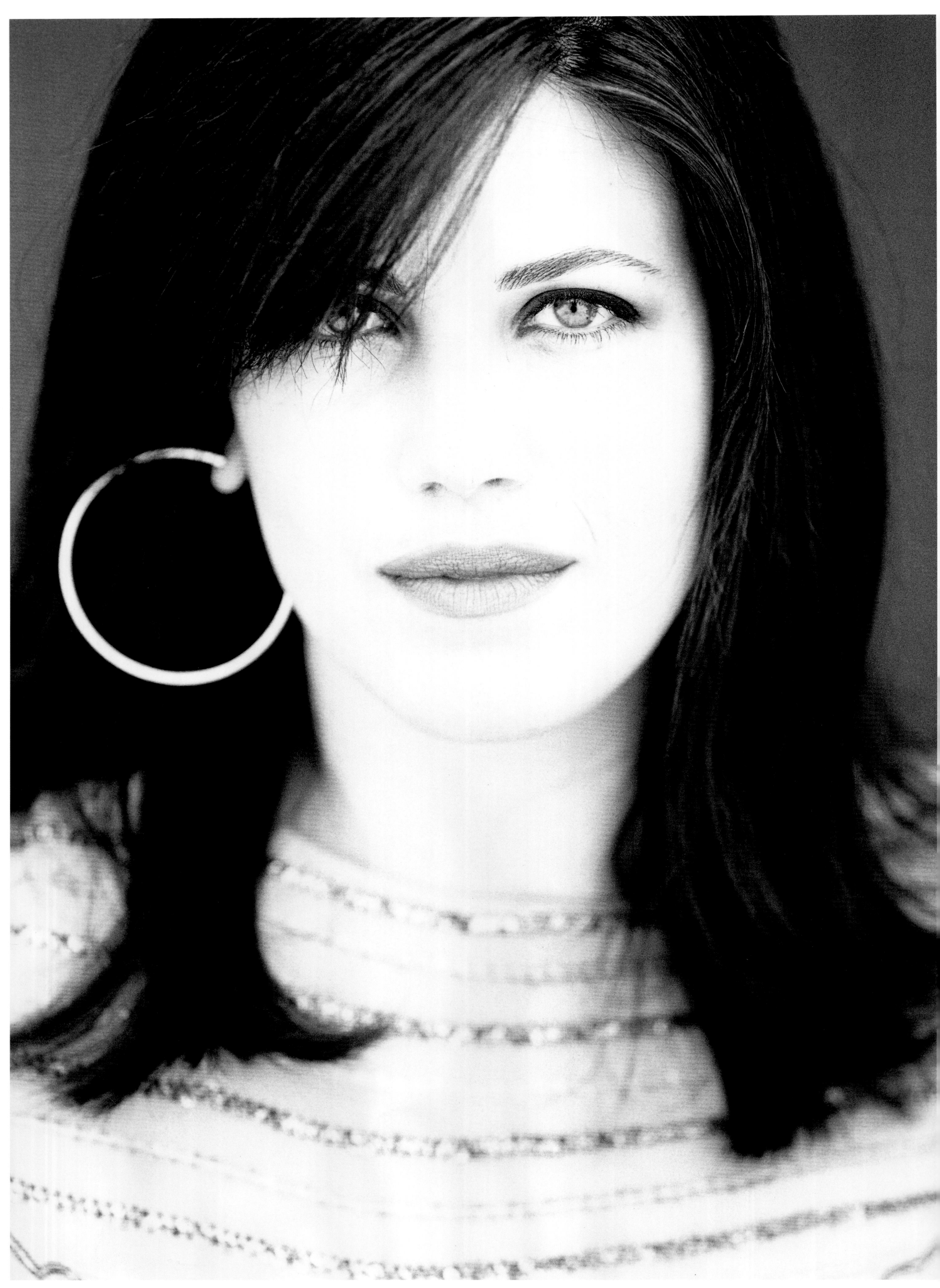

PORTRAITS ON PREVIOUS PAGES

LENNOX LEWIS

EDIE FALCO
BRUCE WILLIS

ED BURNS
HILARY SWANK

BILL O'REILLY
HILLARY RODHAM CLINTON

MARIO BATALI
ERIC RIPERT

WESLEY SNIPES
MIRANDA OTTO

IKE TURNER
GENE WILDER

J.K. ROWLING
ANDRE BRAUGHER

MONICA LEWINSKY

THOSE JACKETS? ...THEY BELONG TO THE MEN WHO DIDN'T MAKE IT OUT...

ACTING CHIEF LADDER 105

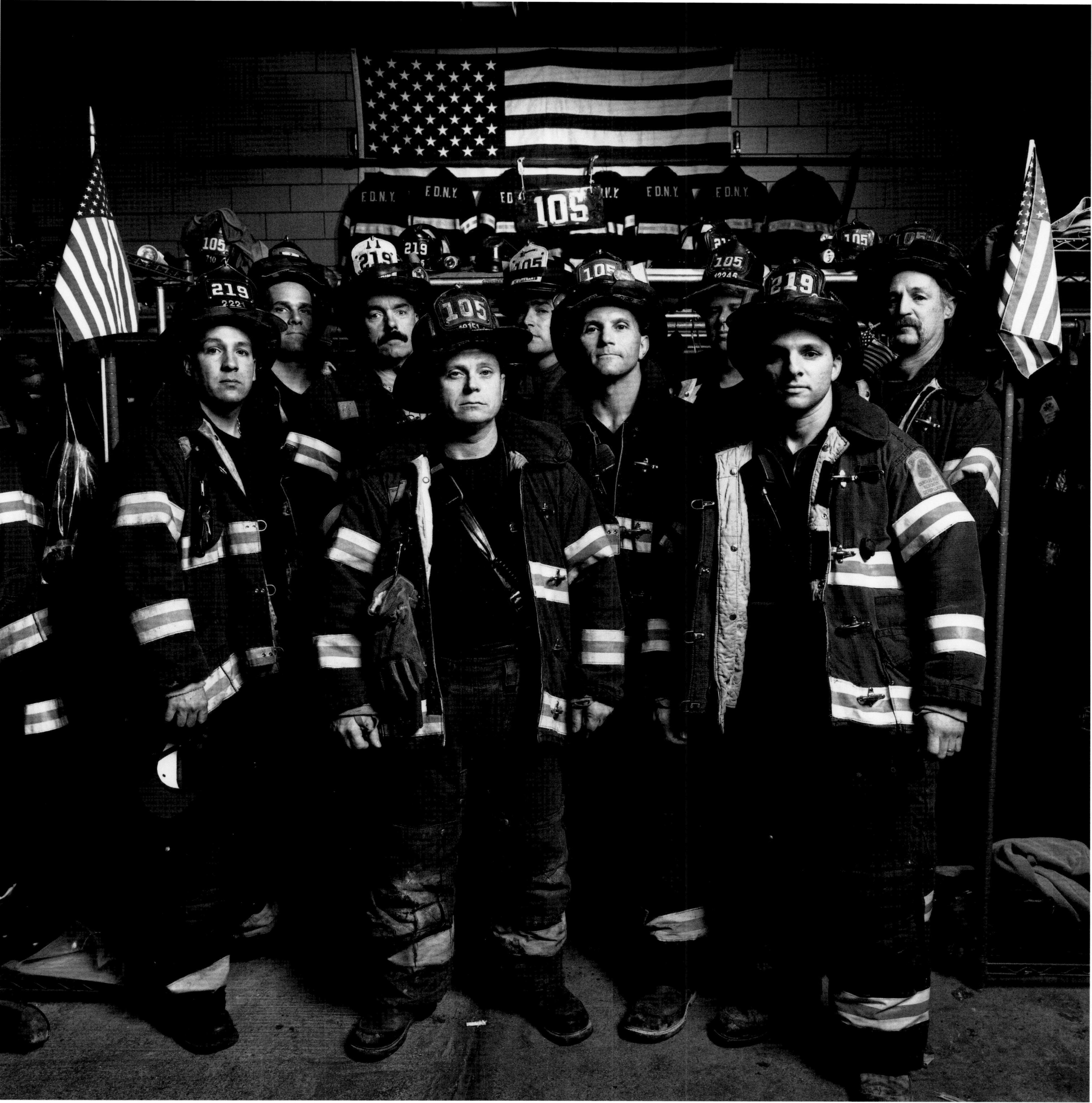
F.D.N.Y.
F.D.N.Y.
105
F.D.N.Y.
F.D.N.Y.
219
105
105
219
105

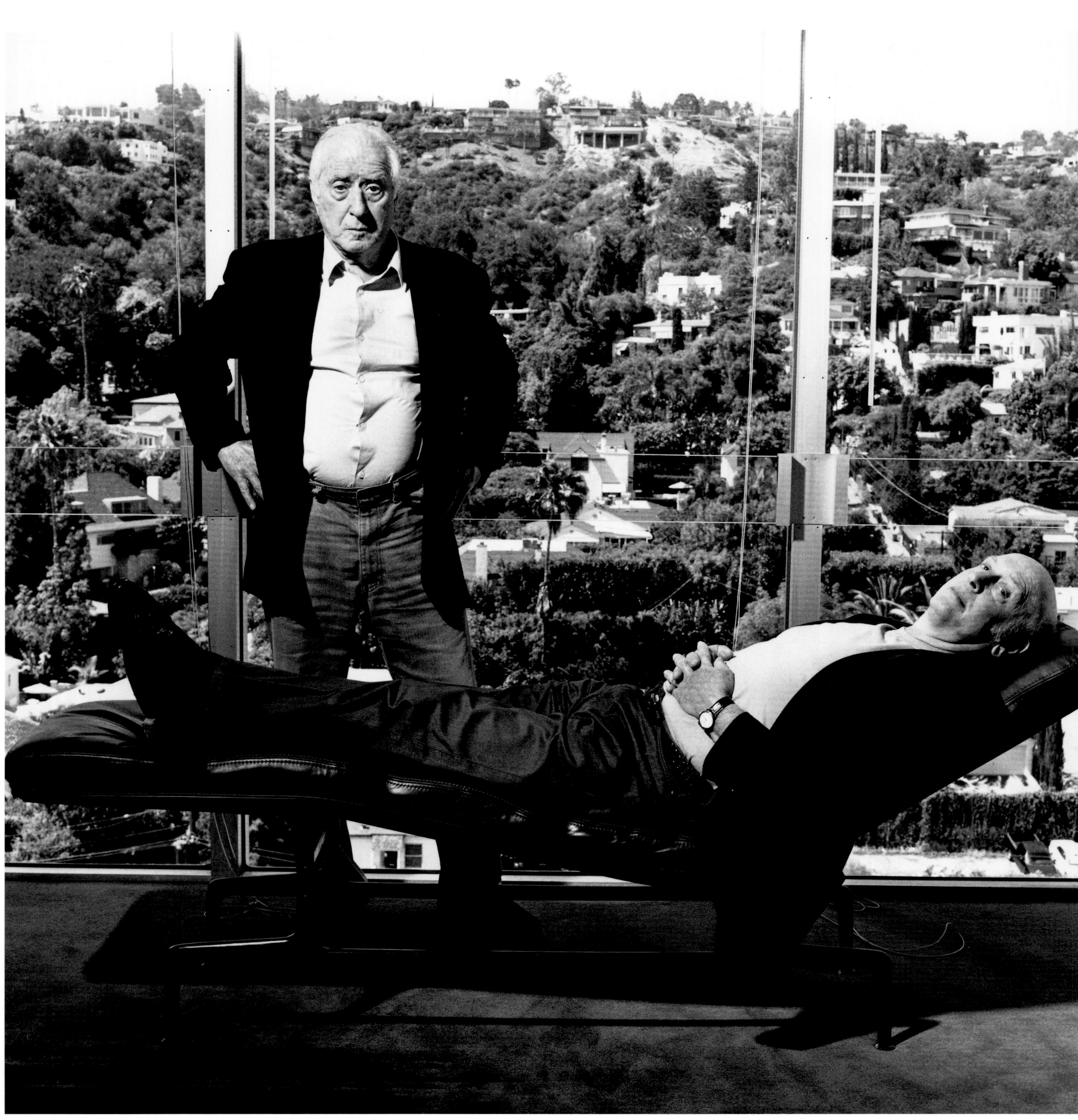

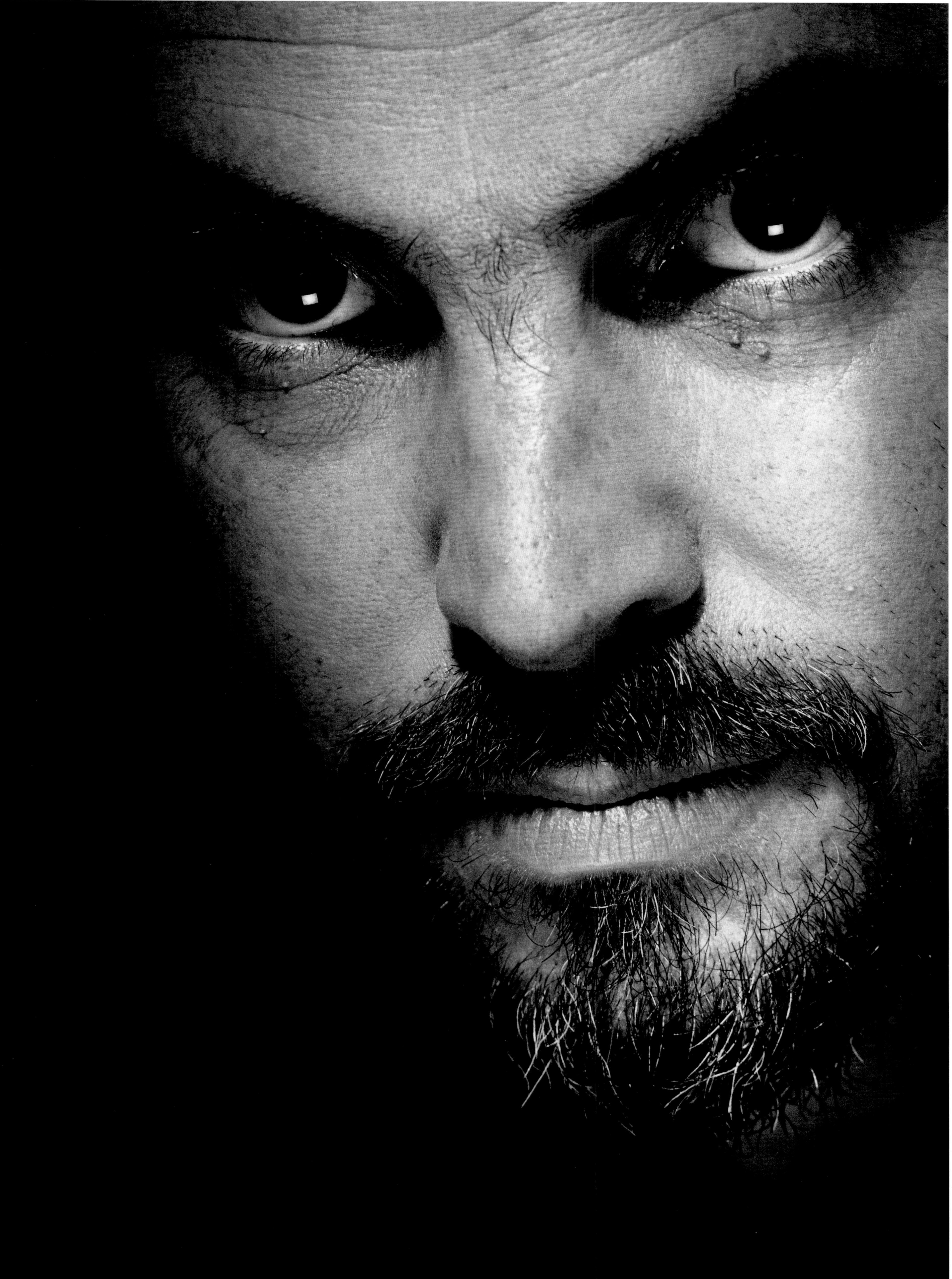

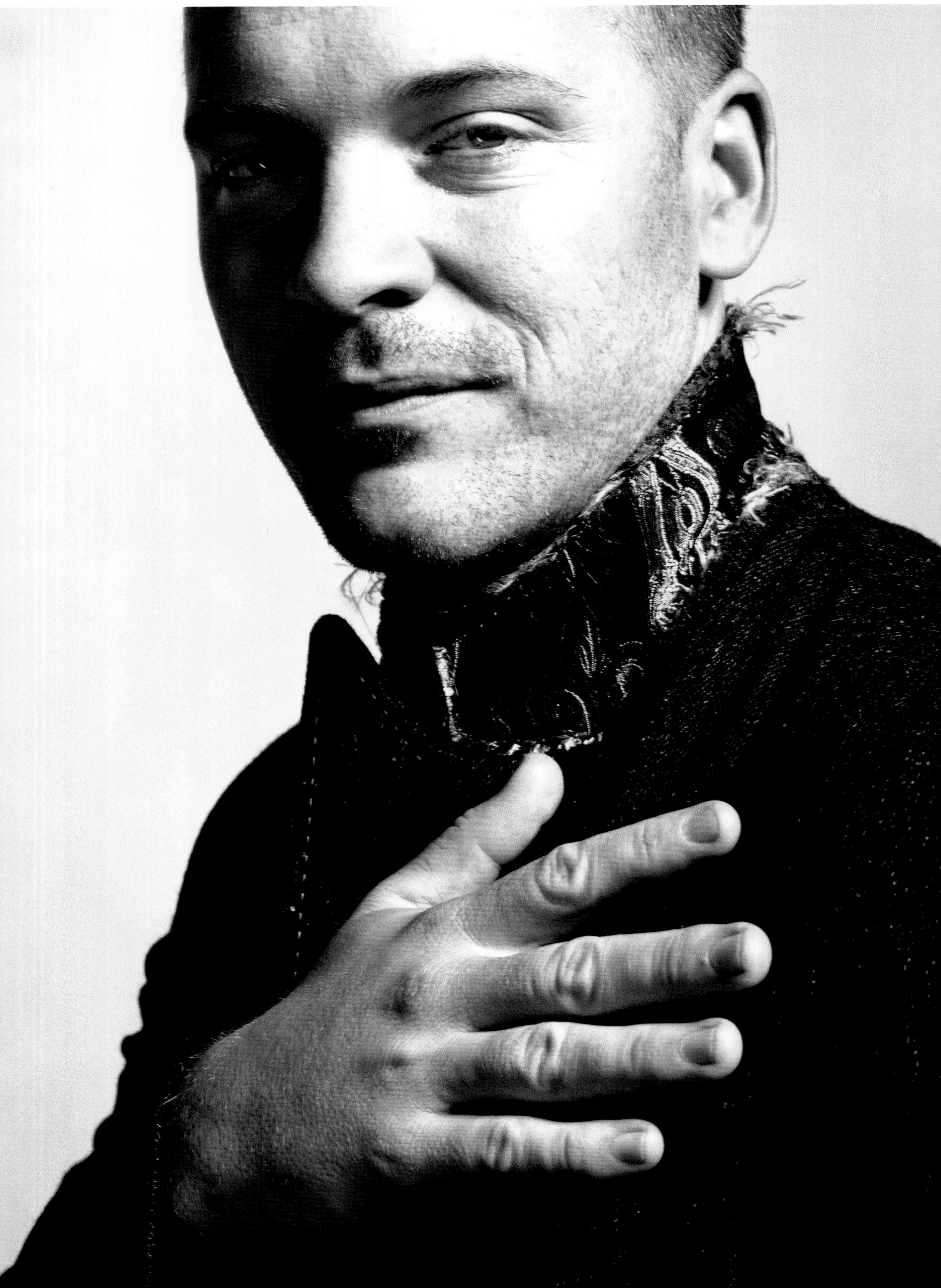

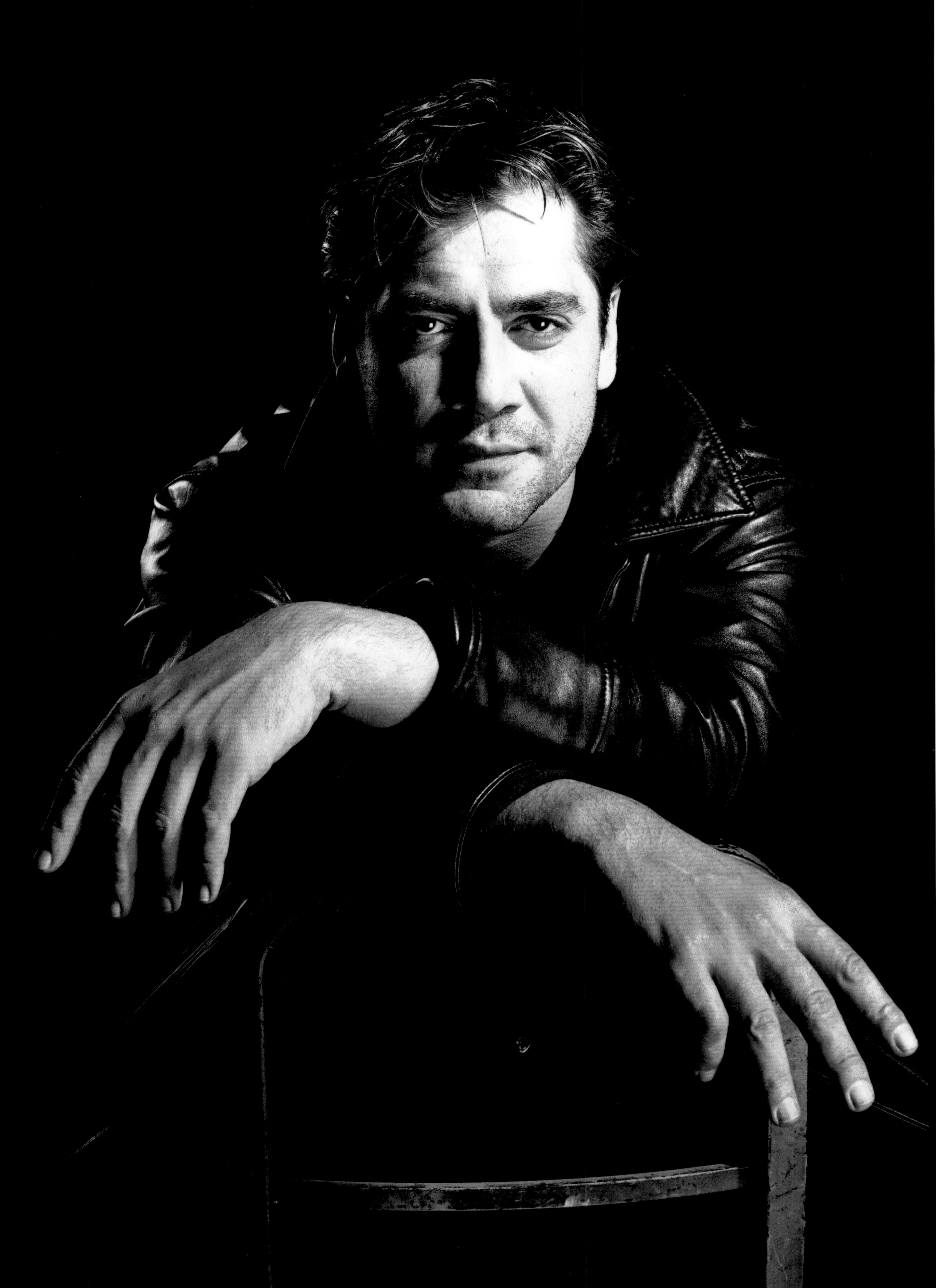

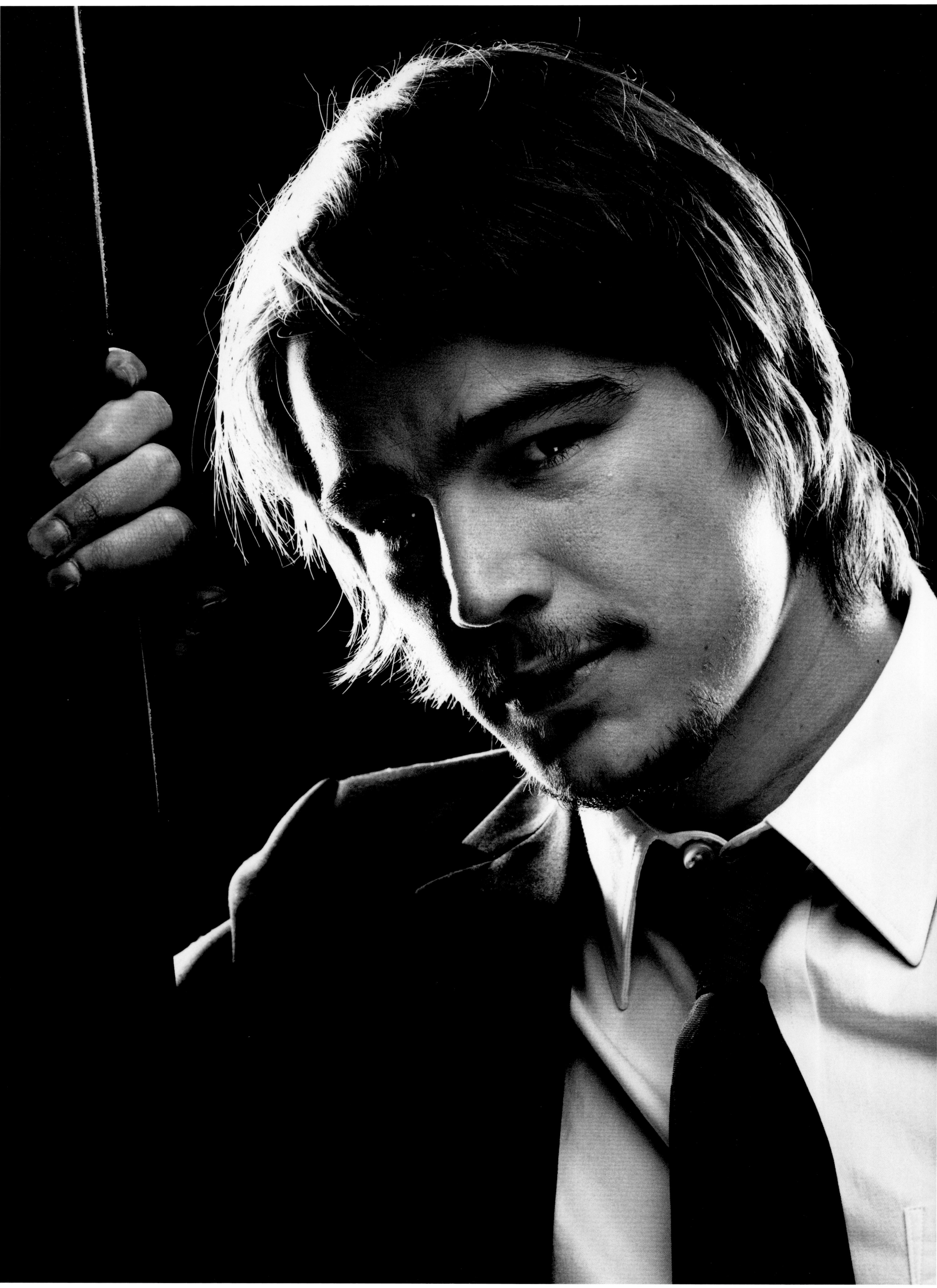

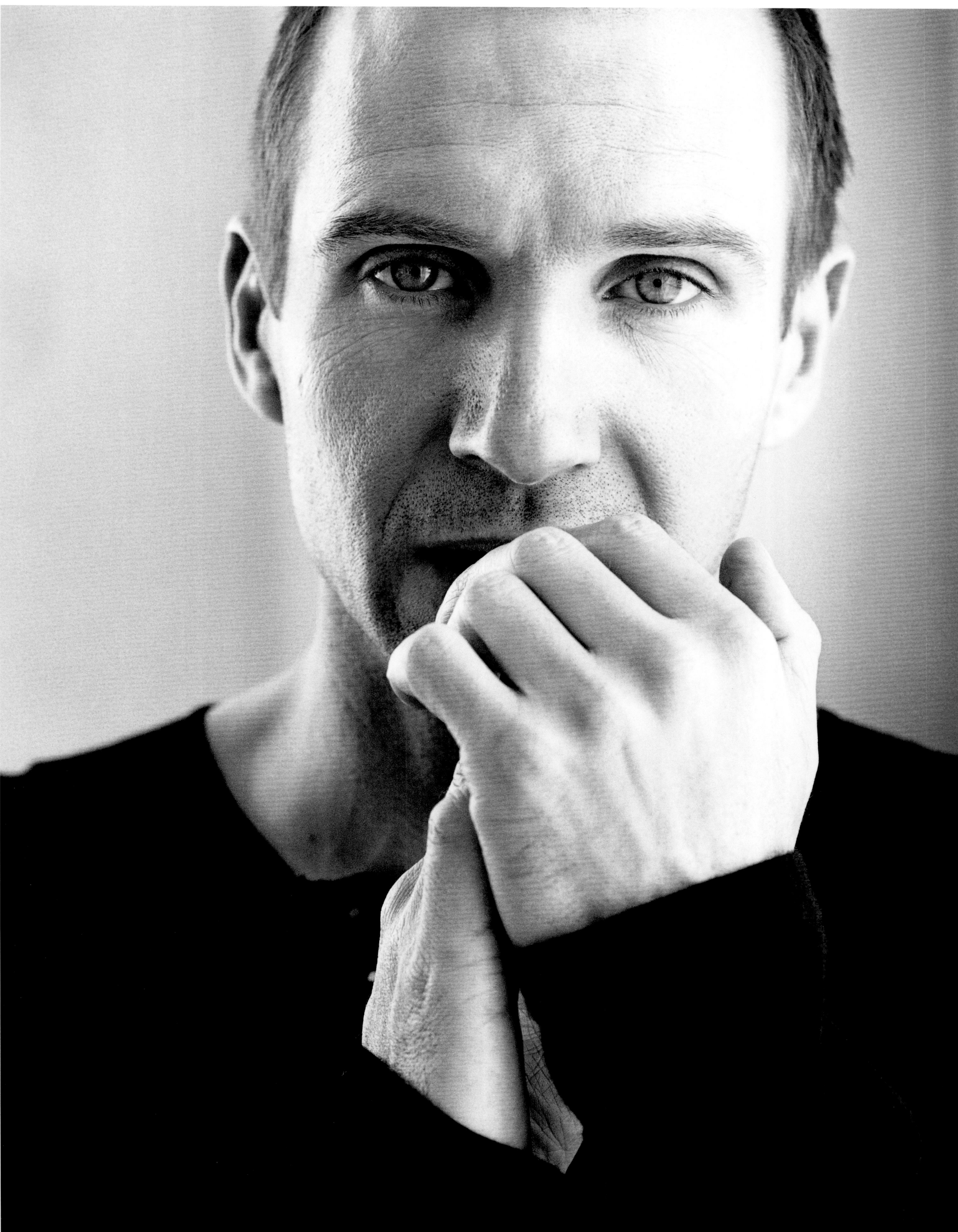

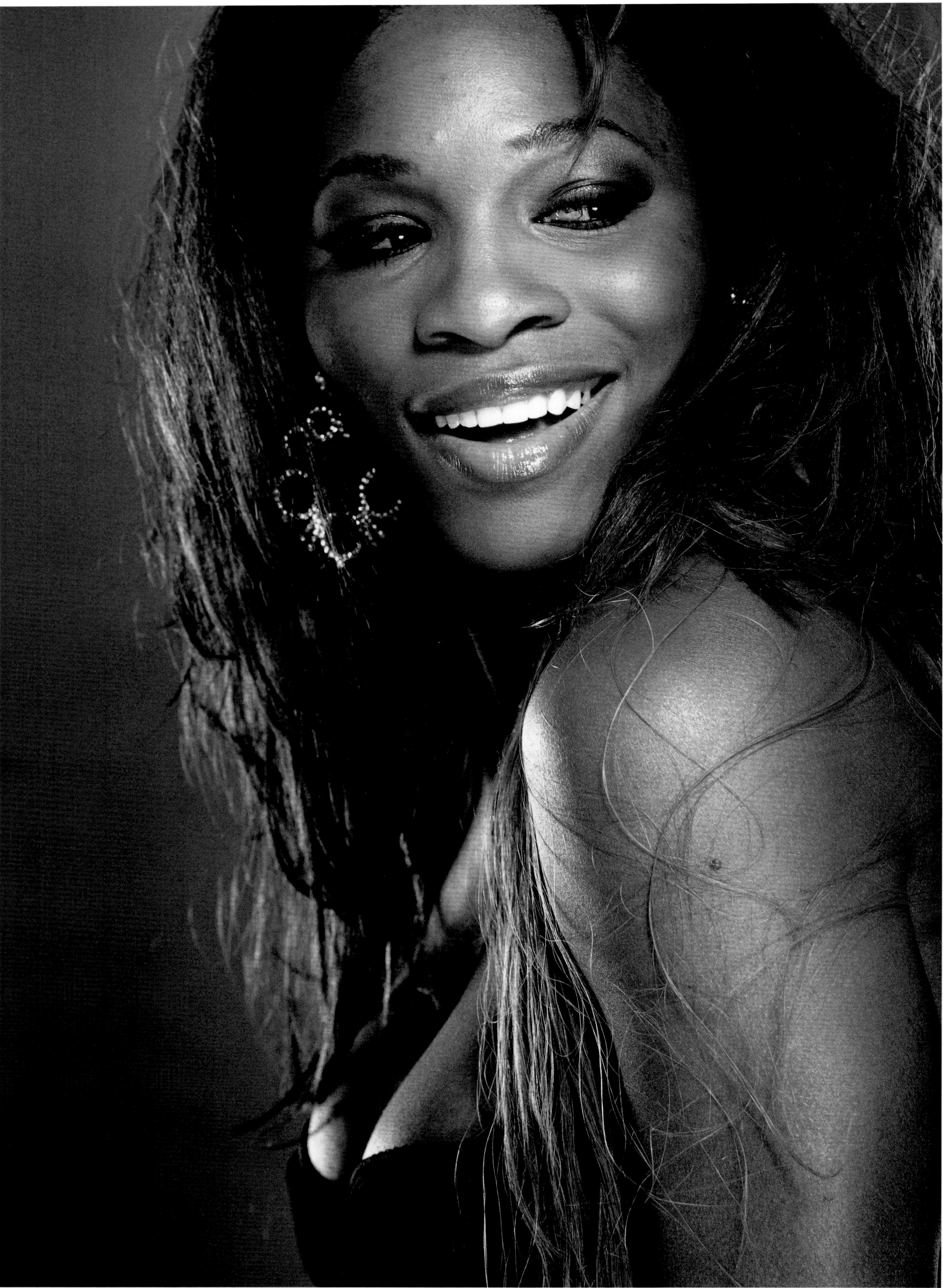

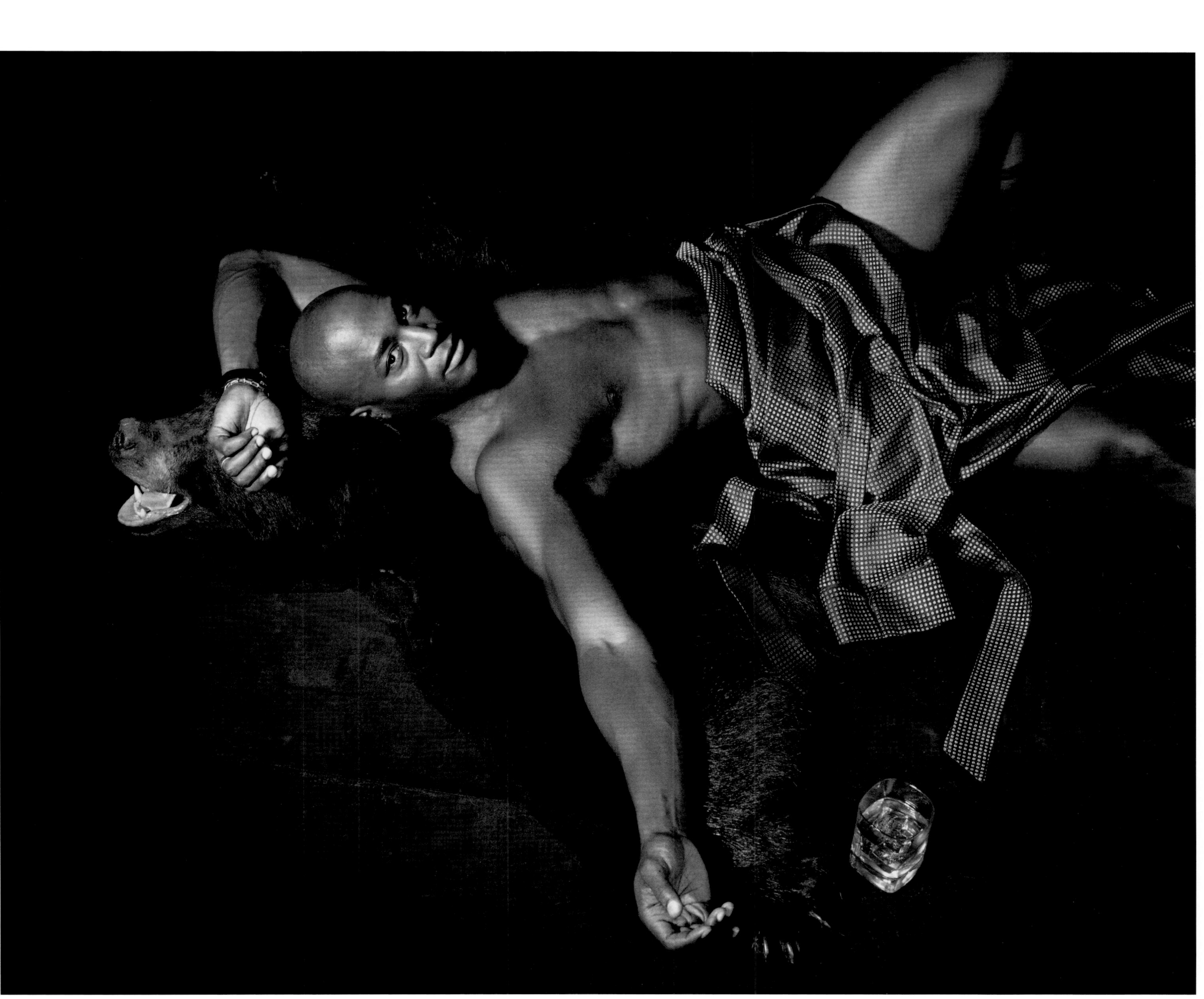

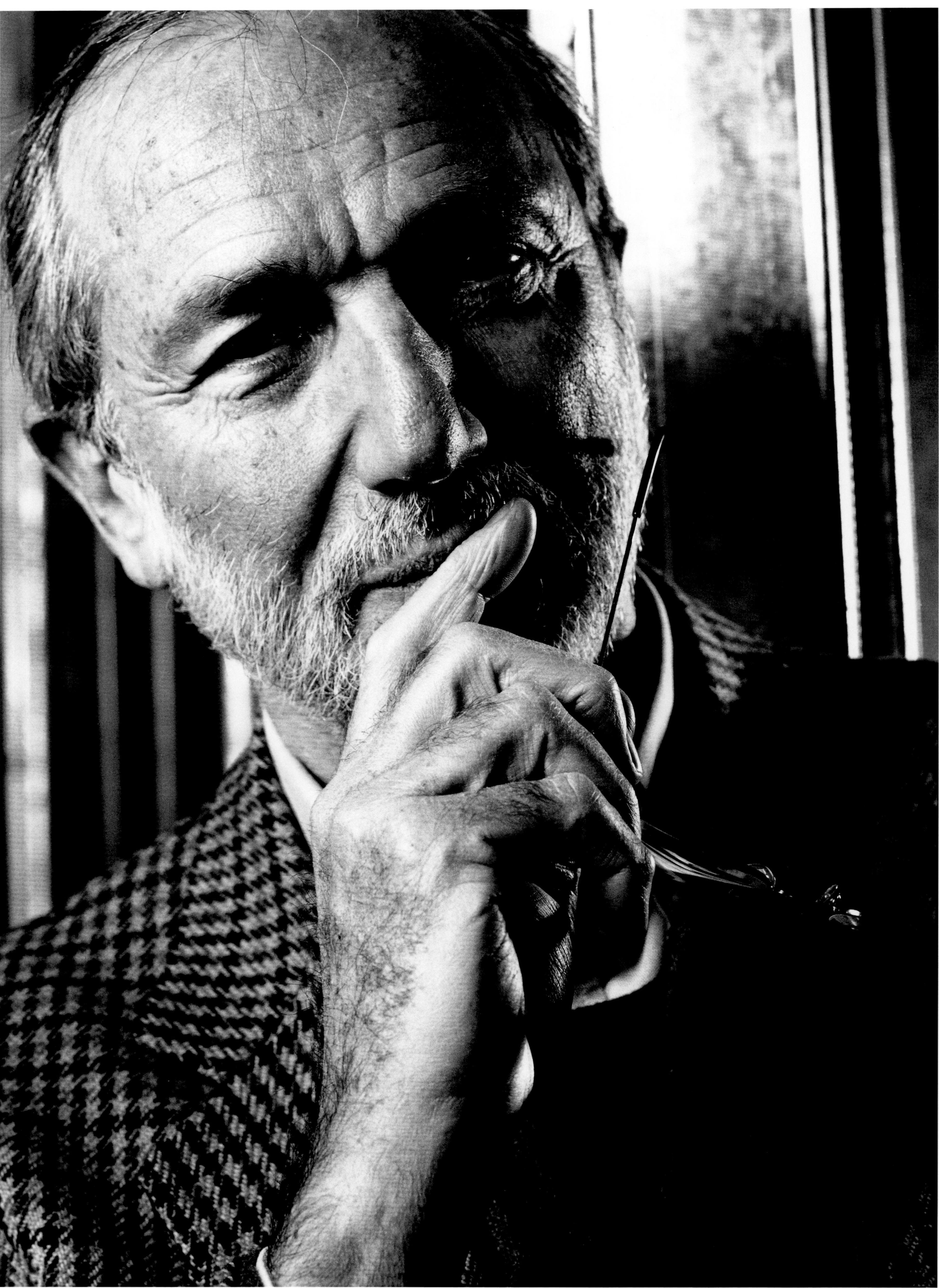

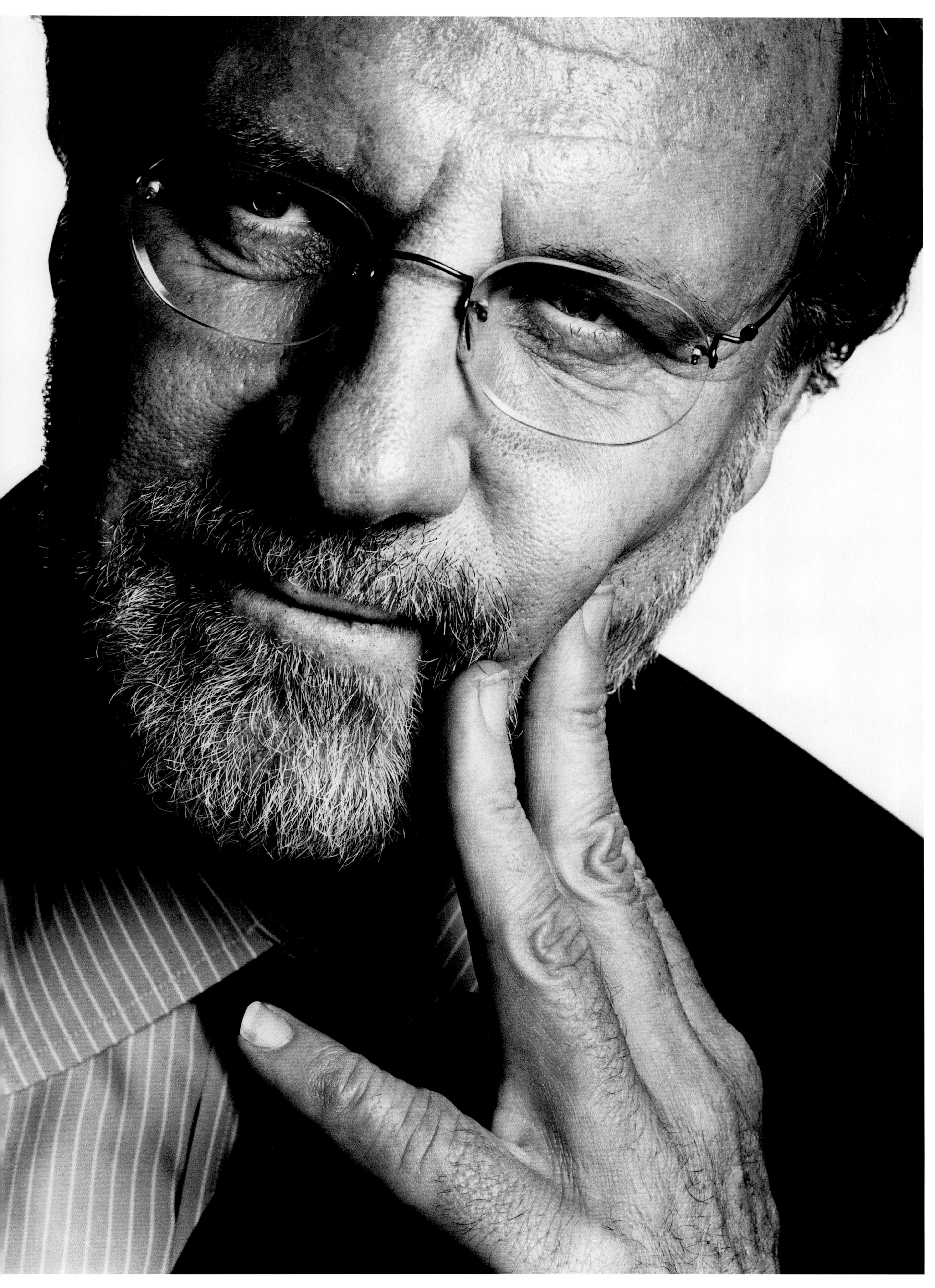

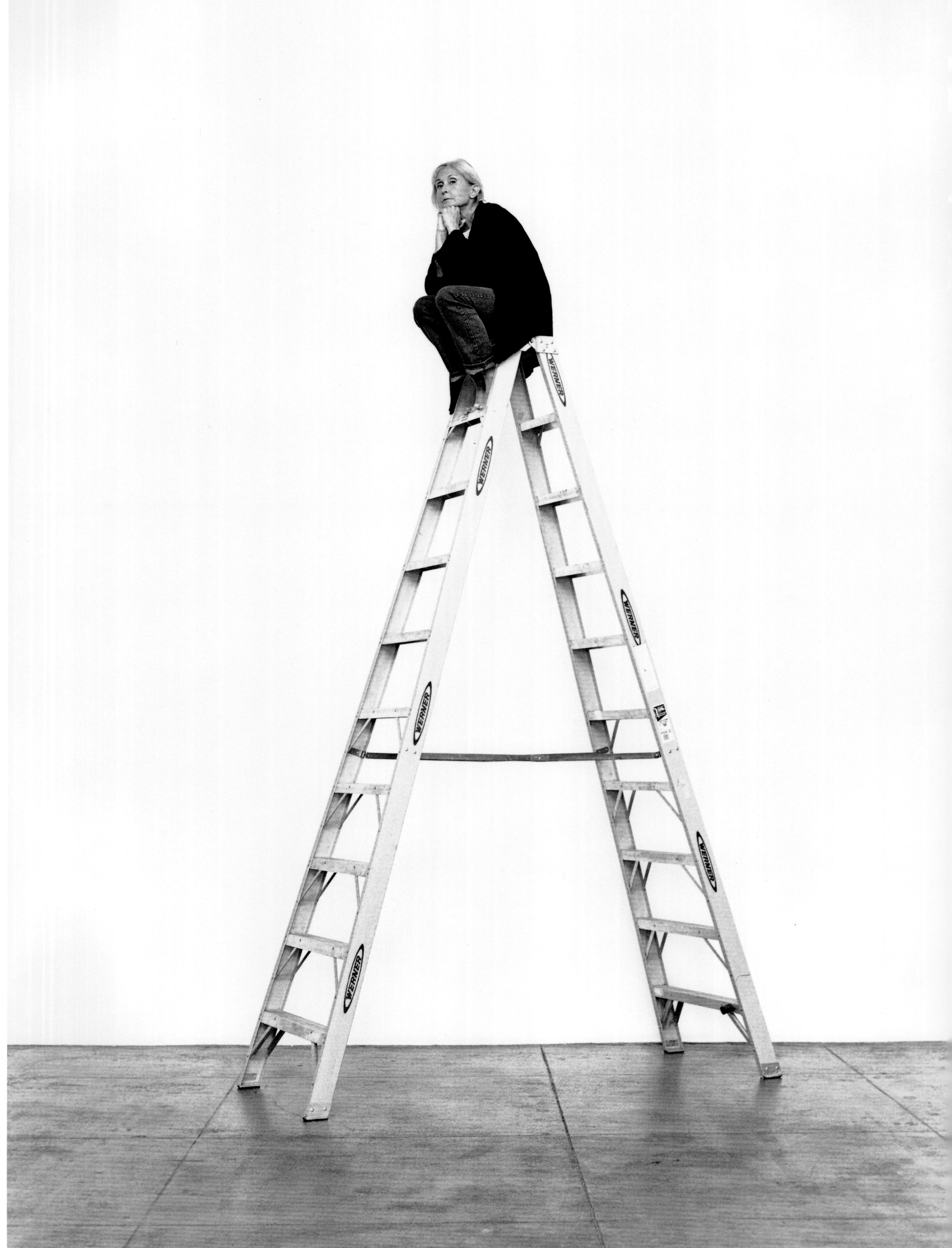
WERNER
WERNER
WERNER
WERNER
WERNER
WERNER

PORTRAITS ON PREVIOUS PAGES

FIREMEN HEROES

JERRY LEIBER AND MIKE STOLLER
ALFONSO CUARON

PETER SARSGAARD
JAVIER BARDEM

JOSH HARTNETT
RALPH FIENNES

SERENA WILLIAMS
TAYE DIGGS

RENZO PIANO
SENATOR JON CORZINE

TWYLA THARP

NOW COME ON GIRLS, LOOK REALLY SAD, AND IT'LL HELP US WITH OUR APPEALS...

CLARA HARRIS COACHING CELESTE BEARD JOHNSON AND LORRAINE LARSON ON HOW TO POSE FOR THE SHOOT. (ALL 3 WOMEN WERE CURRENTLY SERVING PRISON SENTENCES FOR THE MURDER OF THEIR RESPECTIVE HUSBANDS.)

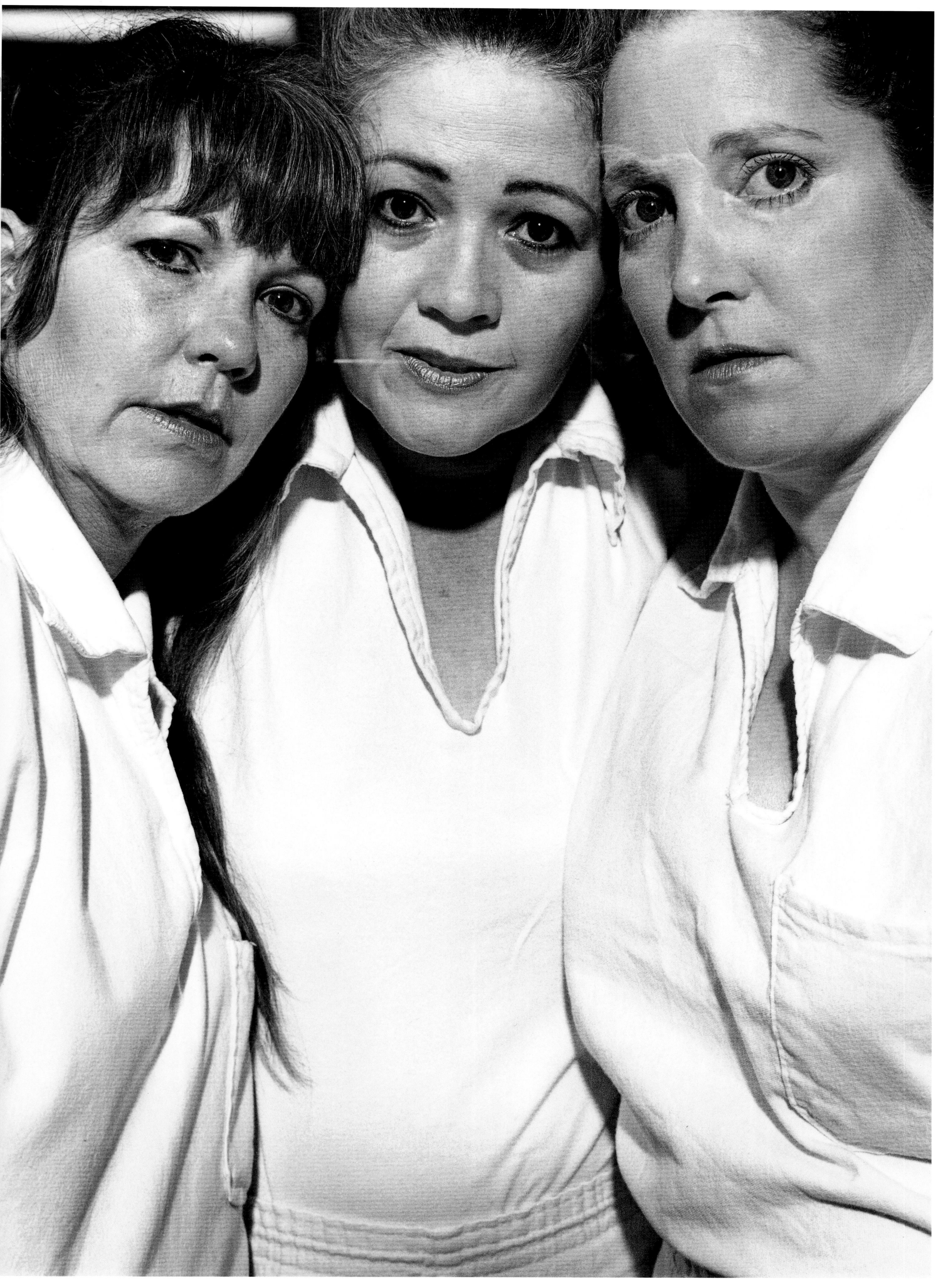

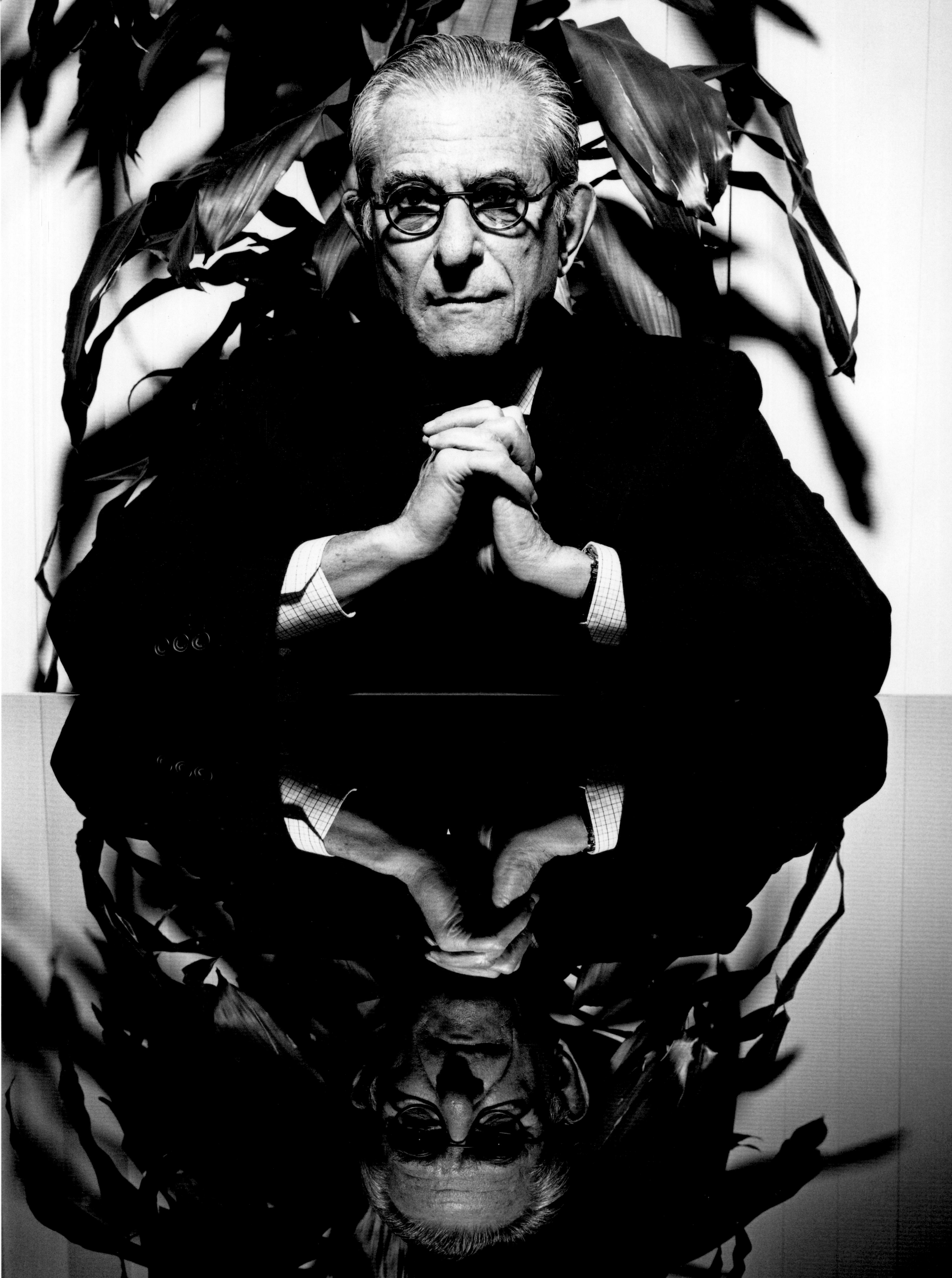

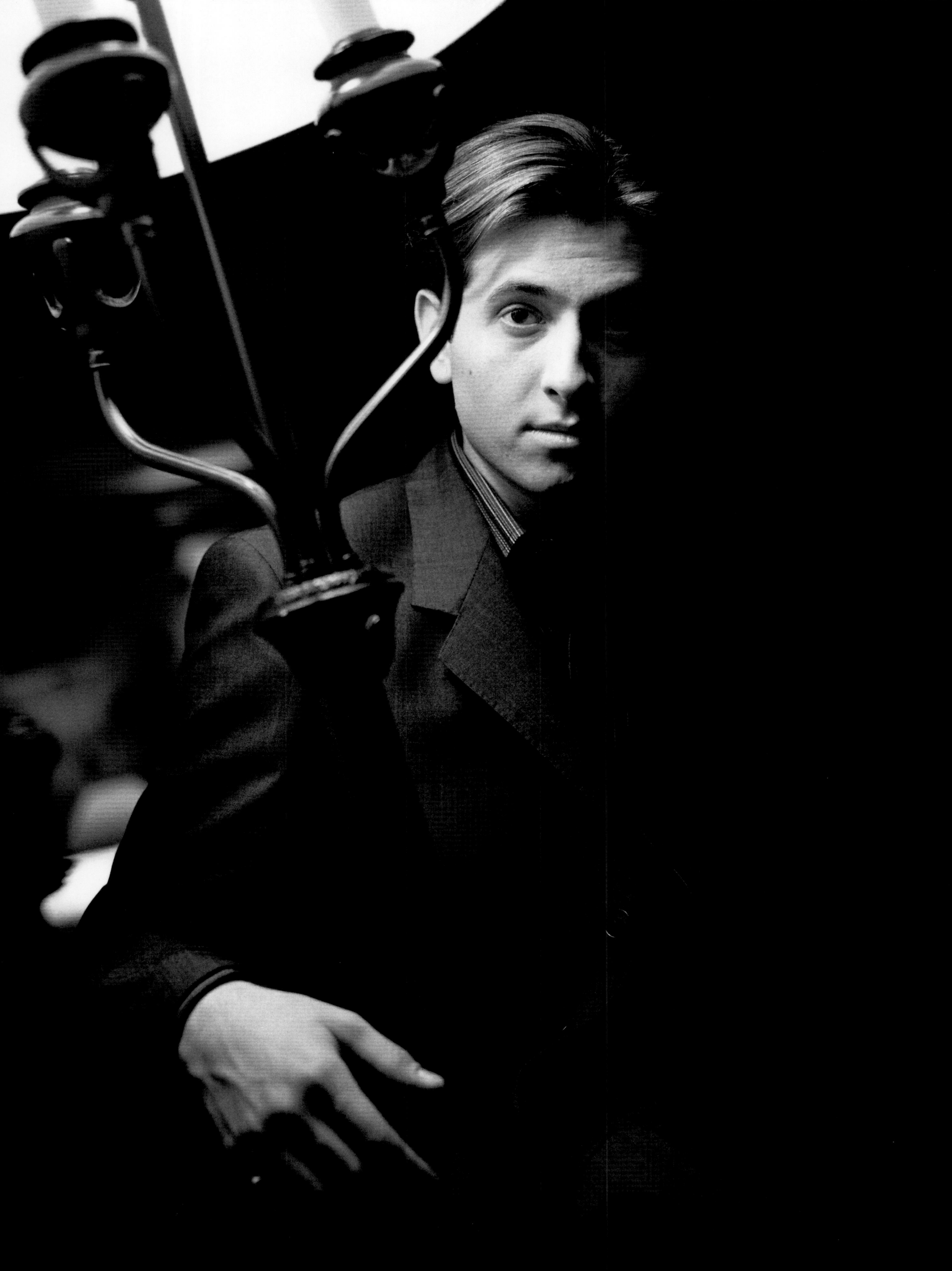

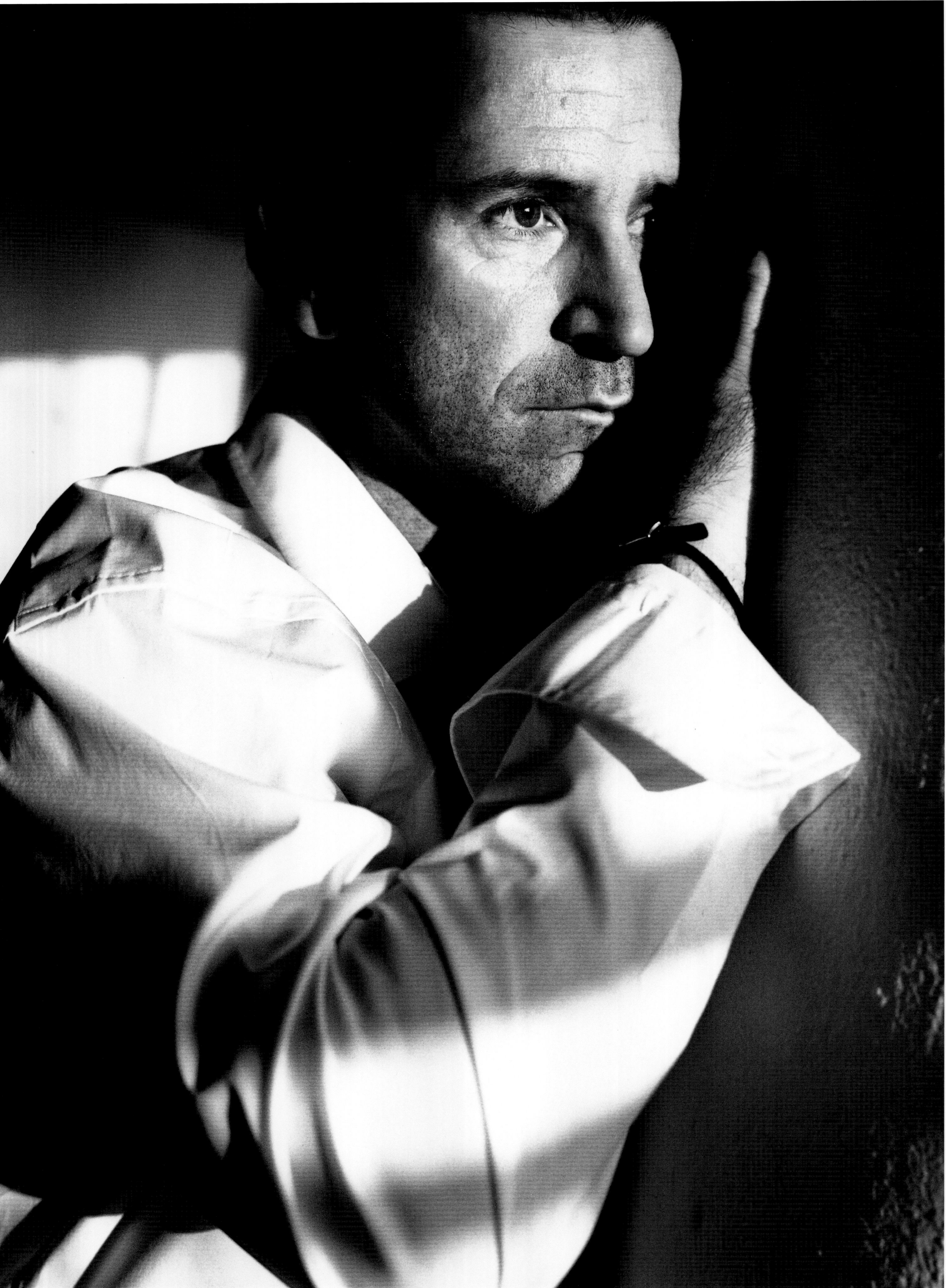

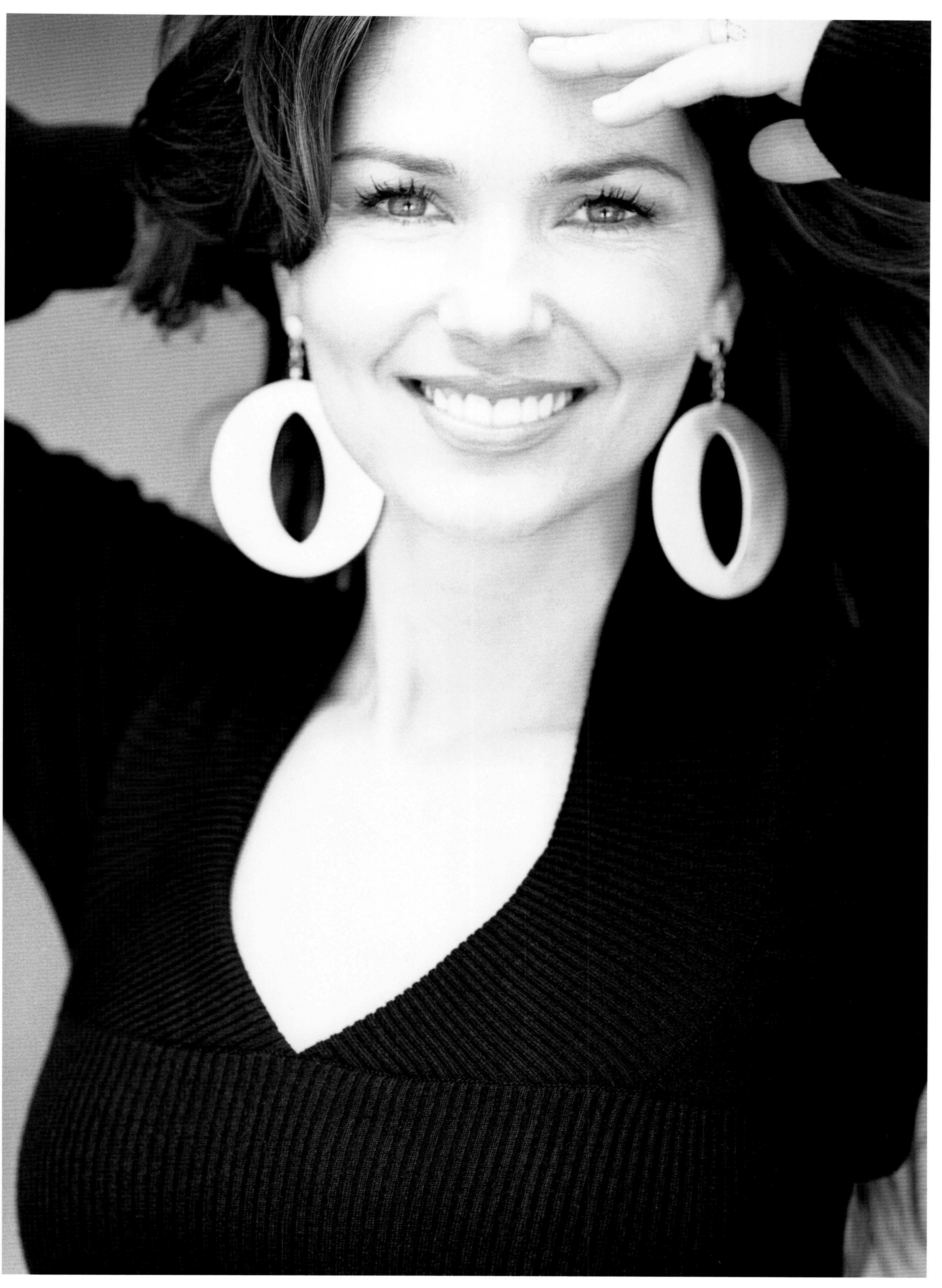

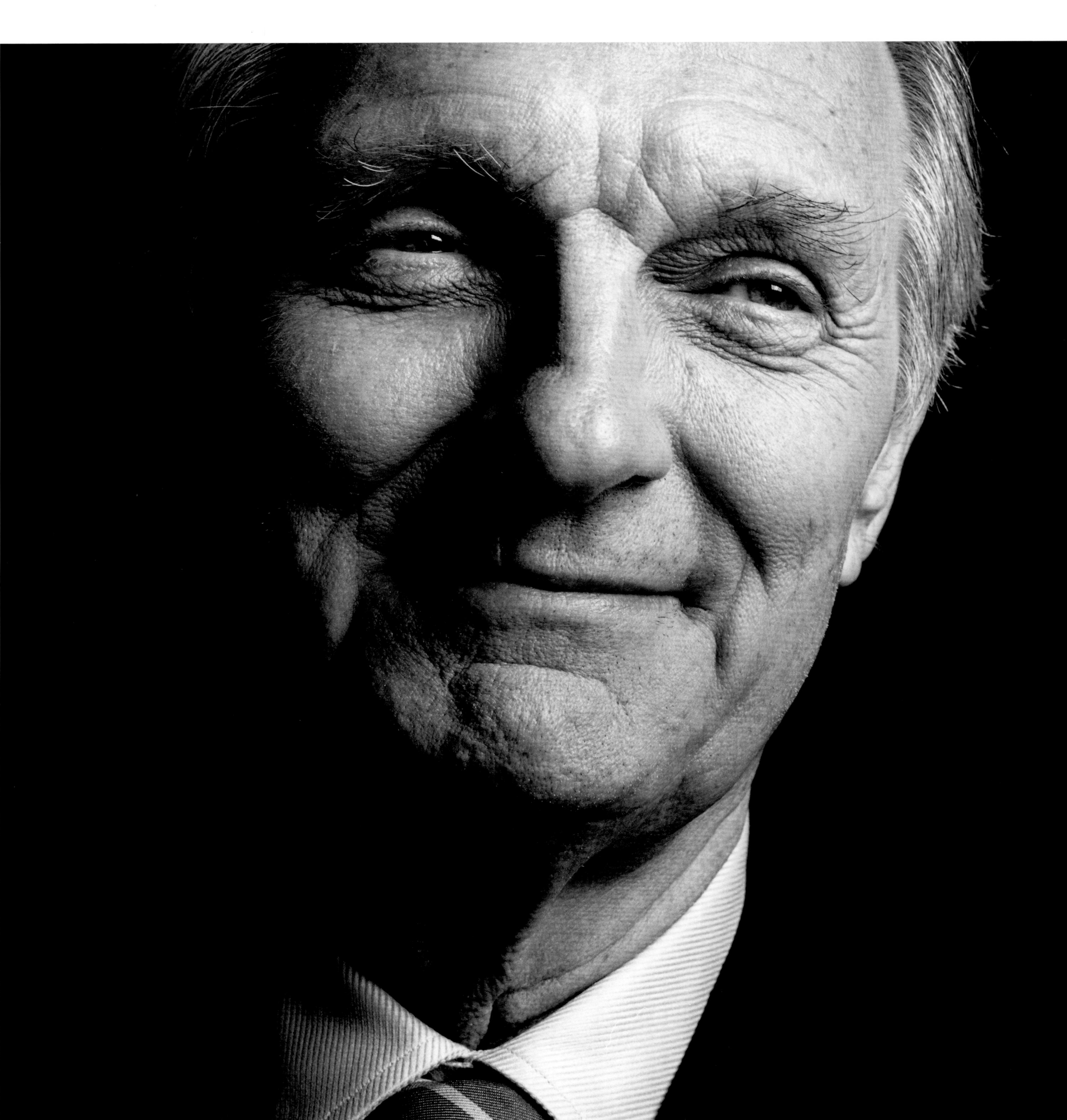

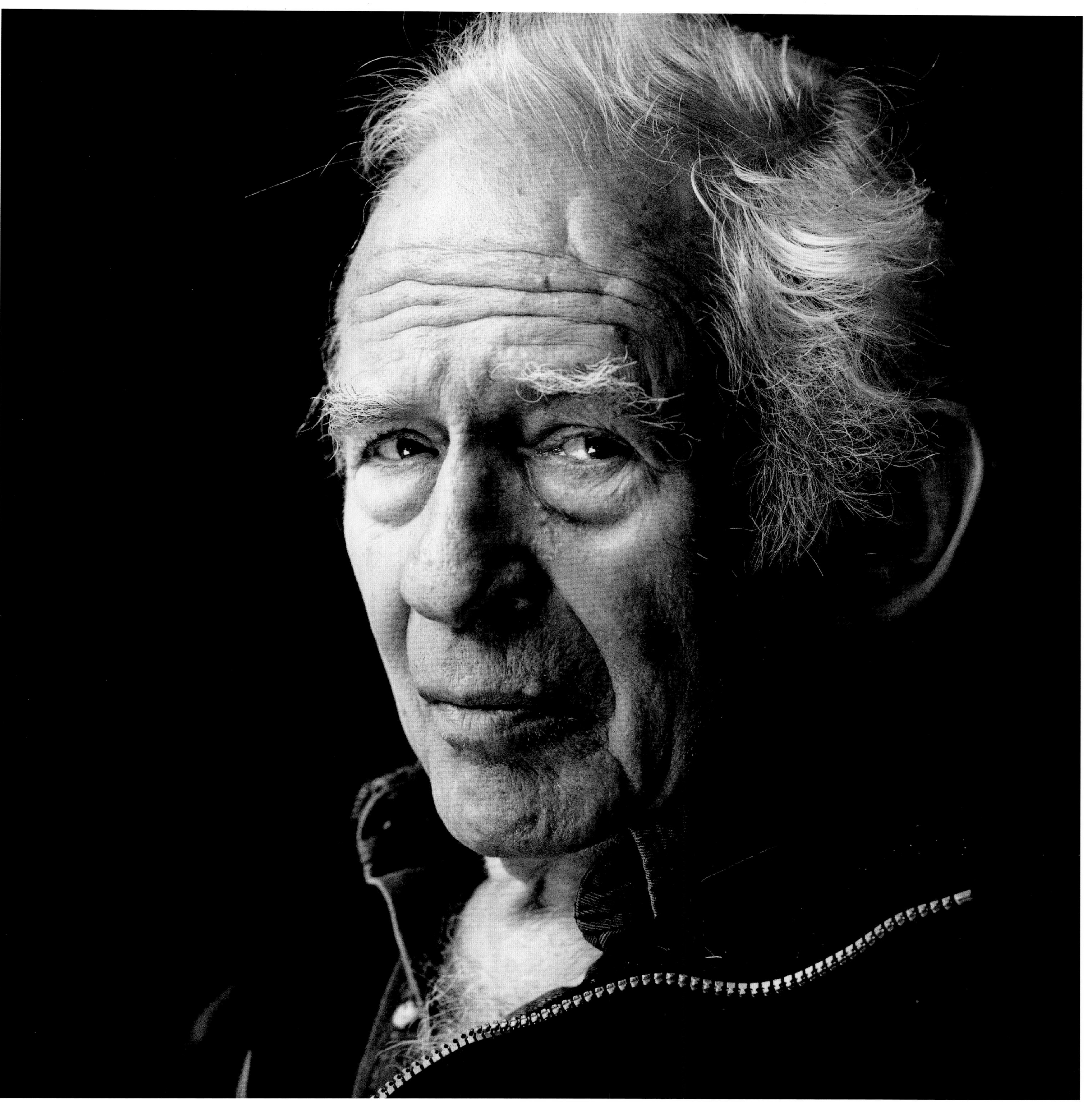

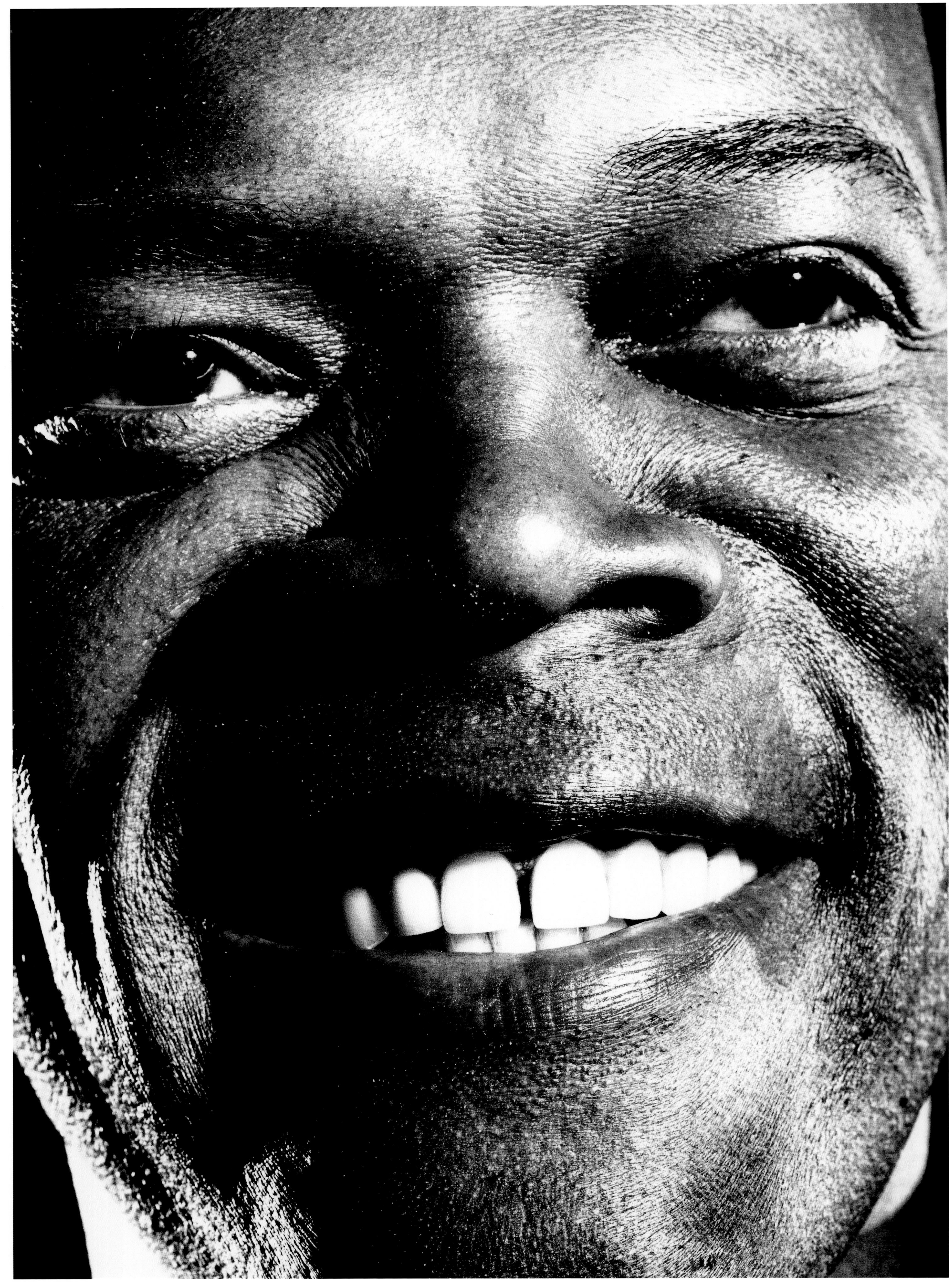

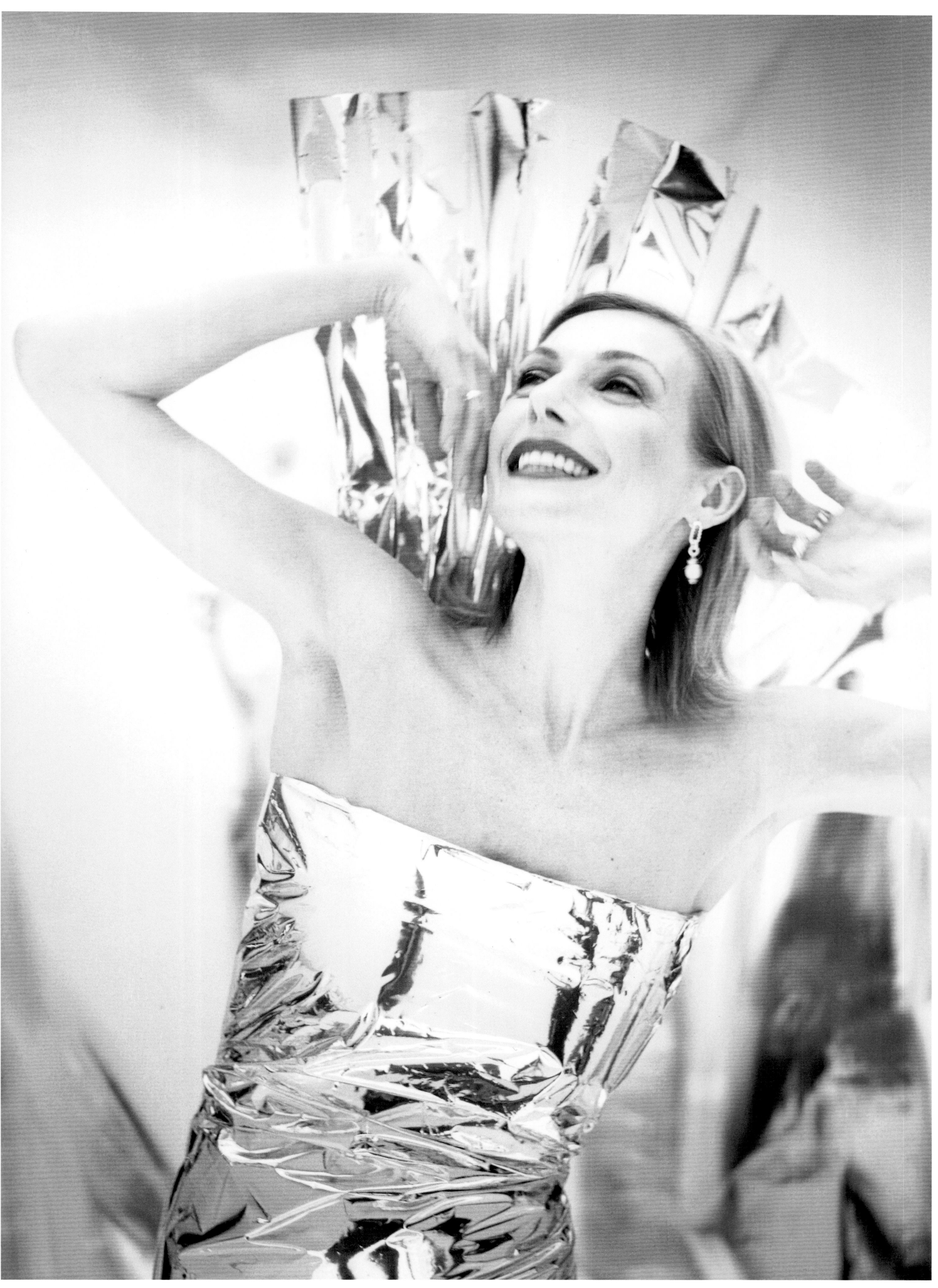

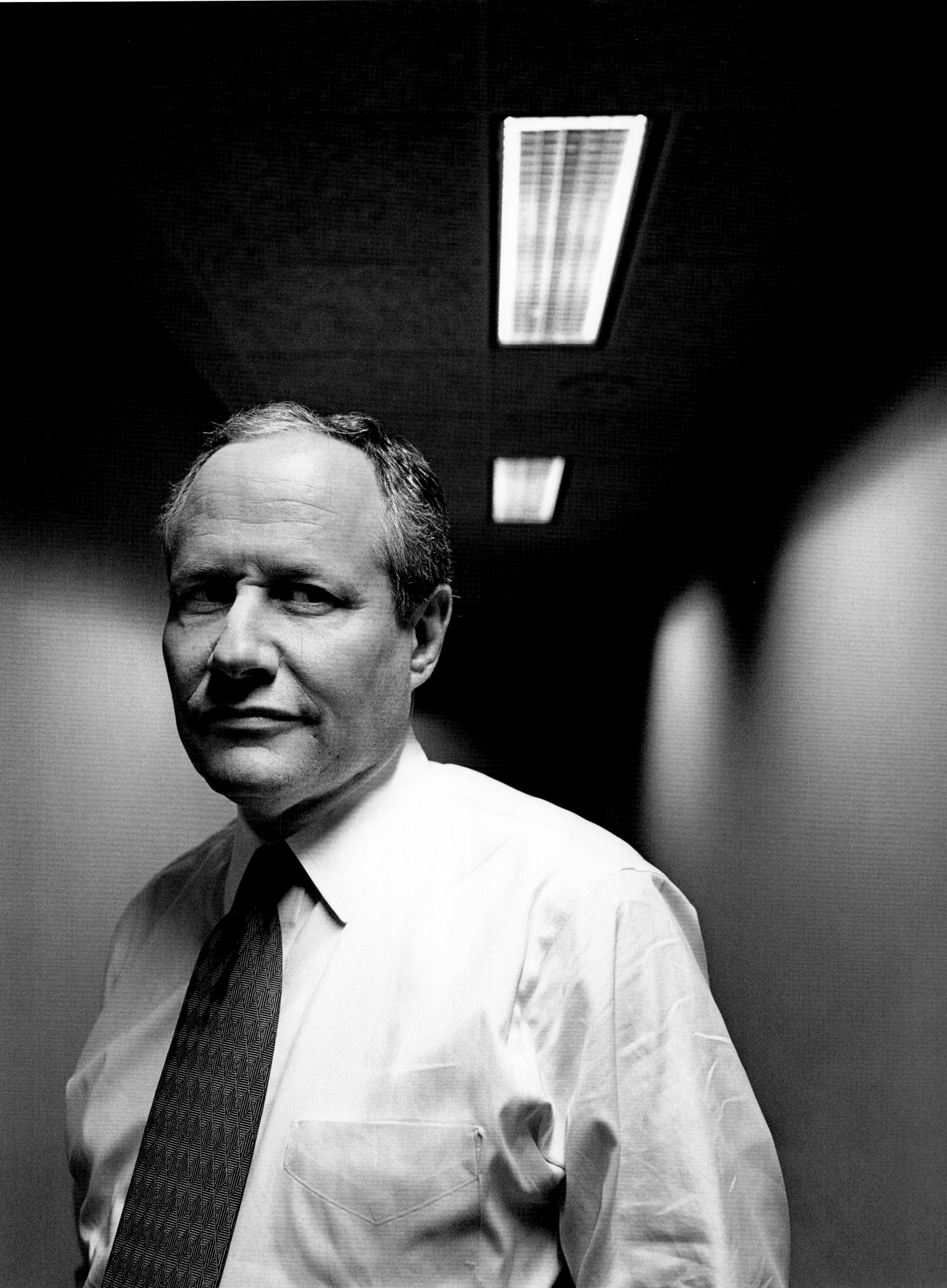

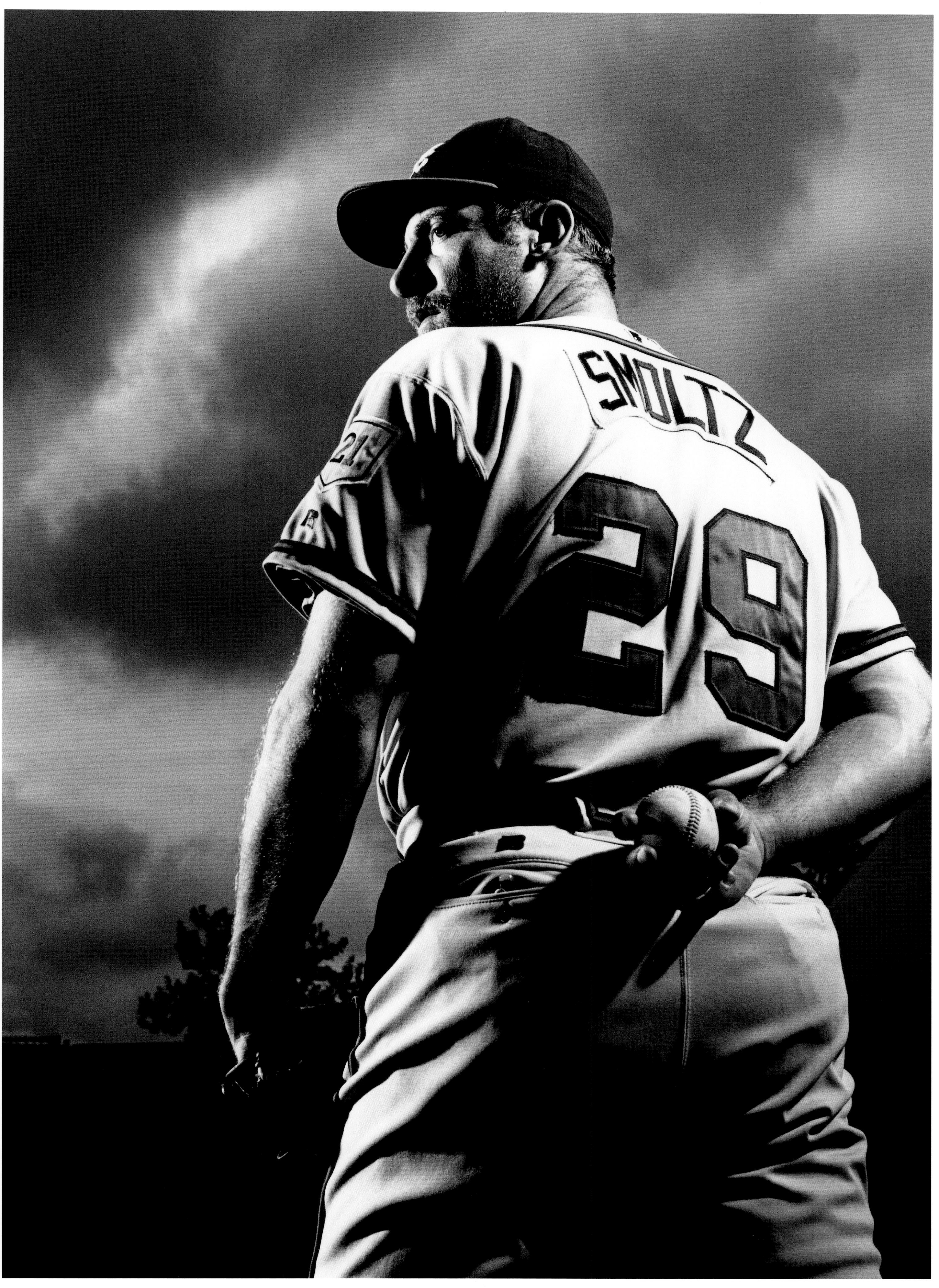
SMOLTZ
21
29

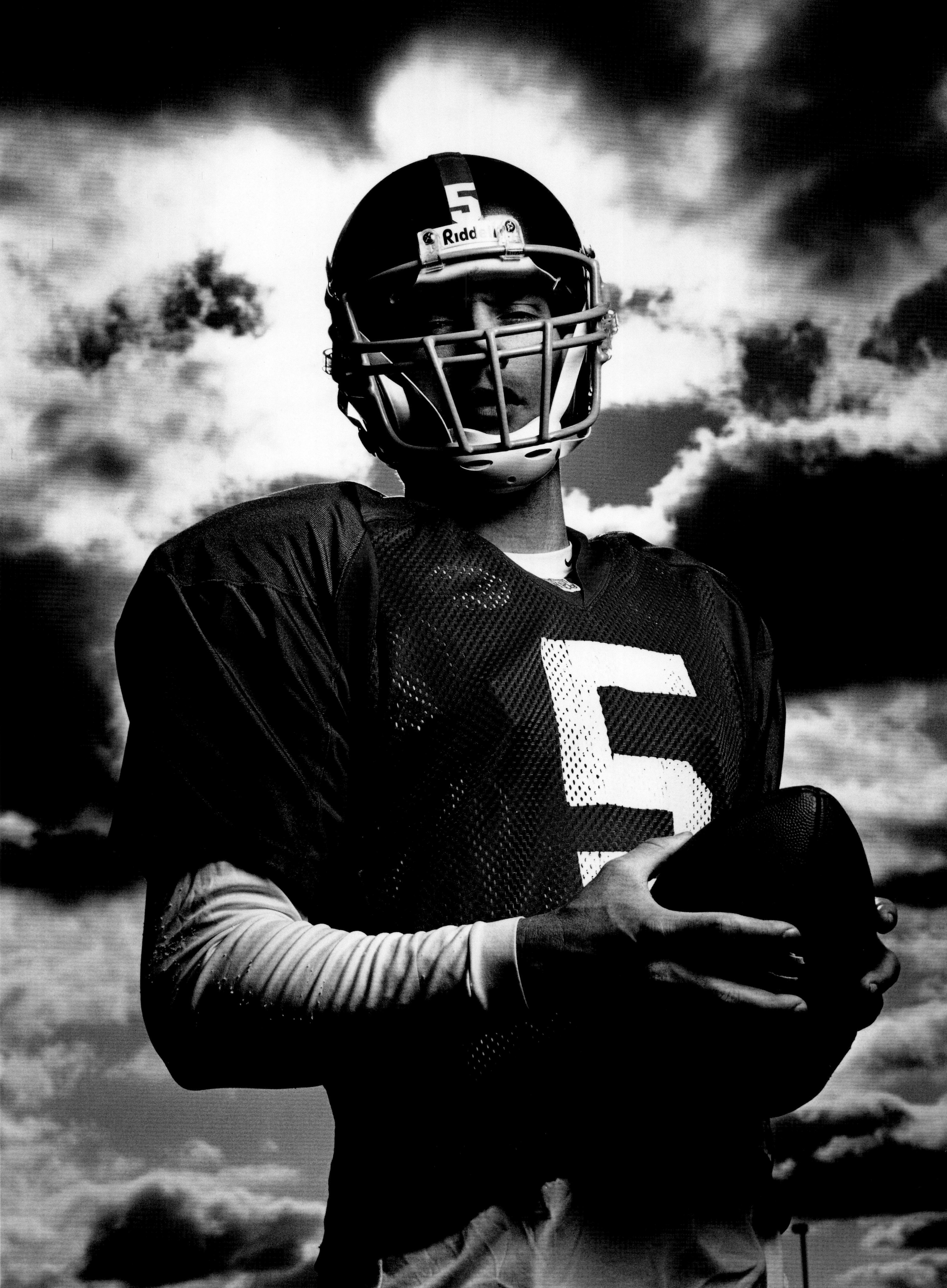
5
Ridd
5

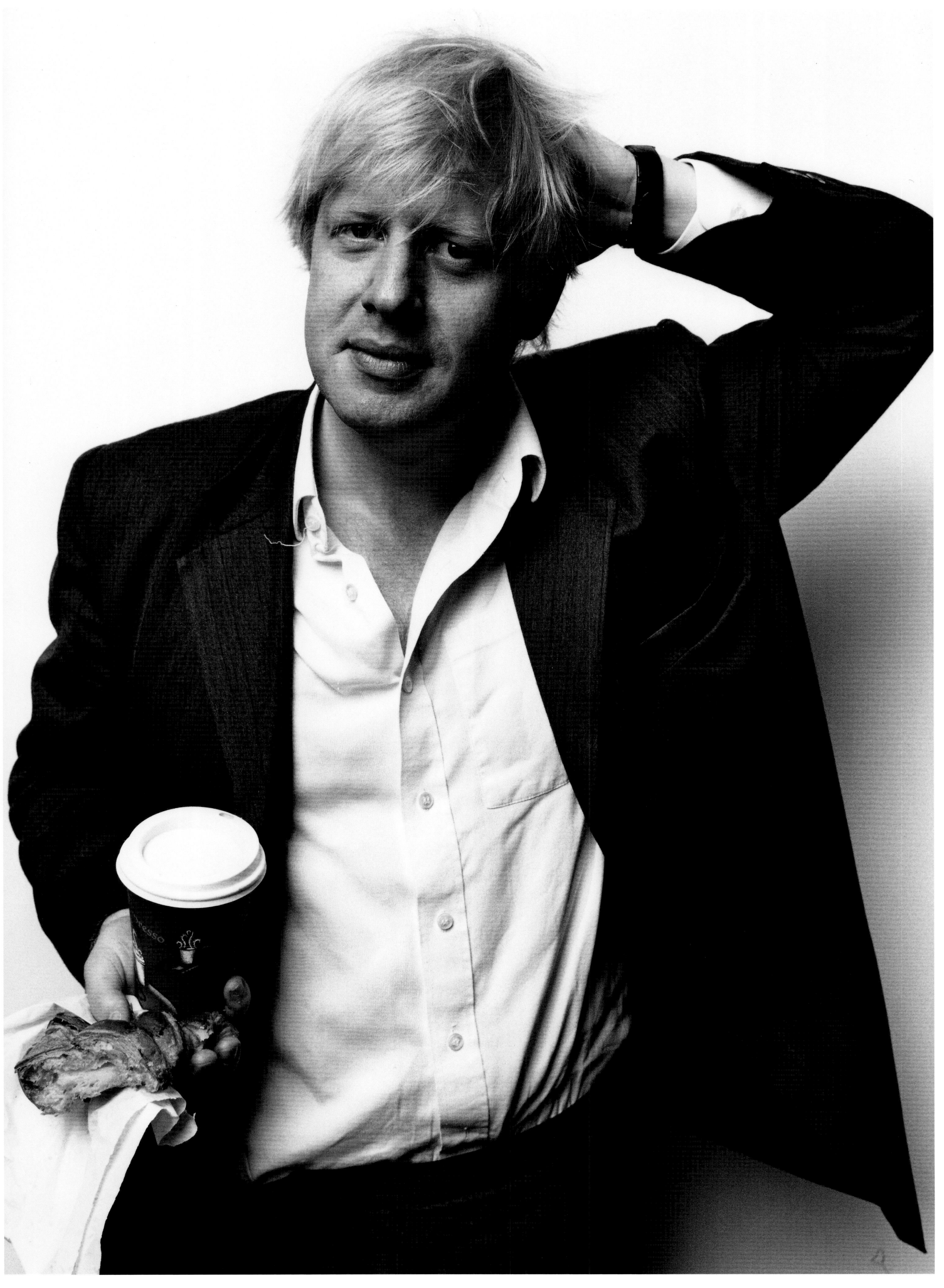

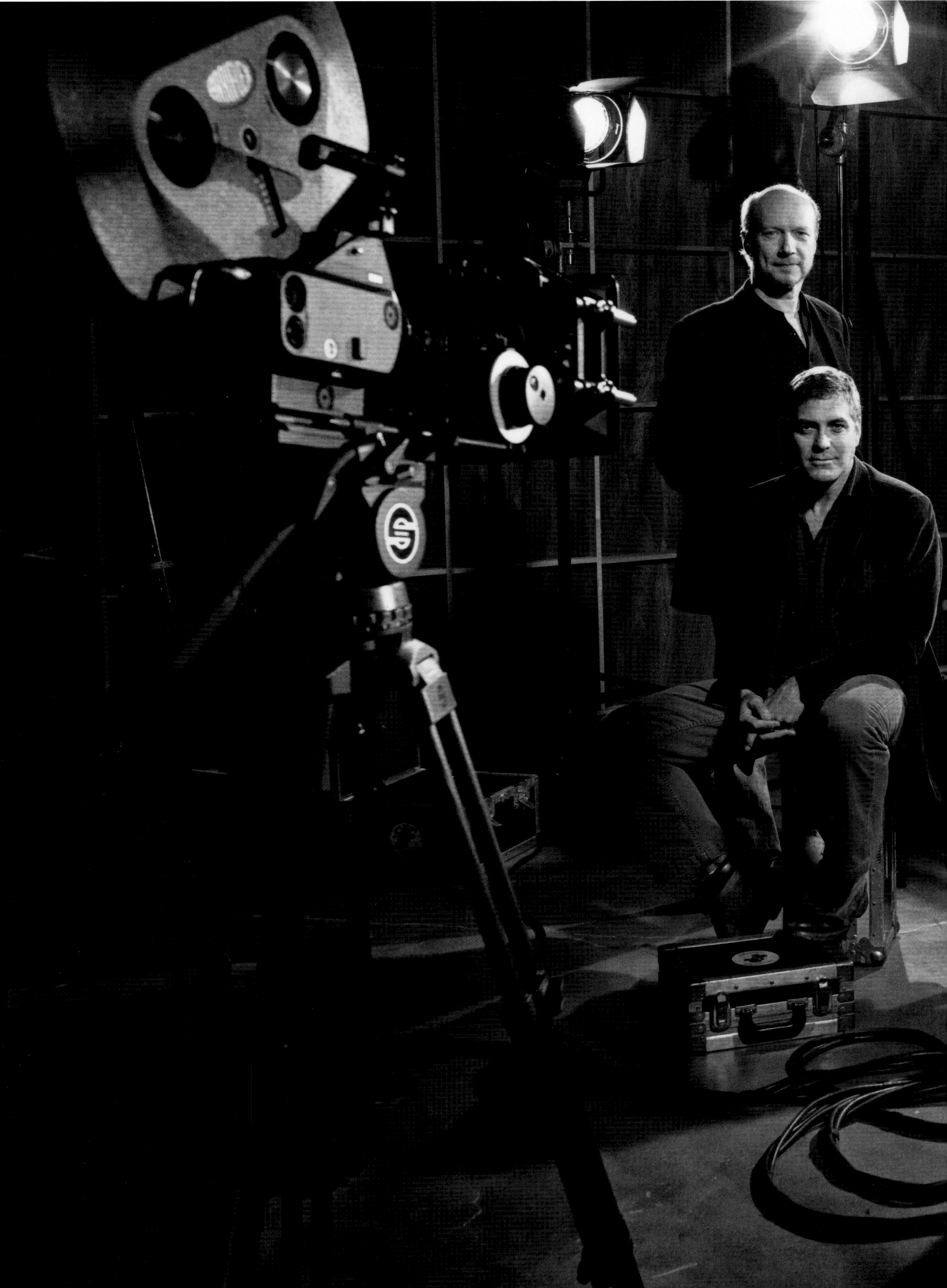

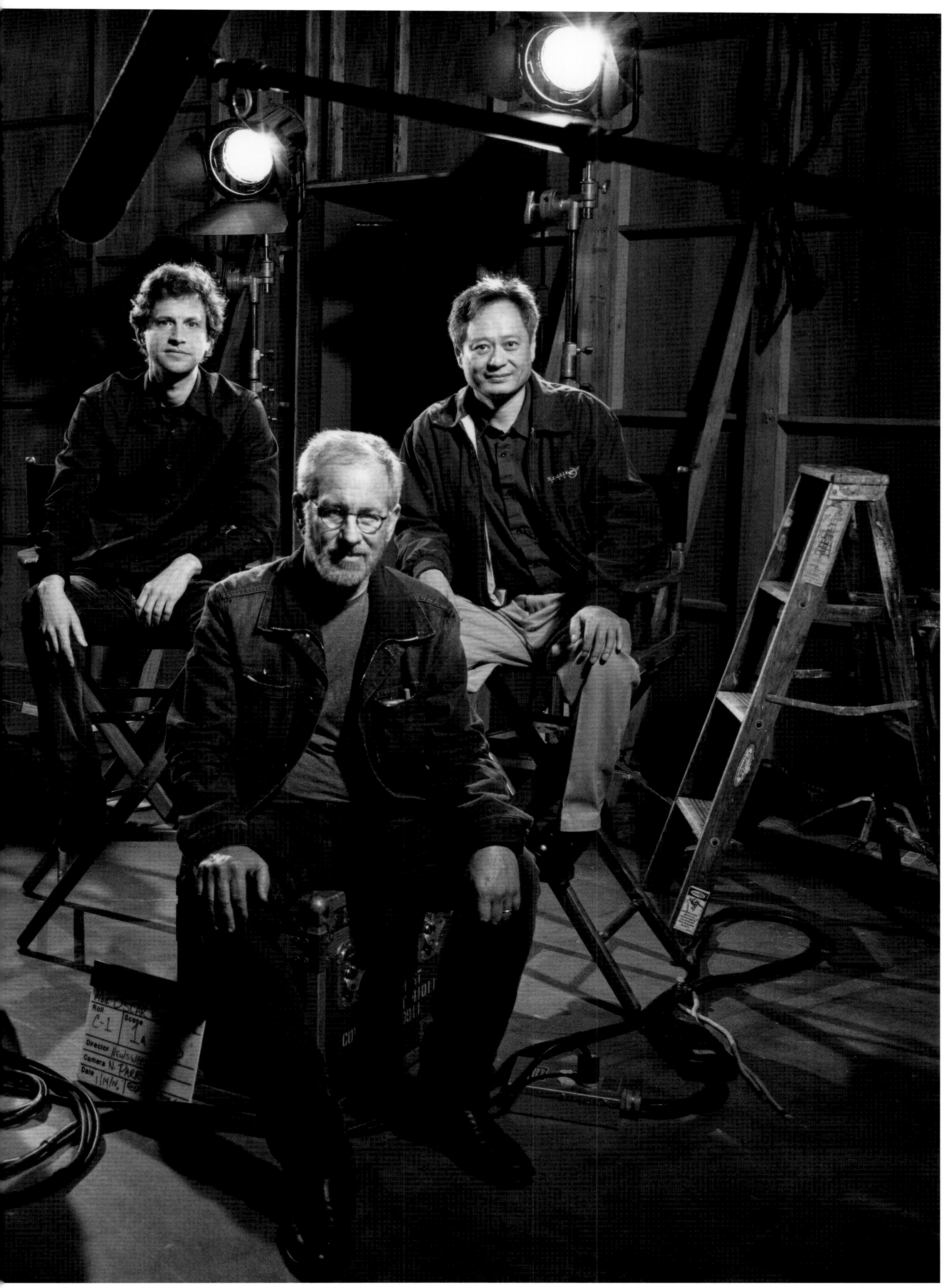
Prod.
Roll
C-1
Scene
Director
Camera
Date

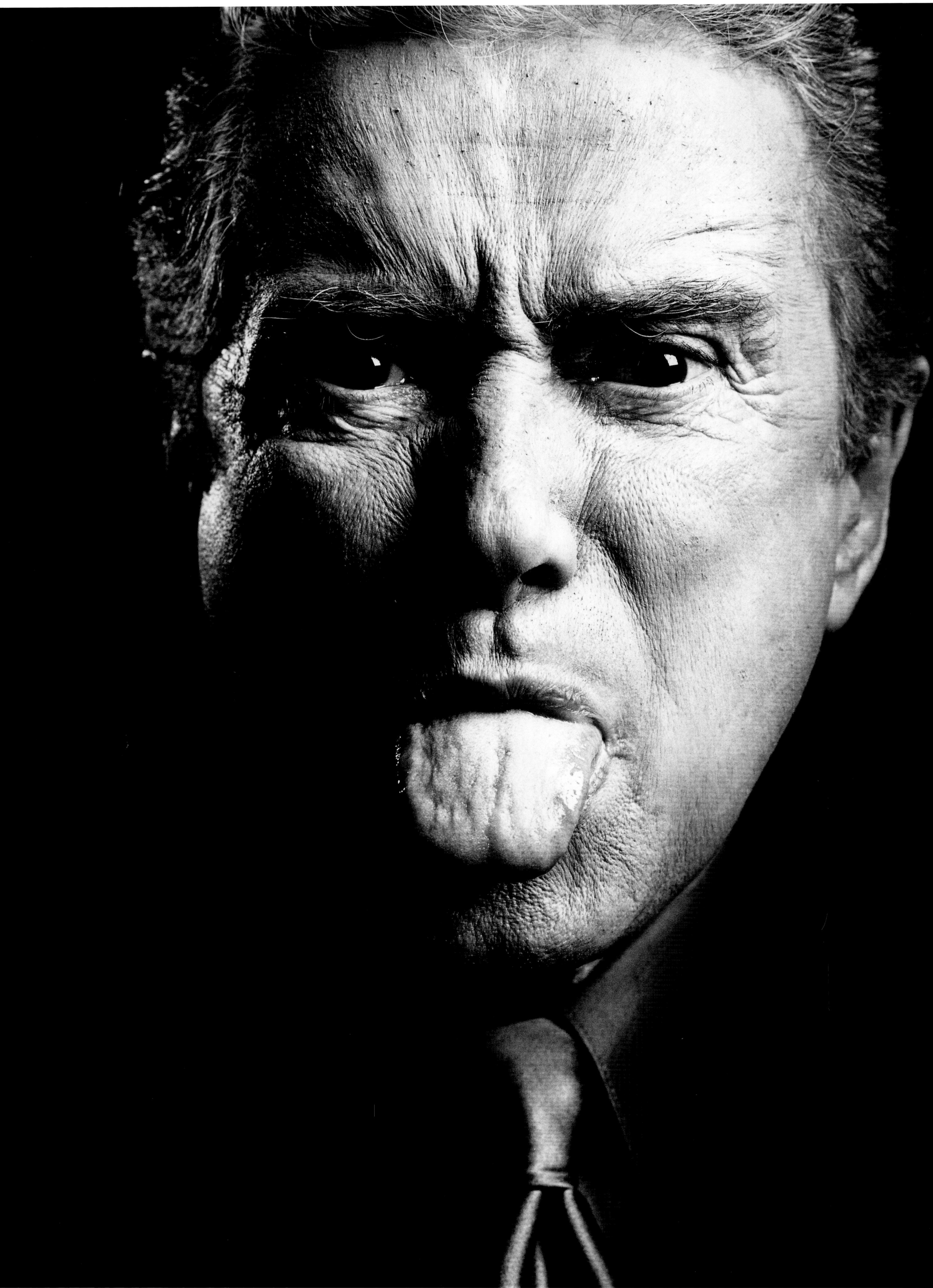

PORTRAITS ON PREVIOUS PAGES

3 INMATES

ROBERT COHEN
PETER CINCOTTI

ANTHONY LAPAGLIA
SHANIA TWAIN

ALAN ALDA
NORMAN MAILER

SAMUEL L. JACKSON
UTE LEMPER

BILL KRISTOL
JOHN SMOLTZ

KERRY COLLINS
BORIS JOHNSON

THE DIRECTORS

REGIS PHILBIN

...AND IN THIS DREAM, EVERYTHING WAS ON FIRE—THE HOUSE, THE FURNITURE, THE RECORDING EQUIPMENT—AND THERE WAS NOTHING ANYONE COULD DO TO STOP IT!
IT WAS AWFUL BECAUSE WHEN I WOKE UP THE WHOLE DAMN LOT WAS STILL HERE!

LES PAUL'S RESPONSE TO COMMENTS ON THE AMOUNT OF STUFF HE HAS ACCUMULATED OVER THE YEARS.

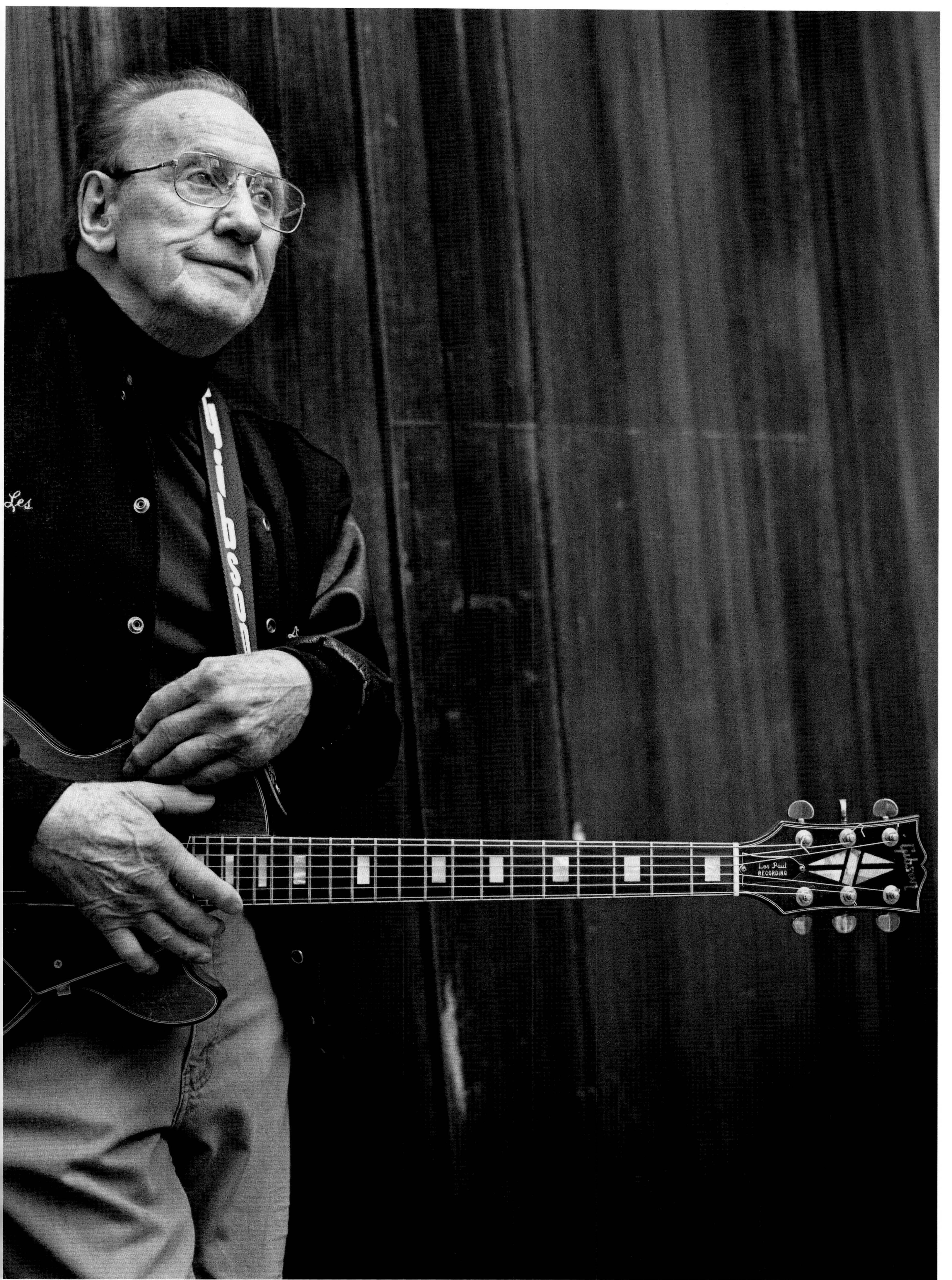
Les
Les Paul
RECORDING

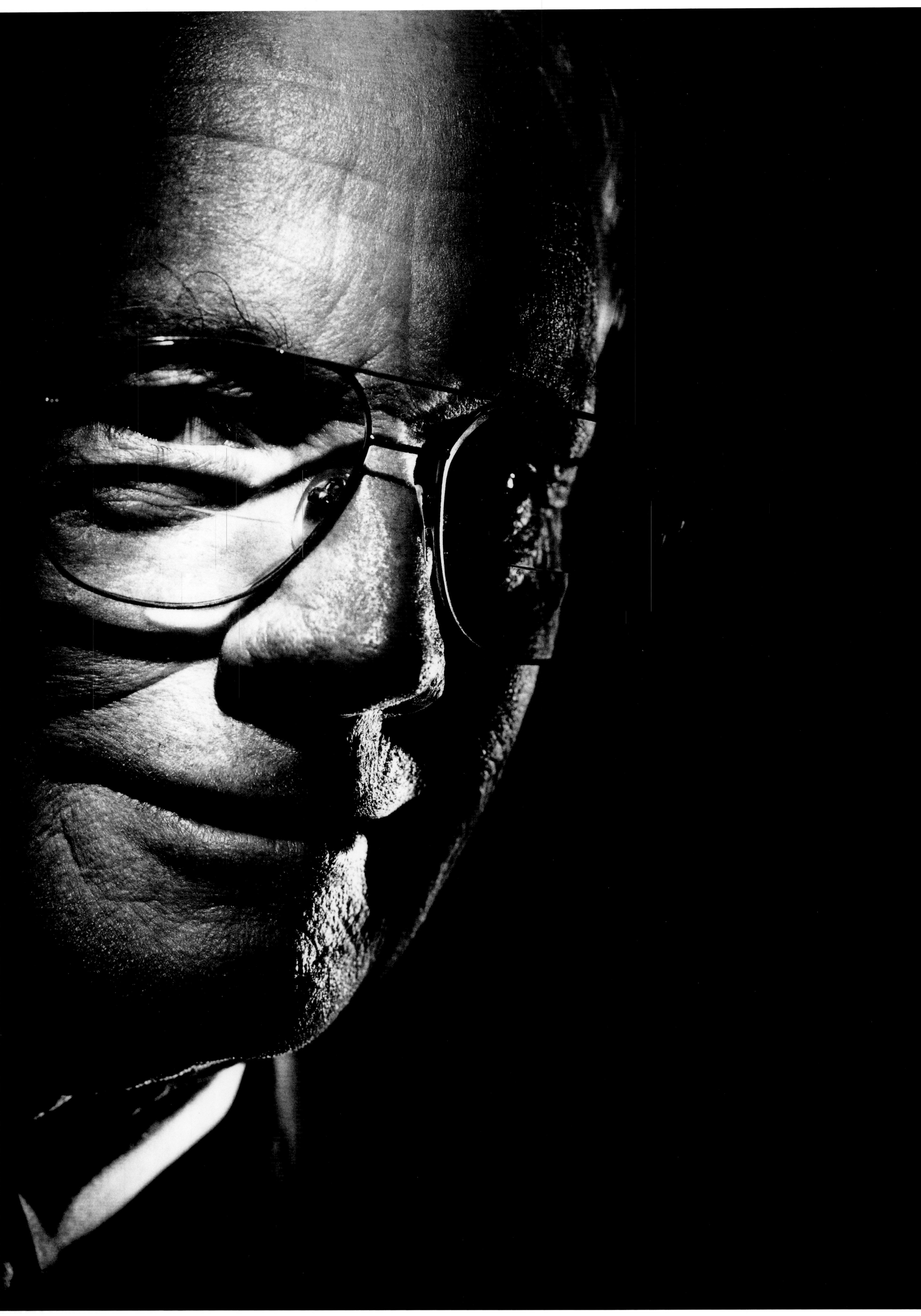

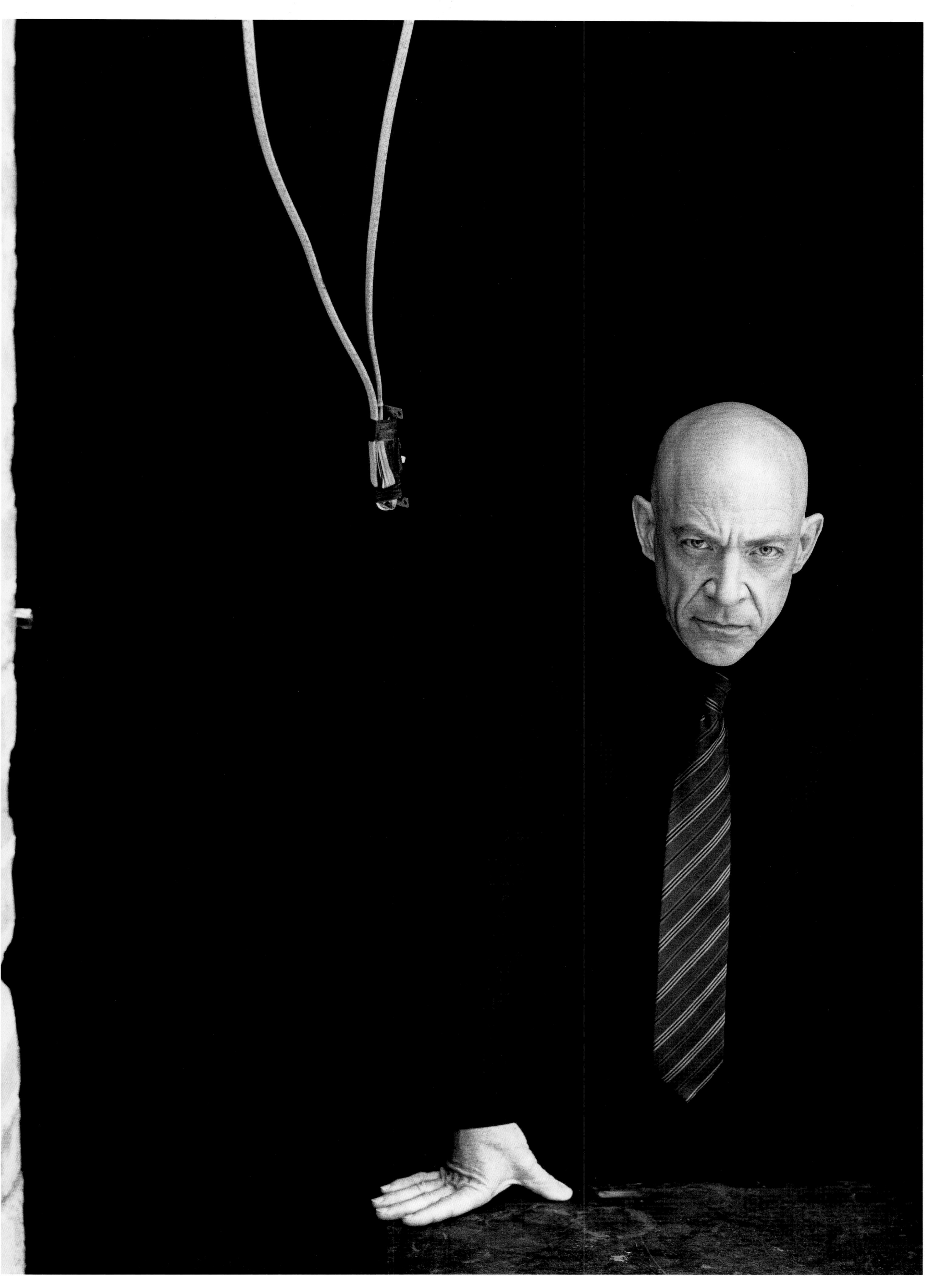

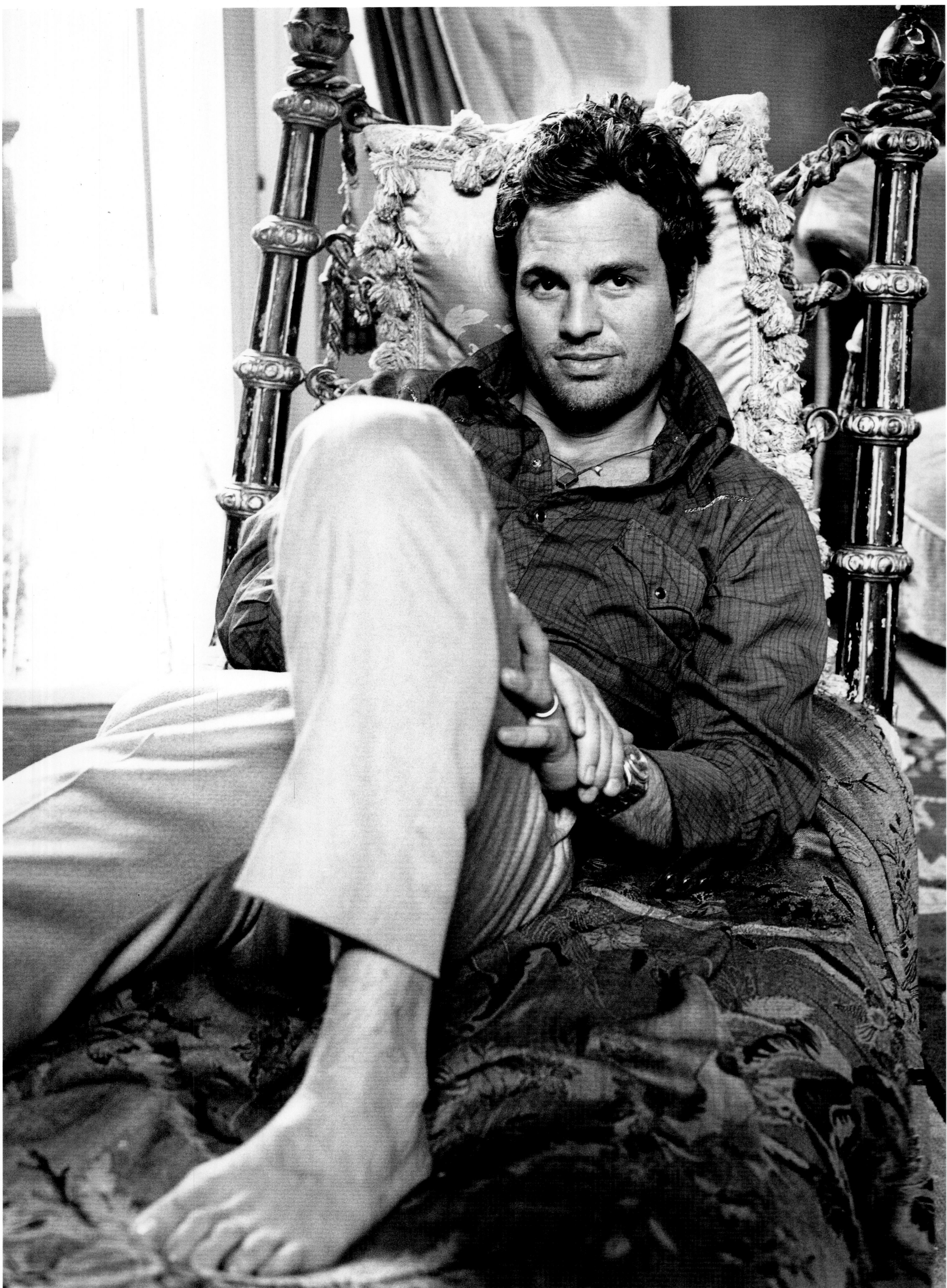

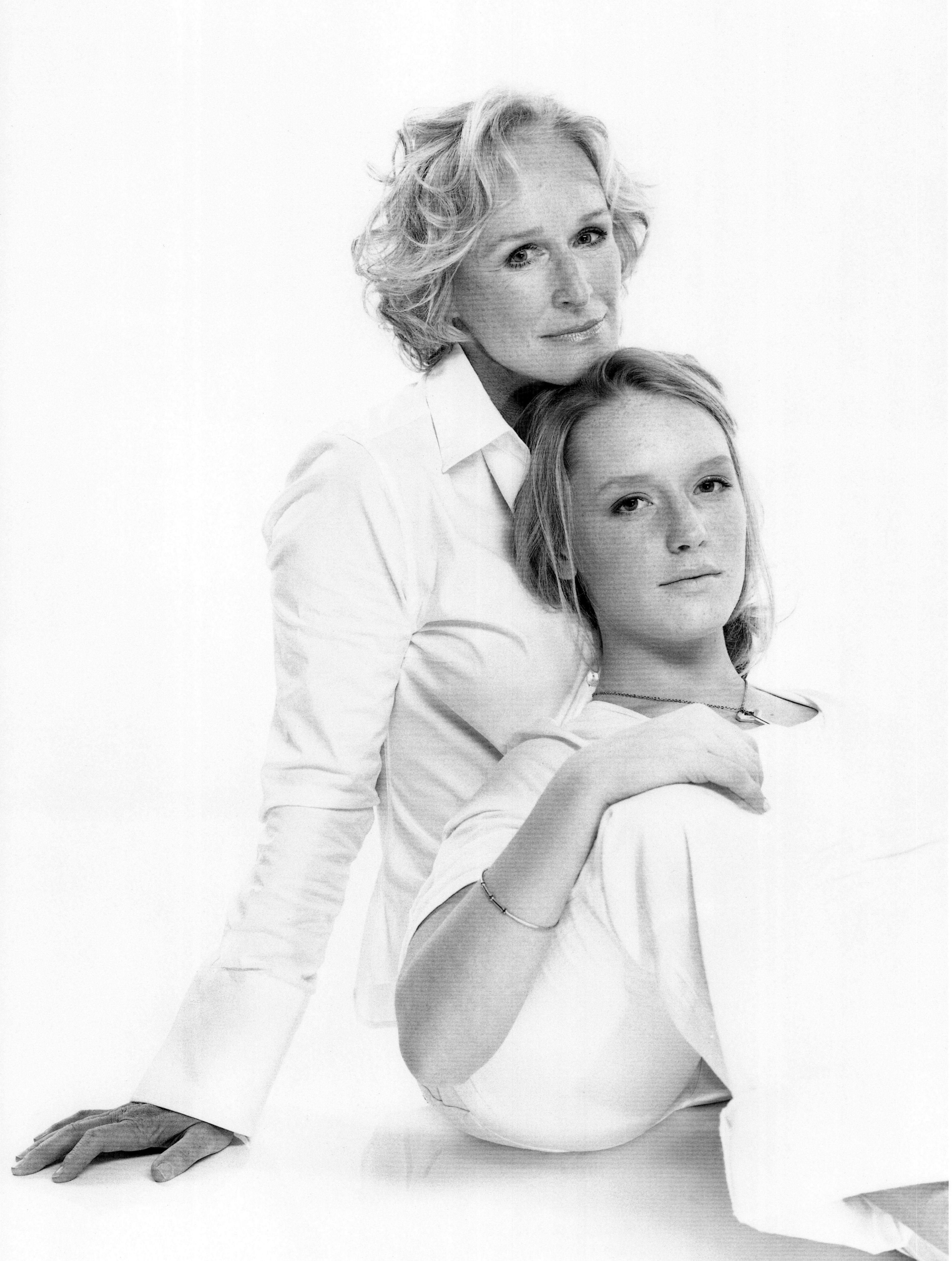

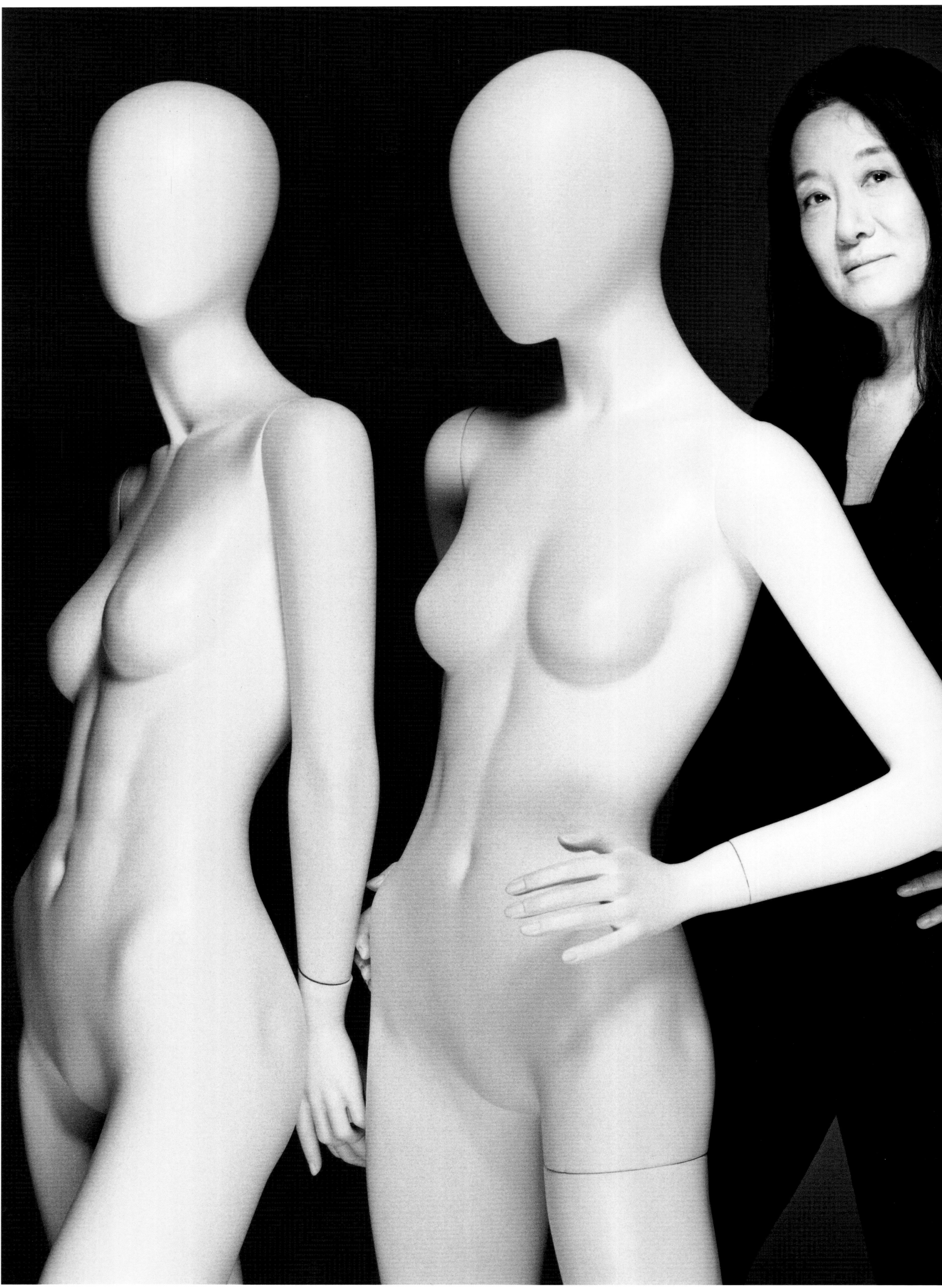

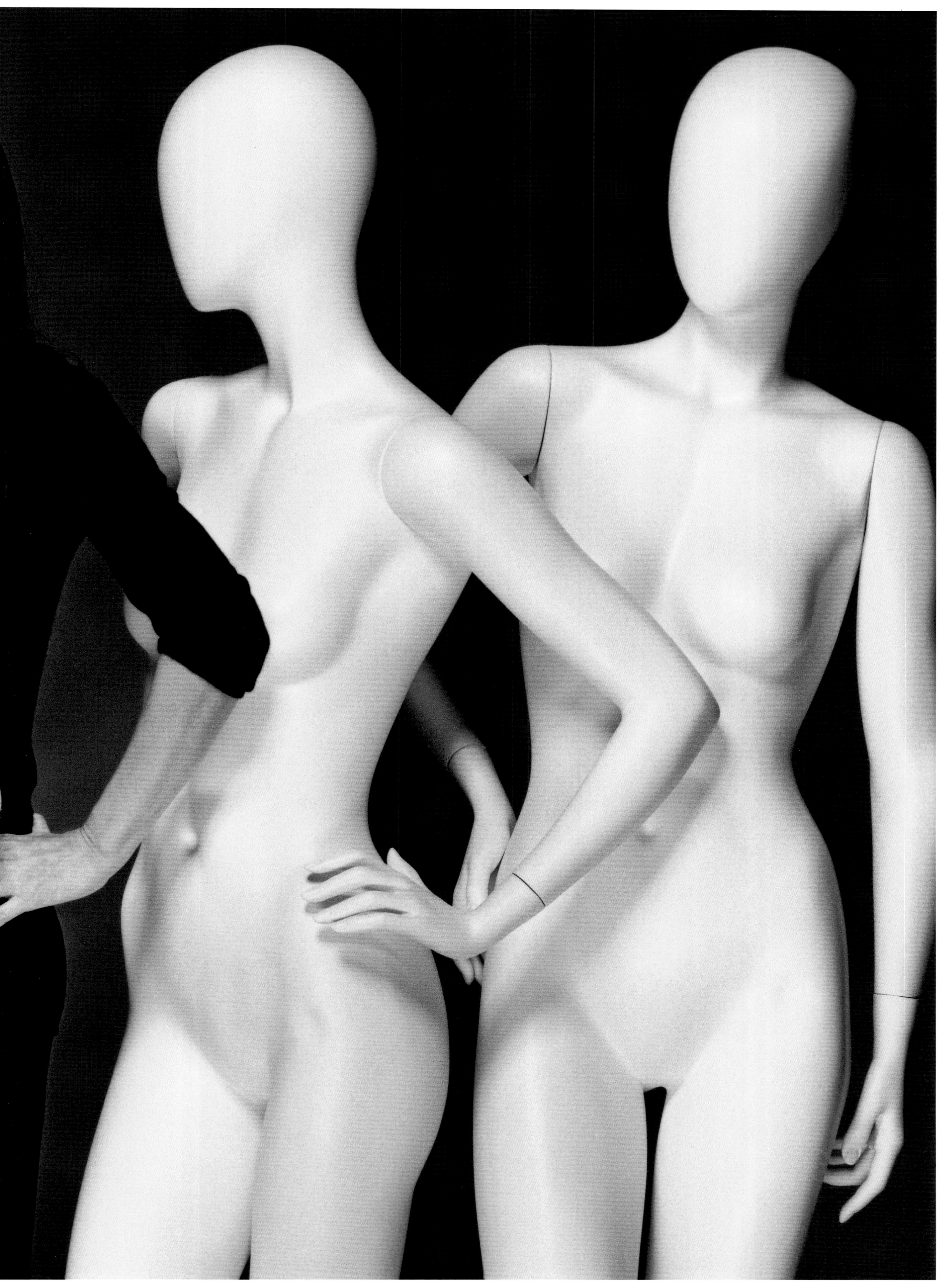

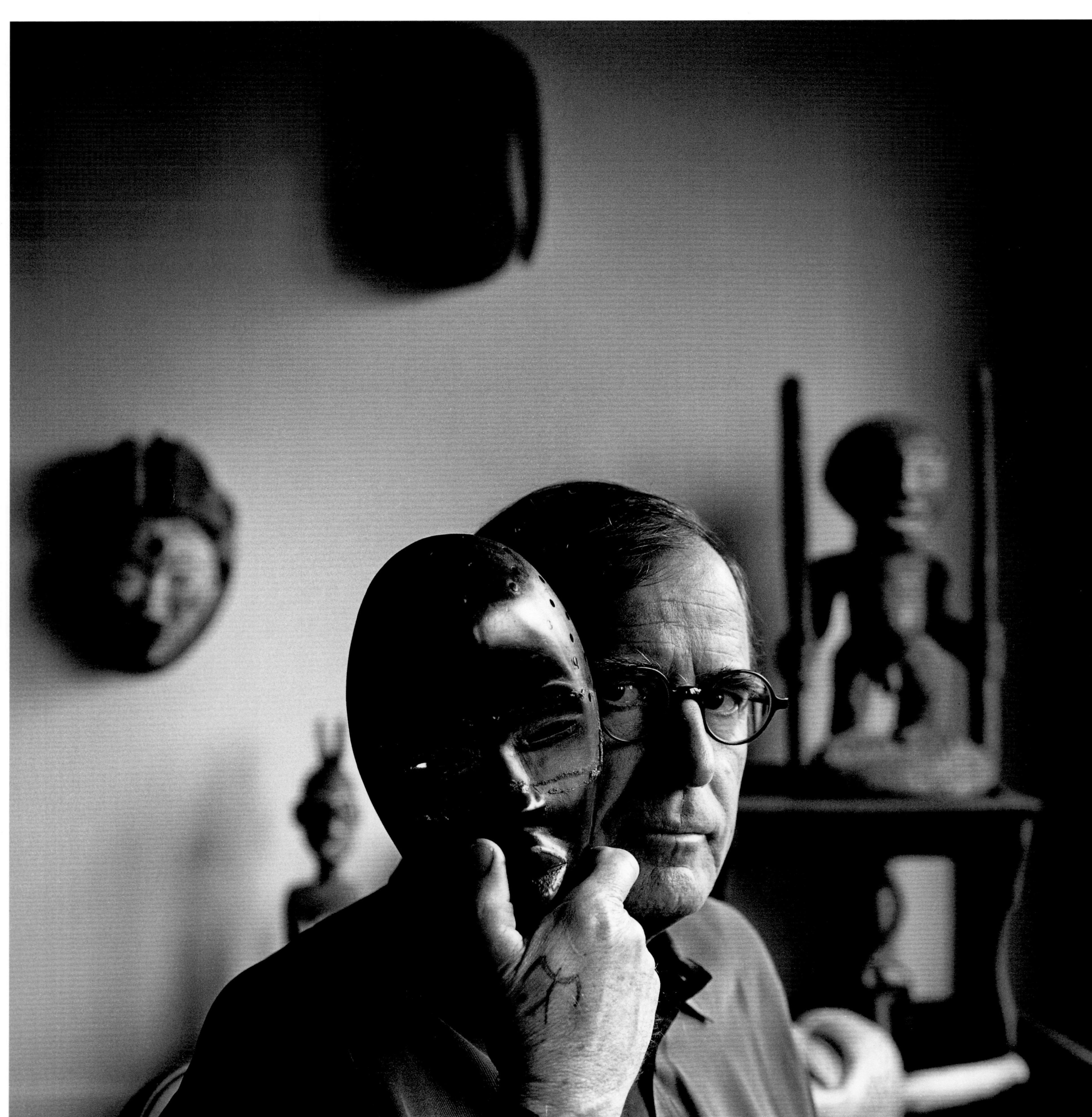

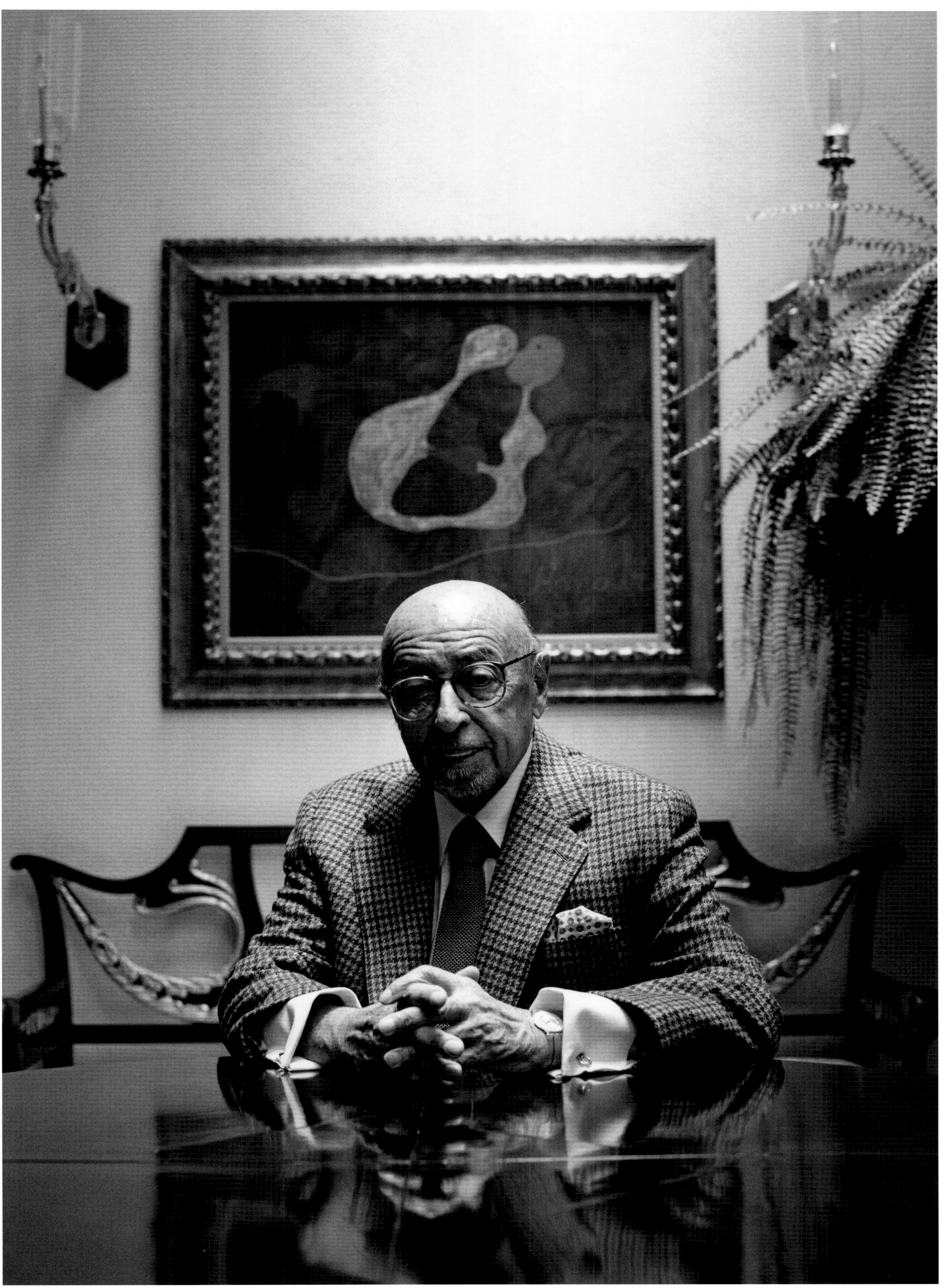

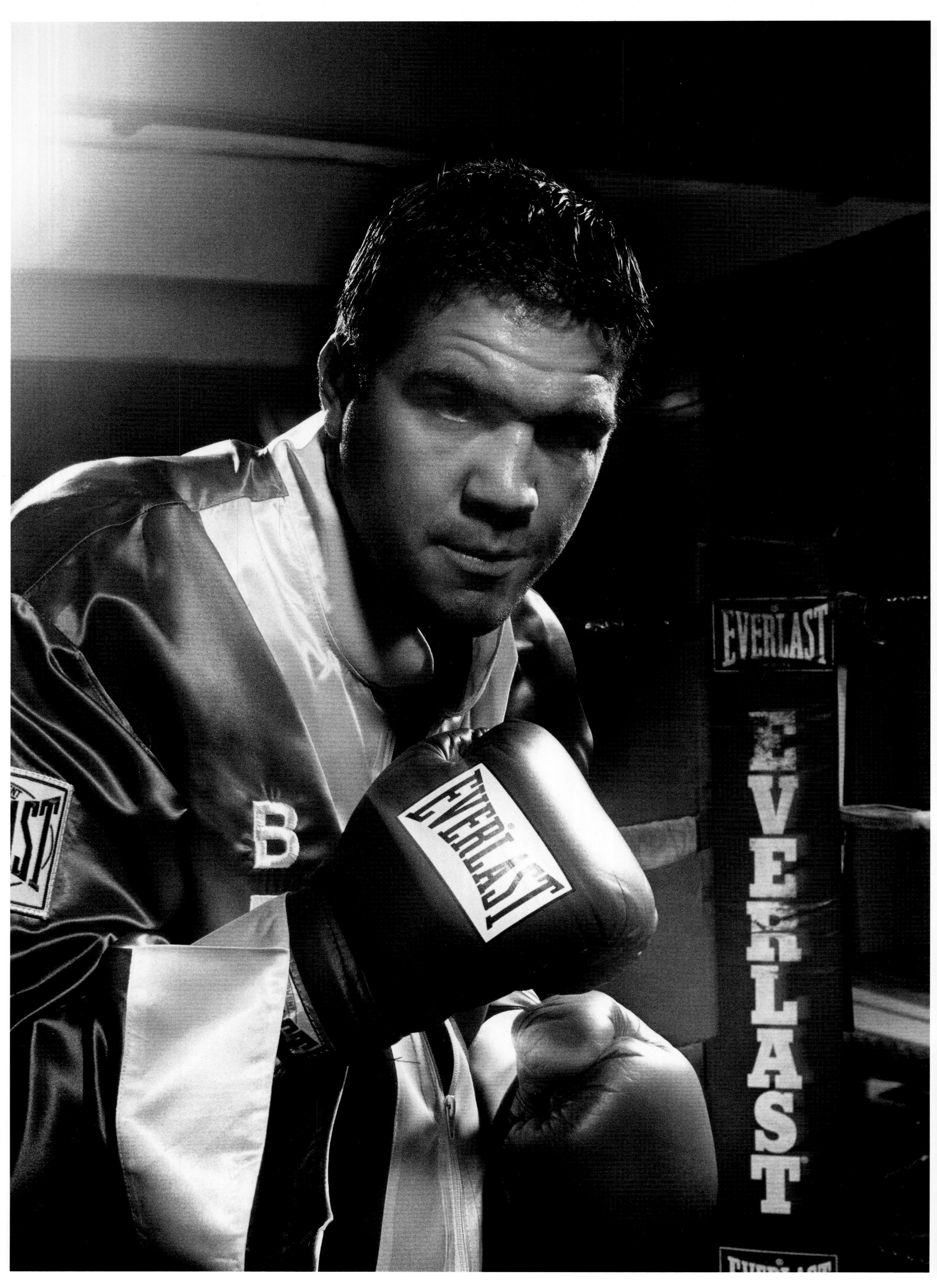
EVERLAST
EVERLAST
EVERLAST
B

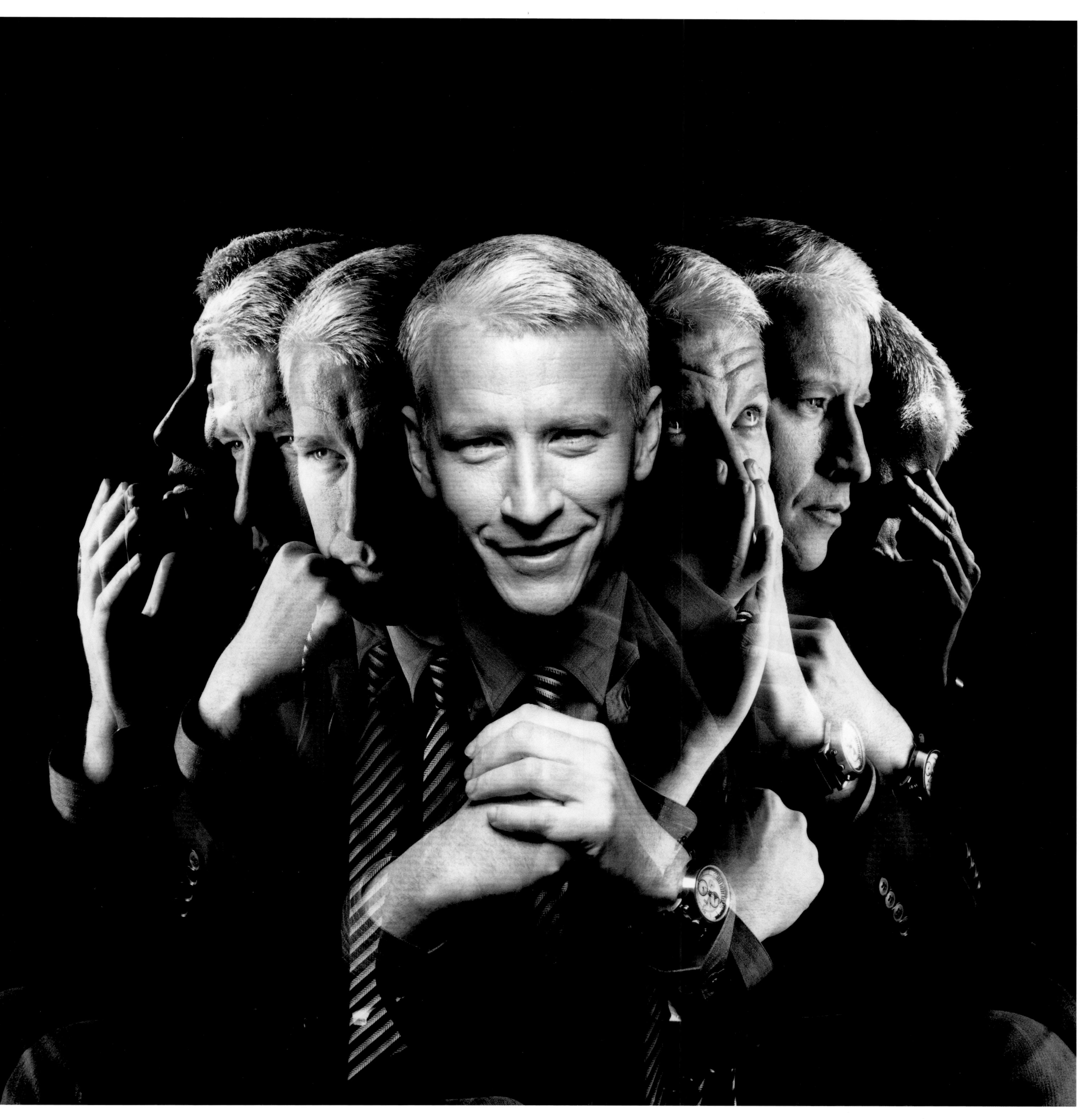

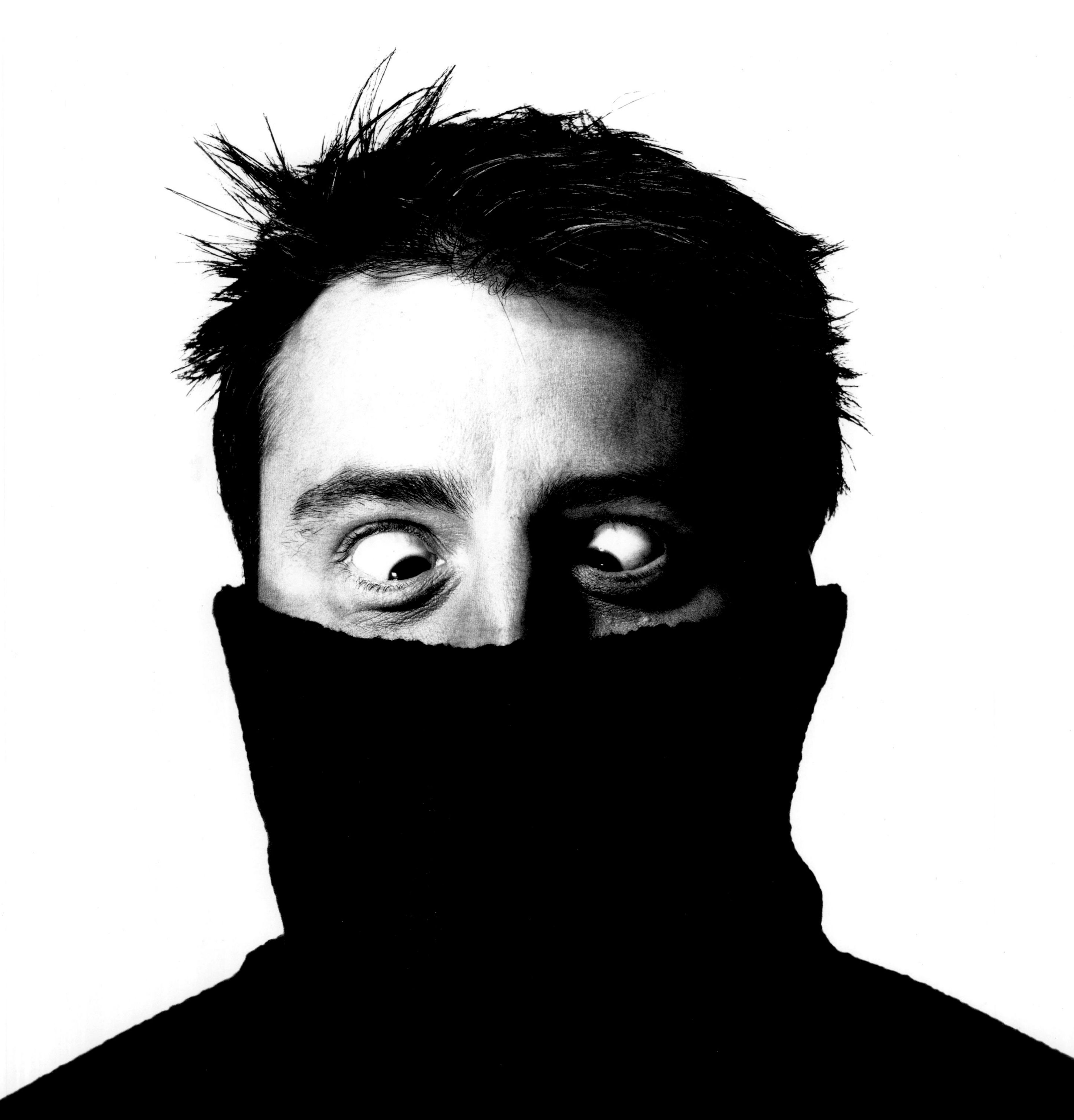

PORTRAITS ON PREVIOUS PAGES

LES PAUL

NEIL ARMSTRONG
J.K. SIMMONS

MARK RUFFALO
GLENN CLOSE

VERA WANG

PAUL THEROUX
AHMET ERTEGEN

JOE MESI
ANDERSON COOPER

MATT LEBLANC

HELLO I'M NIGEL AND I'LL BE YOUR EXECUTIONER THIS MORNING...AND YOUR DENTIST...AND YOUR EVERYBODY-YOU'LL-WANT-TO-RUN-AWAY-FROM. BUT I ASSURE YOU THIS WILL BE A COMPLETELY PAINLESS EXPERIENCE, AND YOU'LL NOT WANT TO LEAVE!

NIGEL PARRY

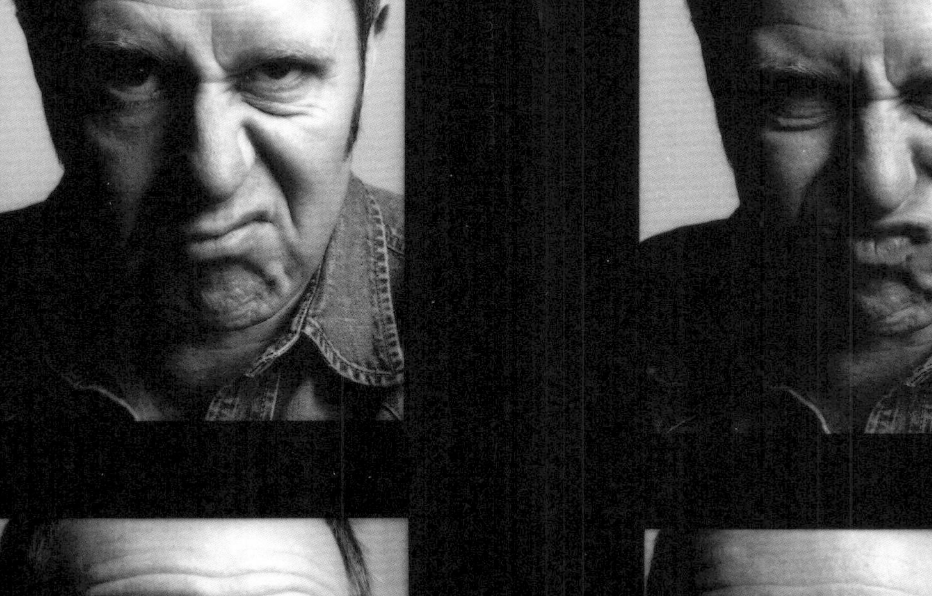
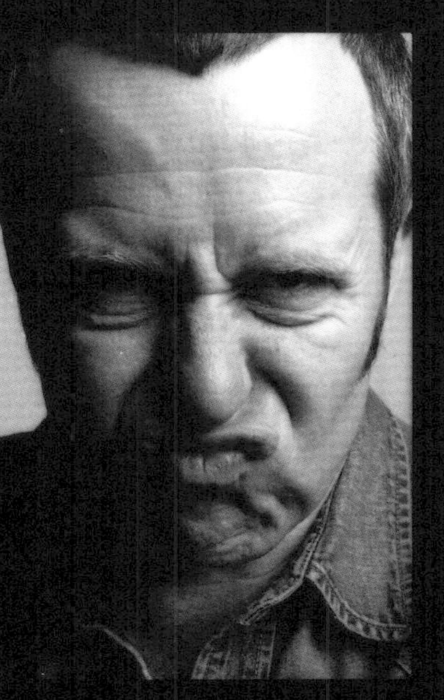
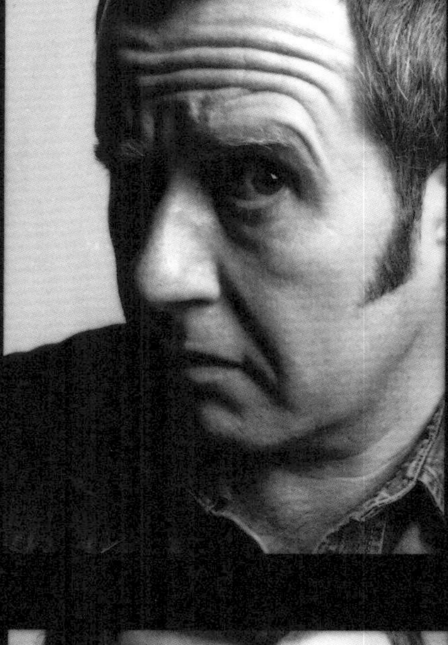
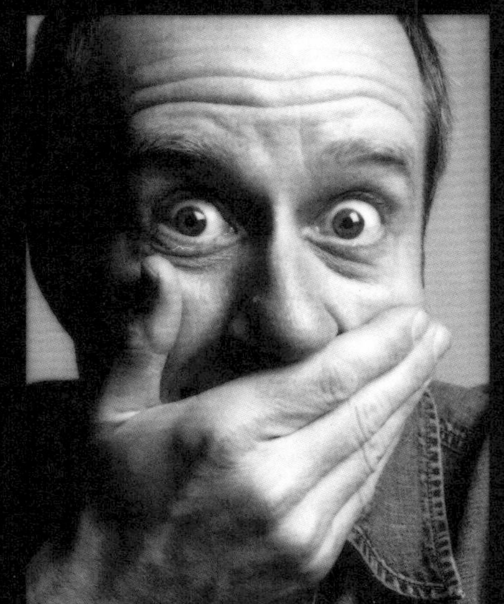
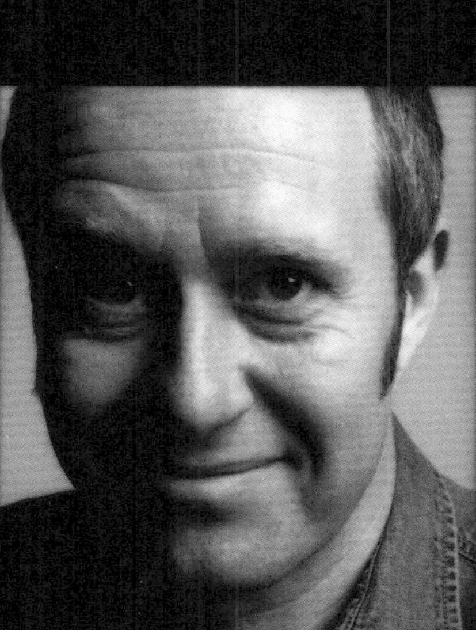
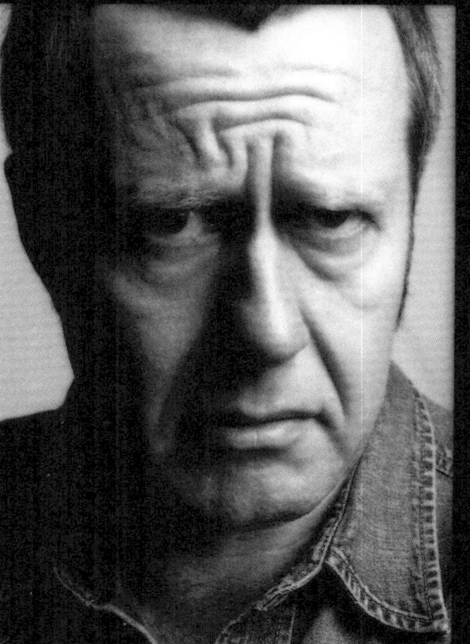
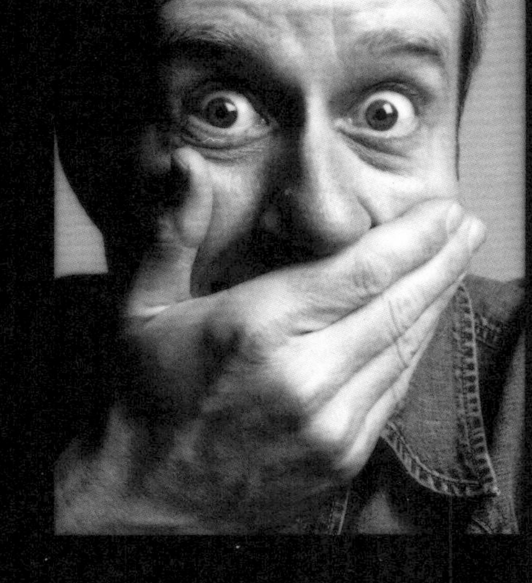
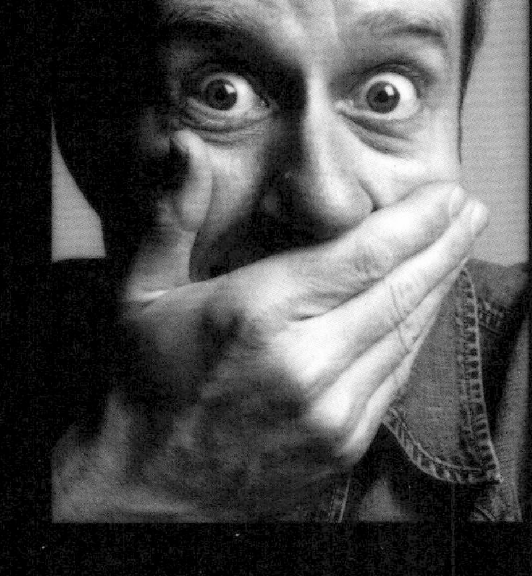
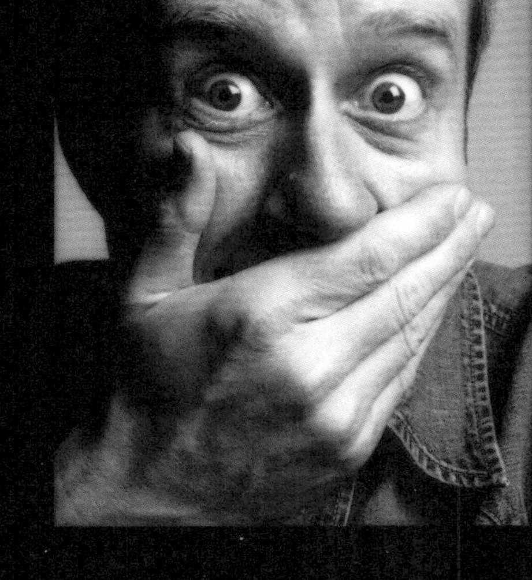
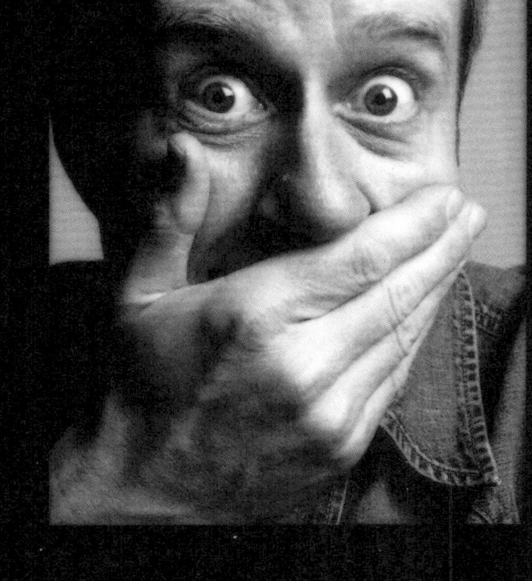
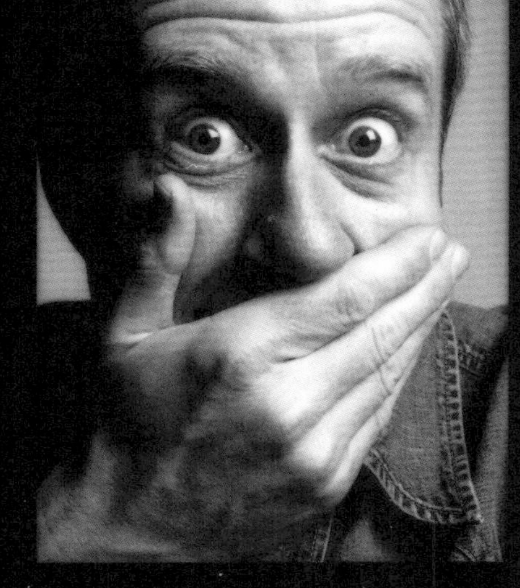
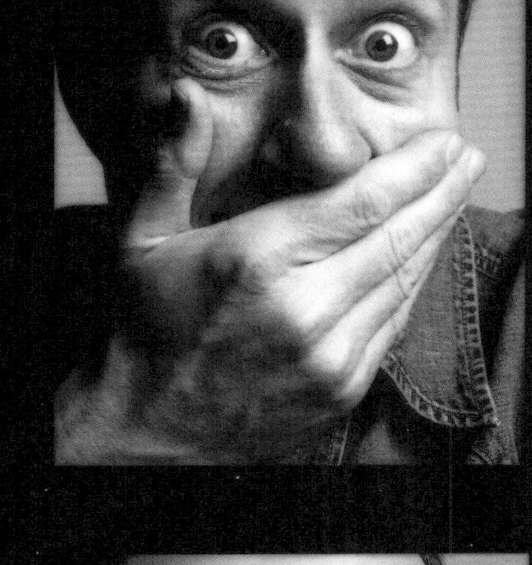
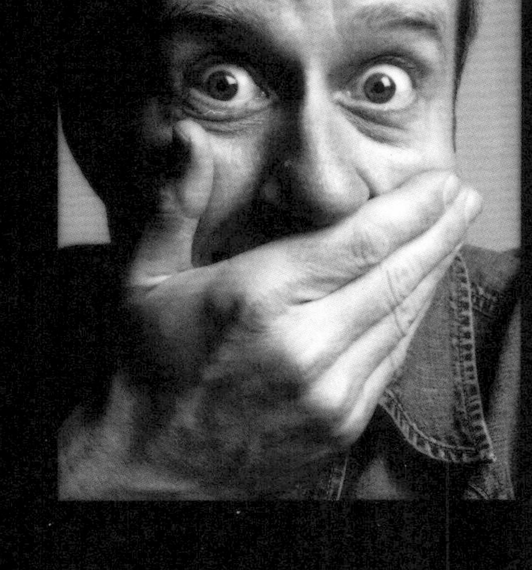
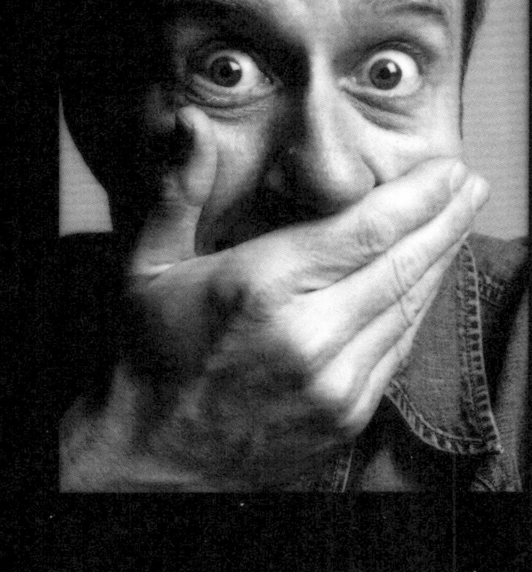
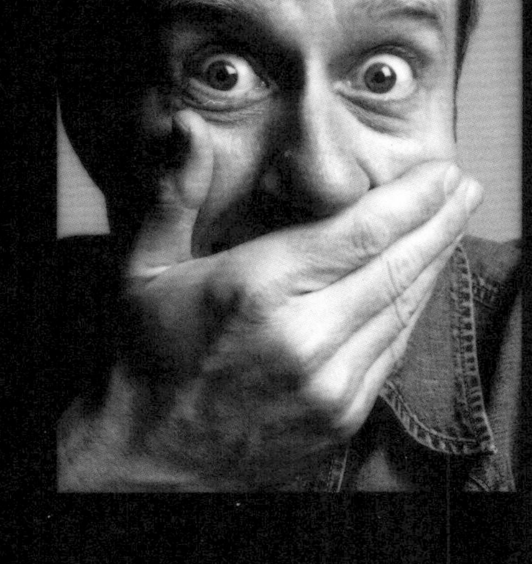
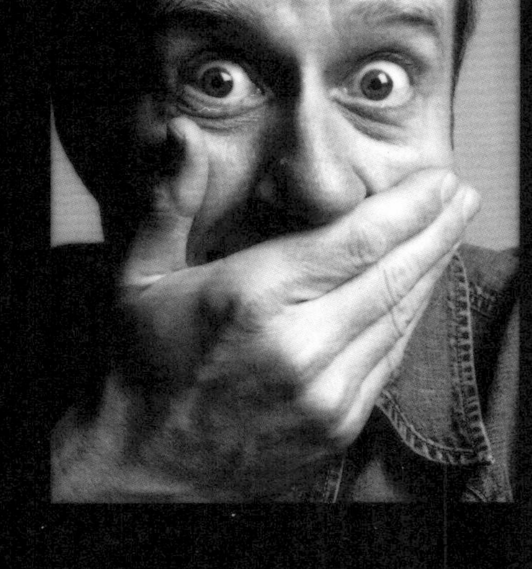
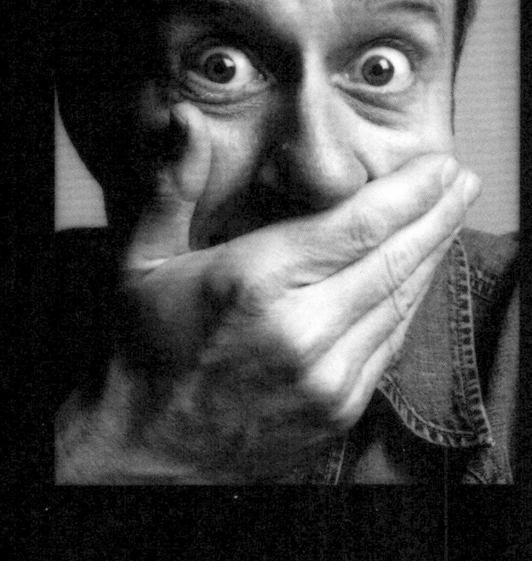
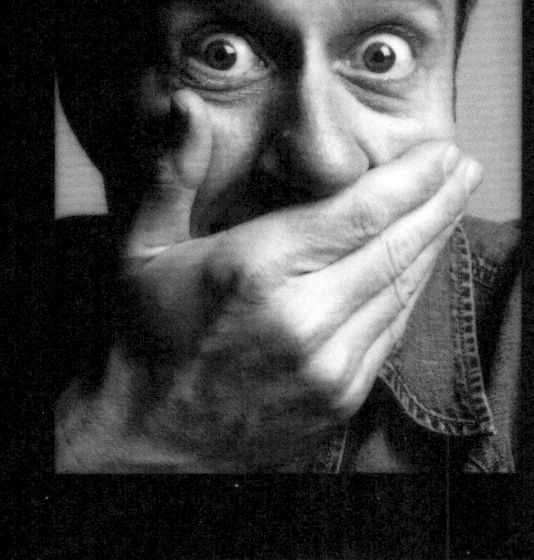
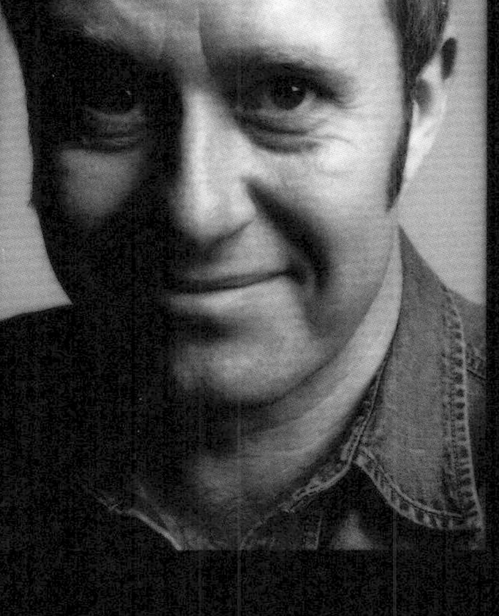
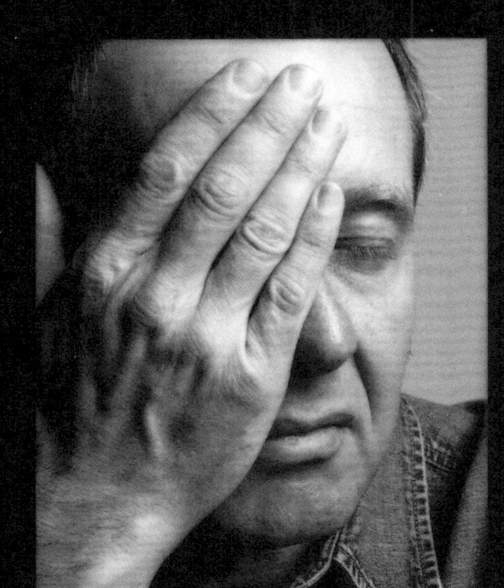
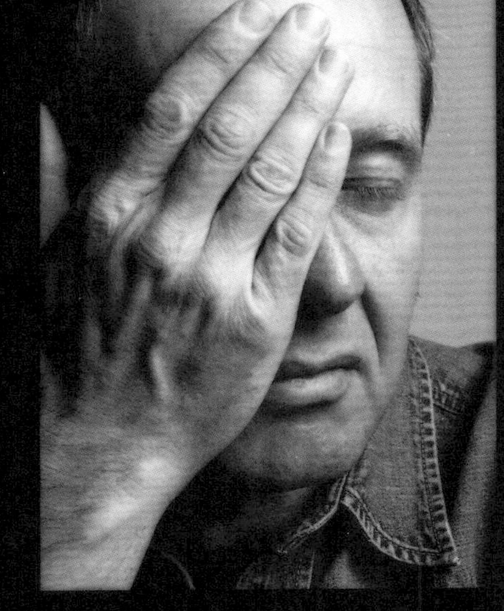
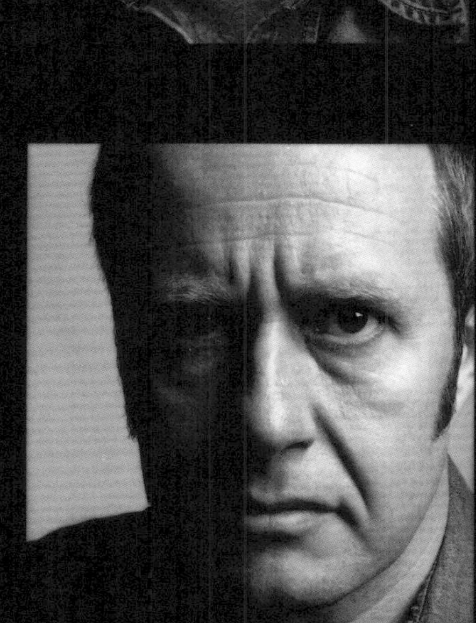
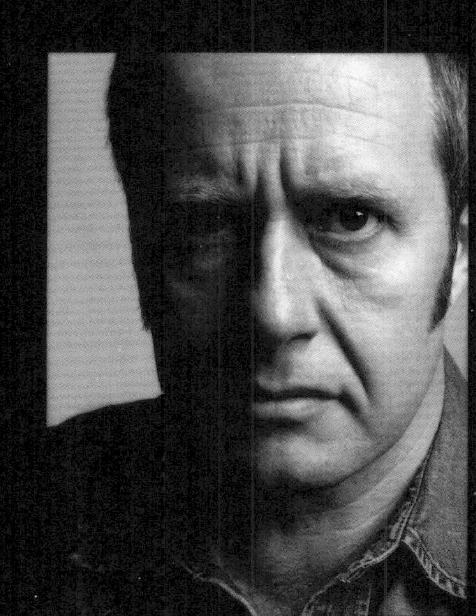
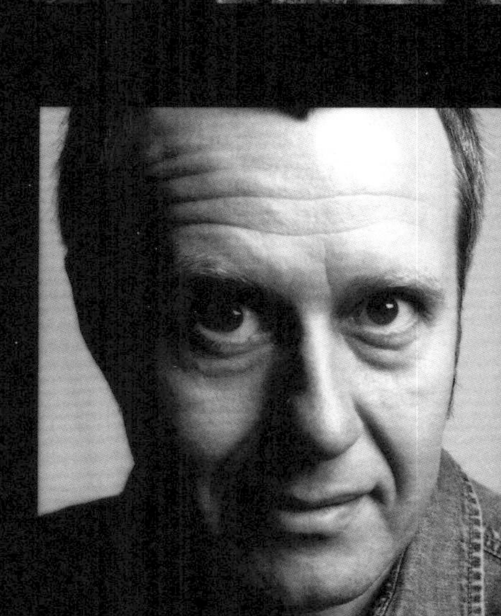
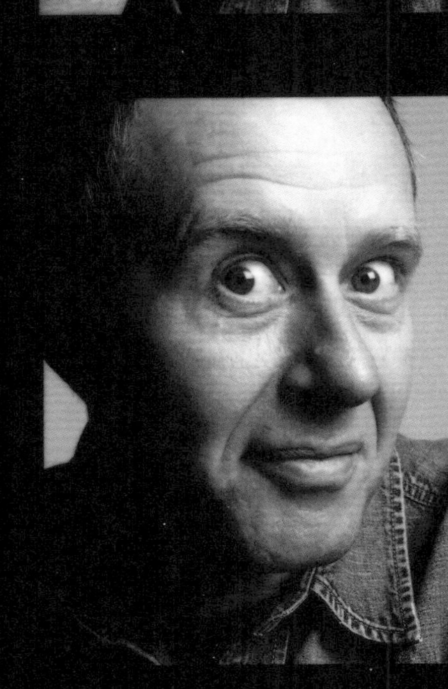
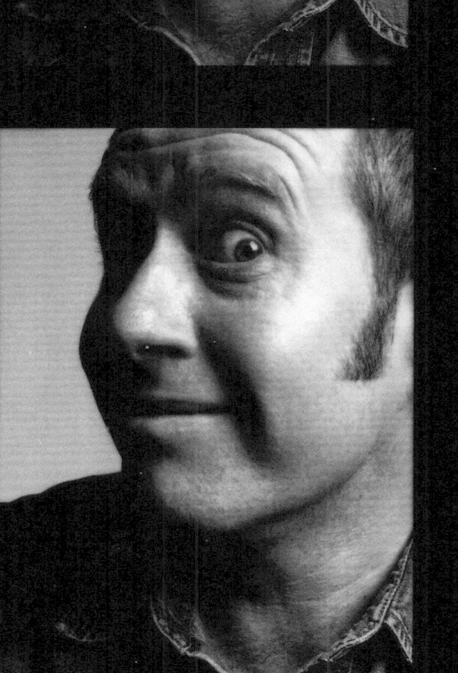
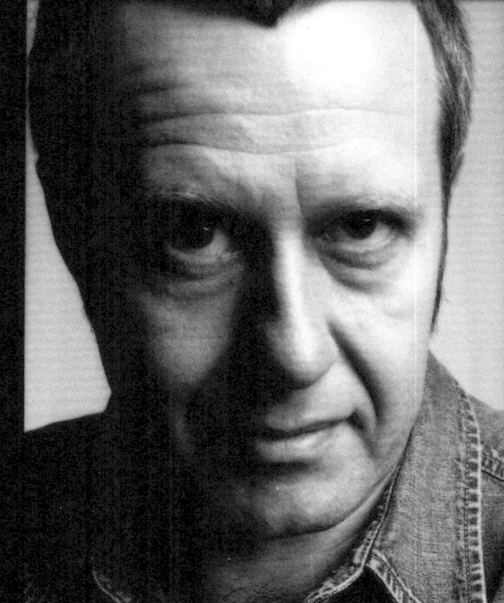

ACKNOWLEDGEMENTS

A HUGE THANK YOU TO ALL WHO MADE THIS POSSIBLE— WITHOUT YOUR ENCOURAGEMENT, ENTHUSIASM, AND ABOVE ALL ASSIGNMENTS, I (WE) COULDN'T HAVE DONE IT!

An even bigger thank you to:
Melanie
Emma and Jack
Paul Giamatti (what a great sport)
Tom Ford
Roger Rosenblatt
Geoff and Pam
Justus and Uta at Pentagram, Berlin
Jennifer and Hugo
Danny, Lisa, Megan, Jeff, and all at CPi
Daniel Power, Craig Cohen, and all at powerHouse Books
Gio and Flo my fashionable friends who always tell it as it is
Gregg
Margo, Fred, Maggie, Dawn, Amber, Mike, Lilius, and all the other assistants who've worked so hard for mere peanuts and beer
Jennifer Crawford, Sydney, Anne Caruso, and all the other wonderful stylists who dress my subjects
Mark Helf for all his genius with props
Nicki, Lisa, Gita, and the other myriad marvelous makeup and hair artists
Mark, Bruce, Simon, Sue, Nicki, and all at Newsweek
Graydon, David, Susan, Lisa, Sarah, Sunhee, Ron, Richard, and all at Vanity Fair
Chris and all at People
Guillaume, Florence, Christine, and all at Elle
Brandon and Nell at Best Life
Maxine and Karen at More
Anne at Modern Luxury Magazines
Jodi at Rolling stone
Jody and all at New York
Michael, Fiona, Richard, Denise, Suzanne, Freyda, and all at Entertainment Weekly
David and all at USA Weekend
Maureen and all at In Style
Dave and Jo at Maxim
Ian at Stuff
American Way, Details, Esquire, Food & Wine, Men's Journal, Premiere, Time, Town & Country
Giovanni Russo, and all at No11
Aidan Sullivan, Laurie Kratochvil, and all who always lend their support
Donna Imbriani, without whom I'd get nowhere
Caroline and Brianne, without whom I wouldn't be organized
Alina, Kimberly, Khaled, Tim, and all at Industria
Everyone at Splashlight
Paula and Justin the digital wizards
Everyone at Quixote, 5th and Sunset, Miauhaus, Smashbox, and Screaming Broccoli
And last but not least, to EVERYONE who graciously stands in front of my lens, and all the publicists and managers who facilitate this great privilege

Published in the United States by powerHouse Books,
a division of powerHouse Cultural Entertainment, Inc.
37 Main Street, Brooklyn, NY 11201-1201
telephone 212 604 9074, fax 212 366 5247
e-mail: info@powerHouseBooks.com
website: www.powerHouseBooks.com

First edition, 2006

Library of Congress Cataloging-in-Publication Data:
Parry, Nigel.
Blunt / photographs by Nigel Parry ; introduction by Tom Ford ; foreword by Roger Rosenblatt.
p. cm.
ISBN 1-57687-326-9
1. Celebrities--Portraits. 2. Portrait photography. 3. Parry, Nigel. I. Title.

TR681.F3P376 2006
779'.2092--dc
2006045699

Hardcover ISBN 1-57687-326-9

Separations, printing, and binding by Oceanic Graphic Printing Inc., China

Book design by Justus Oehler, Pentagram

Nigel Parry is represented in New York by Creative Photographers Inc. (CPi)

A complete catalog of powerHouse Books and Limited Editions is available upon request; please call, write, or bludgeon our website.

10 9 8 7 6 5 4 3 2 1

Printed and bound in China